HALAKHAH

LIBRARY OF JEWISH IDEAS

Cosponsored by the Tikvah Fund

The series presents engaging and authoritative treatments of core Jewish concepts in a form appealing to general readers who are curious about Jewish treatments of key areas of human thought and experience.

Halakhah

THE RABBINIC IDEA OF LAW

CHAIM N. SAIMAN

PRINCETON UNIVERSITY PRESS

PRINCETON & OXFORD

Published by Princeton University Press,
41 William Street, Princeton, New Jersey 08540

In the United Kingdom: Princeton University Press,
6 Oxford Street, Woodstock, Oxfordshire OX20 1TR

press.princeton.edu

ISBN 978-0-691-15211-0
Library of Congress Control Number: 2018936380

British Library Cataloging-in-Publication Data is available

Publication of this book has been aided by the Tikvah Fund

This book has been composed in Arno Pro

Printed on acid-free paper. ∞

Printed in the United States of America

10 9 8 7 6 5 4 3 2 1

To my Rosh ha-Yeshiva Rav Aharon Lichtenstein, zt"l,
who would have never written this book,
but without whom this book would have never been written.

And to my beloved cousin and *Rebbe*, David "Dudi" Goshen,
who taught me Torah as an art that engages all the senses,
and guided me towards my path in the Talmud.

And to my *ḥavruta* and *rav-ḥaver* R. Joshua Weinberger,
who begins raising twenty-four objections,
yet concludes increasing my understanding a hundredfold.

CONTENTS

PREFACE

IN MANY WAYS, the original idea for this book took root in 1990. As a tenth grader in the high school division of Ner Israel Rabbinical College in Baltimore, Maryland, I became immersed in the world of Talmud study and exposed to the idea that a fifteen-year-old boy should spend at least ten hours a day engaged in the intricate details of legal analysis—in addition to general education classes.

In the all-encompassing environment of the *yeshiva*, Sundays were no different from Tuesdays, free weekends were rare, and there were few opportunities to venture off campus and emerge from its controlled habitat. For if the yeshiva's primary message was the centrality of constant Talmud study—an exercise so sacrosanct as to be dubbed "*talmud Torah*," the study of God's Torah—a close second was the ever-looming danger presented by television, movies, music, and other forms of pop culture, all inevitably suffused with the imagery of romance and sexual attraction. Such things, never far from the minds of teenage boys, were seldom spoken of in public. Instead, the guiding mantra was to follow the Talmud's advice, "If you encounter this lecherous inclination, pull him to the Talmudic study hall" (b.Sukkah 52b). True, in speaking with us one-on-one, the more astute rabbis exhibited greater nuance, but in public, the subject was wholly off-limits. Torah study was the only item on the agenda, and those who failed to attend to it with appropriate diligence were castigated for "wasting their lives."

This set the backdrop for one of the most defining and bewildering moments of my life. At the time, our tenth-grade class was studying the first chapter of tractate Kiddushin, which deals with the legal mechanics of how a man betroths a woman. The talmudic discussion here has little practical relevance for today's teenagers or really to anyone outside of a few specialists in the field. Nor is the text in question an obvious choice for a yeshiva striving—with more success than generally assumed—to keep its students oriented toward an austere set of religious pursuits rather than the usual fare of American high schoolers.

Imagine my surprise then, as the lesson proceeded to the following: The Mishnah rules that a woman may be betrothed (formally engaged) to a man either by accepting money from him, by means of a formalized document, or via a sexual union. The Talmud being the Talmud, however, pushes for greater specificity. The following following discussion emerges (Kiddushin 10a):

> They asked:
> Does the beginning of the sexual act effect betrothal
> Or is it the conclusion of the act that effects betrothal?
> What is the practical difference between them?
> Where the male has only initiated the sexual act,
> but the woman has stretched out her hand in the meantime
> and accepted betrothal money from another. . . .
> What is the law?
> Ameimar said in the name of Rava:
> One who engages in the sexual act does so with intention of completing it.

To this day, I recall my utter incapacity to absorb what was expected of me. I was a diligent student, and the yeshiva's worldview mandated I devote all my intellectual energies to understanding the parameters of this talmudic conundrum. And yet, surely, I was not to *actually* think deeply about the issue before us. Was I to envision what the scene might look like, or why the Talmud presents it this way? To consider why the conclusion of the sexual act may be more significant than its beginning? To speculate just how it might come to pass that a woman, having begun intercourse with one man, would outstretch her hand to accept a marriage proposal from another?

But here's the crux. Though the specific content of this passage has ensured that it remains fixed in my memory, from the yeshiva's perspective there was nothing unusual about it. Far from being conceptualized as sexual or graphic, it was simply one more among the Talmud's endless investigations into how various legal relations are created and/or disbanded—no different from asking at what precise moment a debt become due, or how exactly a slave, who is legally barred from acquiring anything, can acquire the document that grants him freedom. These matters, like so many others, were and are approached as pure questions of law—assessed from a clinical distance that dispassionately ignores the psychological state of a woman or man about to become engaged, the morality of slavery, or the disparate economic impact of two approaches to accounting for debt.

Indeed, to focus on such matters is taken as a hallmark of the novice, unfamiliar with how Talmud ought to be studied. More advanced students are quickly acculturated to the view that these lofty matters, which exist solely in the zone of analysis, are divorced from time, space, or lived reality. To riff off the evocative phrase of the seventeenth-century English common lawyers, subsequently repurposed by Bob Dylan and Steely Dan, the Talmud is all "time out of mind."

As years passed, my thoughts continued to wander and wonder. Notwithstanding— or perhaps, because of—the questions it raised, my experience in high school led to a lifetime of love and fascination both with the study of Talmud and Jewish law, and with a quest to understand the nature of that fascination. Though I am now more learned and better read, the essential questions remain the same. Why was I at once to invest my inner soul in thinking deeply about the Talmud's laws, yet at the same time, block off the frames of reference used to inhabit and interpret the world around me? Why do the rabbis insist that Jews not only observe the law in their daily lives but also devote considerable effort and resources to its study? Why search for God in the fine details of talmudic law? If Talmud study is the most sublime of all pursuits, why drill down into subjects seemingly so distant from the sublime? What is the *meaning* of the Talmud's interest in questions of this sort? And what does it signify—for an individual, for a religion, for a society—to be so invested in what the law means?

This book reflects my small contribution to understanding what the study of Talmud—of God's Torah—is all about.

ACKNOWLEDGMENTS

THIS BOOK IS DEDICATED TO R. Aharon Lichtenstein, *zt"l*, for establishing my foundation; to Dudi Goshen, for providing me with depth, insight, and inspiration; and to Joshua Weinberger, for guiding me toward implementation. In different—yet overlapping ways—each of these unique souls is singular in his generation. I am blessed to be counted as their aspiring student in Torah, in *derekh eretz*, and in life.

Beyond these, many other rabbis, mentors, and *havrutot* have developed my thinking on these topics over the years. Rabbis Kalman Weinreb, Michael Berger, Michael Broyde, and Yehud Brandes. *Havrutot* and friends Elli Schorr, Aytan Kadden, Eli Fischer, Betzalel Posy, Rafi Eis, Yehuda Seif, Tzvi Sinensky, Jonny Klahr, Michael Avi Helfand, and Benny Porat. Professors and mentors Louis Michael Seidman, Eben Moglen, Michael McConnell, Charlie Donahue, and Noah Feldman.

I have a debt of gratitude to Villanova University and the Charles Widger School of Law that have supported me and served as my academic home while writing this book. I have also greatly benefited from students and research assistants who have found the unfindable, sharpened my arguments, and provided the necessary pushback: Isaac Roszler, Daniel Shulman, Josh Stadlan, Yizchak Shmalo, Michael Shulman, Leead Staller, and, in particular, Charlie Wollman and Yaakov Ellenbogen. Special mention to Judy Greenwald, whose keen editorial eye caught many mistakes that had escaped me, and to Menachem Butler for finding the unfindable, and keeping me up to date of the latest in every imaginable field.

Thanks go out to the visionaries at the Tikvah Fund who have supported this project from its inception. I am indebted to the Fund's legendary editor Neal Kozodoy who made every paragraph tighter, sharper, crisper, and more penetrating (and would certainly have shaved words off this sentence).

Professor Robert George and the Madison Program at Princeton University not only provided time and support to write this book, but assembled thinkers and scholars from across legal and religious traditions who pushed me to present my thoughts in a framework comprehensible to a variety of readers.

Last but hardly least, is family. I extend deepest gratitude to my parents, whose gifts I am only learning to appreciate as I wade deeper into the role of parent myself. And to my beloved Shari, who is strong where I am weak, kind where I am rash, wise where I am obtuse, consistent where I am impulsive, insightful where I am stubborn, caring where I am aloof, and calm when I am unsettled. All that is mine is surely hers, yet all that she has done is to her credit alone.

Introduction

The Academy of Heaven

What happens in heaven? The question grabs the attention of everyone from ancient theologians to modern *New Yorker* cartoonists. It continues to fascinate because it touches on the timeless matter of truth. What is perfect? What are the secrets of the universe? What explains who we are and why we are here?

In the Bible, the familiar image of heaven is the divine throne. The book of Ezekiel describes the angels and heavenly creatures singing God's praises amidst chariots, lightning, and fire. The Christian book of Revelation contains some twenty chapters drawing on these themes.

For their part, the rabbis of the Talmud frequently describe heaven with images of God's throne and the sovereignty over all that is created. In one text, however, the Talmud presents a view of heaven without any precedent in the Bible, an image that is unthinkable, if not blasphemous, outside the rabbinic context. It opens as follows: (b.Bava Metzia 86a).

| They were arguing in the Academy of Heaven:

Sit with these words for a moment. First, focus on the noun. In this talmudic passage, heaven consists not of angels, halos, lyres, pearly gates, or fluffy clouds, nor of chariots, smoke, lightning, or thunder. Heaven entails an academy—a yeshiva—a place of Torah study. Now the verb, "arguing." This heaven is not a place of peace and tranquility, but of intellectual debate and argument.

What is being argued about in this academy? The mysteries of the cosmos? The answers to life's true meaning? The secrets that emerge when theology meets physics? Is this where God's ultimate purpose is revealed from the divine throne itself?

Not at all. The Talmud continues:

> If the blotch on the skin preceded the white hair,
> he is impure.
> If the white hair preceded the blotch on the skin,
> he is pure.

Skin? Hair? Blotches! Not only does the Academy of Heaven forgo any discussion of the cosmos, but it studies halakhah, which is nearly always translated as Jewish law (more on this term below). And not just any of Judaism's laws, but some of the most obscure and technical issues found in the entire rabbinic canon. The question debated at this ultimate institution of higher learning relates to the laws of *tzaraat*, the skin malady outlined in Leviticus 13, and commonly translated as leprosy.

Here is the background: if the skin develops a white blotch and *then* the hairs inside the blotch turn white, the affected individual is diagnosed with *tzaraat* and deemed impure. But if the hair turns white first, and then the skin blotch appears, the infection is benign and the individual is pure.

But now a complication arises:

> If there was doubt as to which came first . . .

Apparently, there is not only law and arguments in heaven but doubt as well. Yet surely any doubt must be fleeting. After all, we are studying law from the mouth of the Almighty . What doubts could possibly emerge?

> The Holy One, blessed is He, says he is pure,
> While the rest of the Academy of Heaven says he is impure.

What's this? One might think that in a well-functioning heavenly academy, God would be sitting on a throne teaching authoritatively, while the angels sit in rapt attention below. But the Talmud's Academy of Heaven is different, for when it comes to debating the nuances of Jewish law, the angels have the audacity to challenge God, and God treats them as equals.

The Talmud then goes one step further. God is not even the final authority. That role is instead assigned to a talmudic rabbi who must be called up to the Academy to adjudicate.

> They asked: "Who will judge this issue?"
> It was decided that it would be Rabba b. Nachmani
> As Rabba b. Nachmani said:
> "For I have singular knowledge in the laws of leprosy . . . "
> They sent a messenger to get him.

What we have seen here is surely not the only view of heaven in the Talmud, but it is a view of heaven that only the Talmud could fathom. And in a few short lines, the Talmud has told us quite a bit about how it understands both heaven and halakhah.

First, note how the natural state of halakhah is an argument about rules that have meaning regardless of whether they are used to decide a case. We can only presume that there are no mortals and certainly no lepers in heaven—and even if there were, God certainly knows whether blotch or hair came first. But the legal rule reflects something important beyond its applicability to a given case or controversy. That is why God and the angels debate these incredibly specific details.

The second point follows: law is something intrinsically worthy of study—so worthy and important that it is the central activity that takes place in heaven. To the Talmud, ultimate perfection is God and the angels arguing over the intricacies of halakhah.

What exactly is halakhah, then? It is almost universally translated as Jewish law, but in its literal sense, the word means something akin to "the path." The common translation prevails because halakhah presents itself as a regulatory system that governs virtually every aspect of the life practiced by observant Jews for centuries. Take for example the influential sixteenth-century work known as the *Shulḥan Arukh,* usually dubbed the *Code of Jewish Law* (literally a "set [or ready] table"). This compilation begins with the "Laws of Arising in the Morning" and carries on right through to the "Laws of Retiring to Bed," followed by the "Laws of Modesty" (sexual intimacy) and covers everything from the laws of childbirth to the laws of mourning. Elsewhere, this work instructs not only to eat matzah on Passover, but legislates *when* one should eat it (after nightfall but before midnight) how *much* one must eat (one, or maybe two, olive's worth), in what *position* one should be while eating it (reclining—but to the left) and the *length of time* one has in which to eat it (about ten minutes). The same is true for what to wear and when to wear it, how to do business and with whom—not to mention the laws of *Shabbat* (the Sabbath), Jewish holidays, prayers, blessings, marriage, divorce, inheritance, and thousands of other familiar and lesser known Jewish practices.

Committed Jews observe these laws by (among other activities) ceasing all travel and work-related activity before sundown on Friday evening, eating only kosher food, and maintaining separate sets of dishes for meat and milk-based foods. Each spring, Jews restock their kitchens with food that is especially kosher for Passover, and haul out two *additional* sets of milk and meat dishes reserved for the holiday. Whether measured in time, energy, or money, many of these practices come at great expense, yet Jews adhere to them because halakhah so demands. And though less common today, Jewish communities were once empowered to punish those who flagrantly violated halakhah's rules.

These are just some of the compelling reasons to translate halakhah as Jewish law. But the problem with this translation is that it both overestimates and underestimates the role of halakhah and how it functions.

On the overestimating side, the modern ear hears the term "law" and assumes halakhah is the Jewish version of American law, German law, or Uruguayan law: that is, a legal system established by an independent state with the authority to make and enforce its rules within the relevant territory. Halakhah, however, has not generally functioned in a specific country; it is the law of a people, not of a place, which operates outside of (and at cross-purposes with) the power structures of the state or principality where Jews have resided.

Furthermore, halakhah has rarely maintained the autonomy needed to enforce the full range of its regulatory regime or, putting it more bluntly, to be solely "in charge" of Jewish life. Throughout their history, Jews have been subject to political and legal systems that compete with halakhah, and to which halakhah has often accommodated itself. This point will be explored in later chapters; for now, the key idea is that both halakhah's authority to govern and its method of governance are quite different from how American, German, or Uruguayan law regulates those respective countries.

On the *under*estimating side, translating halakhah as Jewish law does not begin to grasp the role it plays in Jewish life. This point is best illustrated by another tale about the study of halakhah, this one very much on earth.

A few years ago, on Shabbat, a flyer was posted on the synagogue of an upper-middle-class Orthodox community outside New York City whose congregants tend to be doctors, lawyers, real-estate developers, businesspeople, and white-collar professionals. The flyer publicized a lecture to be delivered that afternoon by a guest rabbi visiting from another community. Most of the information provided was routine: the rabbi's name, the time and place of the lecture, and the names of the sponsors who made it possible.

On any given weekend, similar announcements can be found in thousands of churches and community centers across the country. Two things however set this flyer apart. One was the topic of the lecture: "Bidding Competitively on Goods or Properties when Others are Previously Involved"—an issue vaguely related to what lawyer's call tortious interference with contract. The other was the rabbi's title: dean of an advanced institute of talmudic study specializing in business and commercial law. It is as if, say, the chair of Harvard Law School's forum on corporate and financial regulation had been invited to share his recondite expertise with the parishioners.

For a law professor who teaches the subject of contract law, these details might be fascinating. But aside from professors of contract law, this is hardly a matter of general interest, and is certainly of dubious appeal to a lay audience—much less to anyone searching for spiritual fulfillment. Indeed, in any other setting in contemporary America, a lecture bearing this title would be delivered by a law professor speaking to students or academic colleagues, or by an attorney addressing practitioners or clients. Further, while these particular congregants saw themselves as bound by halakhah, neither the topic nor the style of presentation was designed to set forth the rules directly relevant to common scenarios of religious observance. Yet on that Shabbat afternoon, nearly 150 laymen—none of whom was an academic specialist and few of whom would ever draft an agreement under Jewish law—came out to hear the rabbi guide them through the byways of the talmudic discussion.

Why? For the 150 people involved the answer is clear. They did not see this as a lecture on law, but rather as an opportunity to participate in a quintessentially spiritual act: the study of Torah. For as the Talmud sees it, the study of Torah, a study often centered on picayune particulars of halakhah, is one of the most pristine forms of divine worship. This activity of *talmud Torah* competes not only with other spiritual pursuits such as prayer and good works, and not only with other intellectual interests like studying philosophy, art, or science, but with virtually every other human activity—up to and including the basic human need of earning a living!

The content of that lecture on Shabbat afternoon dealt with the talmudic rules of contract and property law—many of them indeed similar to what is taught in American law schools. But to those present, the deeper meaning of the discussion could not have been farther from the concerns of business or commercial life. Following the example of God and the angels in the Academy of Heaven, they were engaged in a devotional act of religious worship, connecting to God through debating and analyzing the multifarious legal details contained within the divine Torah.

Nor is studying or sweating over the minutiae of halakhic discussion unique to one New York City suburb. Every day, thousands of men, and increasingly women, around the globe gather in synagogues and office parks, sit in trains or buses, or log in online, to study a double-sided page of Talmud. The program, known as *daf yomi* (a page a day), takes seven-and-a-half years to complete the entire Talmud. In August, 2012, more than 90,000 people crammed into MetLife Stadium—home to the National Football League's two New York City-based teams—to mark the completion of another cycle. (By way of comparison, the stadium held

82,500 people for Superbowl XLIII.) The gathering, however, was neither a sports game, a rock concert, a political rally, or anything remotely akin to what usually draws 90,000 Americans to an event space. Improbable as it sounds, the occasion was the joyous celebration of an enormous and enormously technical legal work of more than 5,400 pages studied each day as a religiously prescribed "hobby."

Roughly 1,600 years ago, a Talmudic sage predicted that "in the future, the stadiums of the Gentiles will be used by Jewish leaders to teach Torah in public" (b.Megillah 6a). For the vast majority of intervening epochs, this declaration could only have been understood as a messianic hope—or a tone-deaf display of delusional hubris. But by 2012, the commitment to Torah study—the very opposite of popular entertainment—could fill one of America's massive colosseums to celebrate the Torah in public.

Though packed stadiums catch our attention, the unique status of Jewish law is even more evident in life's quieter moments. When a parent is critically ill and the child wants to beseech God for a cure, Torah study is an appropriate response. Should the parent pass on, Torah study is a time-honored way to commemorate the departed. The same is true of joyous occasions—weddings, bar mitzvahs, newborn celebrations, graduations, and birthdays—are all commonly punctuated with words of Torah.

It should be clear now why the term "Jewish law" fails to do justice to halakhah. Imagine substituting American law for Jewish law in any of the descriptions above. I have spent a decade and a half among accomplished legal scholars, and am fortunate to know very successful lawyers. Yet I have never been to a stadium full of people celebrating the Constitution, much less the Tax Code; have never heard a law professor address a church group on the details of contract law; and have never seen a parent faced with the joy of new life, or a child with the tragedy of a parent's death, whip out the Uniform Commercial Code in search of inspiration or insight. By contrast, it is hard to imagine *any* private, public, social, religious, or institutional setting where it would not be appropriate to pull out a book and expound on some finer point of Jewish law.

As for the heavens, the typical American view was summed up by Grant Gilmore, one of the twentieth century's best-known law professors (and incidentally, co-author of the Uniform Commercial Code). Gilmore ends his classic book on American legal history as follows:

> The better the society, the less law there will be. In heaven there will be no law.... The worse the society, the more law there will be. In hell there will be nothing but law, and due process will be meticulously observed.[1]

What for the Talmud is heaven, for Gilmore is hell. The difference could not be starker.

So while halakhah is undoubtedly law, it is also something else. What makes identifying that additional quality difficult is that it is not well-theorized in Jewish sources; nor are there many useful parallels in Western systems. This book will argue that halakhah is not only a body of regulations, but a way, a path of thinking, being, and knowing. Over the course of several chapters, we will see how the rabbis use concepts forged in the regulatory framework to do the work other societies assign to philosophy, political theory, theology, and ethics, and even to art, drama, and literature. While halakhah's regulatory ideals are realized through observance of its laws, access to the broader social and religious aims is gained through its study, through *talmud Torah*.

But what happens to law when it is also a foundation for social and theological thought? And what does it mean for speculative reason to be carried out in legal categories? How are legal texts transformed when recited as prayers or read for religious inspiration? How are spiritual teachings transformed when encoded into law? What results when the study of law may take precedence over its practice? And what does it mean for legal analysis to connect man to God? The ensuing chapters constitute an attempt to answer these questions.

Conceptual Introduction to Halakhah

As an introduction, this book is aimed at readers who might not know much about either Jewish law or the state of academic scholarship on the subject. As such, I have considerably simplified halakhic discussions and attempted to provide the necessary background to follow the argument. Similarly, I have kept overt references to academic scholarship and notations rather sparse, even on the many occasions that I have profited from the thinking of other scholars or when the matter is more nuanced than space allows. The same goes for the relatively modest number of endnotes. Instead, I have included a topically organized selection of *Further Readings* at the end of the book designed to point the interested reader to additional resources on the relevant topics.

This book offers a conceptual introduction to halakhah. First, it is conceptual in that it is not doctrinal: that is, it is not an effort to present and explain correct halakhic practice. It does not catalogue or clarify the laws of Shabbat or *kashrut* (kosher laws), or weigh in on current controversies regarding their contemporary application. It is not so much a book *of* halakhah as a book about *how to think of* halakhah.

Second, it is conceptual in that it aims to define the basic parameters of the concept of halakhah. The core argument is that halakhah exists on a spectrum or continuum. At one pole, it functions similarly to how law is classically understood—a system of rules designed to govern human behavior. I refer to this as the conventional, or halakhah-as-regulation view. But the book's central concern is the opposing pole, which is far more difficult to describe. Here, halakhah functions as Torah, as an object of Torah study, and even as literature—with "Torah" used as a catchall phrase to refer to religious teachings and instruction that are broader than what is usually conveyed through the term "law."

The metaphor of opposing poles also suggests that each side exerts a magnetic pull on the range of halakhah as a whole. While there is an undeniable appeal to casting halakhah as law-like rules of regulatory conduct, the countervailing pressures of Torah study pull in the opposite direction and transform concrete rules of behavior into wellsprings of philosophical and religious thought. In a sense, we can think of the two poles as establishing the goalposts, while the "game" of halakhah, and indeed its lived history, plays out on the field between them.

Halakhah-as-Torah is surely the less intuitive approach, and I place more emphasis upon it precisely because it is in greater need of explaining. For while there is often disagreement as to how to apply rules in a given scenario, from a conceptual perspective the idea of halakhah-as-regulation easily corresponds to common understandings of law and its purpose. By contrast, when legal ideas are pursued in the service of broader social and cultural goals, the paradigm of "law" becomes decreasingly useful, and more elaboration is required.

Still, to be clear, I do not argue that every individual mishnah, or every line in the Talmud, or subsequent work of halakhah adheres to the thesis of "halakhah as Torah," in its pure form. There is little doubt that this approach is more dominant in later layers of the Talmud than earlier ones, and that in the medieval period it is more characteristic of northern Europe than North Africa, or that as modernity approaches it is more typical of the Lithuanian school than of either hasidic masters or the worldview of Sephardic halakhists. Rather, the claim is that halakhic discourse moves dialectically between its two poles, and that even when halakhah does tend toward the conventional view, the force of the opposing pole can be detected in the background. The opening chapters elaborate on the idea of halakhah-as-Torah as manifested in the Talmud. Later chapters show how even as the thrust of halakhic analysis moves towards the halakhah-as-law pole, the pull of halakhah-as-Torah continues to register.

Conceptual and Historical Methodology

Lastly, this book is conceptual in the sense that it is neither a historical survey nor a work of history. At the basic level, it does not document the central times, personalities, or places of Jewish law; the degree to which legal doctrines change over time; what were the causes or who were agents of such change; how communities differed from each other or interacted with non-Jewish society; or (with the exception of the final chapter and the Conclusion), even the degree to which Jews have observed the laws of the Talmud and its intepreters.

The purpose of this book is not to document how Jewish law was lived.

Likewise, I have made scant reference to such central figures as the eleventh-century commentator Rashi, arguably the most important commentator on the Talmud, nor devoted much discussion to Sephardic halakhists who came to prominence after the sixteenth century, or to classic works of the nineteenth century, such as R. Israel Meir Kagan's *Mishnah Berurah* or R. Yechiel M. Epstein's *Arukh ha-Shulḥan*. To state the obvious, these omissions are not a comment on the centrality of these works or figures to the halakhic tradition as a whole. The specific persons or historical examples discussed were chosen with one central criteria in mind: to show, in a relatively concise book, how the concepts of halakhah-as-Torah and halakhah-as-regulation played out at critical junctures in the development of halakhic thought.

More significantly, this book approaches halakhah and its history from a legal and phenomenological perspective, rather than the historical one that dominates academic treatment of the subject. The difference between these perspectives was best expressed by the great English legal historian, Frederic W. Maitland (1850–1906), who asked why the English—who had been teaching the history of Roman law in their universities since the High Middle Ages, and who were enthusiastic historians of other legal systems—had not written the history of their own law.

In an essay titled, "Why the History of the English Law Is Not Written," Maitland answers this question by noting that lawyers and historians have different views on what counts as evidence or argument.[2] Historians want to understand the past *qua* past, whereas lawyers always read the past as continuous with the precedents and principles of the present. Maitland cites the example of the thirteenth-century Statute of Merton. To the historian, the meaning of that statute is determined by examining the prevailing political and economic factors and considerations that caused the law to be enacted. For the lawyer, the meaning of the statute depends less on events of the thirteenth century and more about how eminent later judges read and applied it. Where the historian finds records, personal correspondence, and other evidence from the thirteenth century highly probative, these are of limited use to a lawyer who must craft legal arguments. In Maitland's memorable phrasing:

> But is it really the statute of 1236 that [the lawyer] wants to know? No, it is the ultimate result of the interpretations set on the statute by the judges of twenty generations. . . . That process by which old principles and old phrases are charged with new content is from the lawyer's point of view an evolution of the true intent and meaning of the old law; from the historian's point of view it is almost of necessity a process of perversion and misunderstanding. Thus we are tempted to mix up two different logics, the logic of authority and the logic of evidence.

In the latter half of the twentieth century, legal theorists pointed to a similar distinction by contrasting "internal" versus "external" viewpoints of the law. H.L.A. Hart and Ronald Dworkin, two influential scholars who conducted a decades-long debate regarding the central issues of legal theory, nevertheless agreed that the goal of jurisprudence was to make sense of the legal and interpretive practices native to the law itself, commonly called the internal point of view. This perspective is, at the very least, committed to taking the law's categories seriously and offers an account that lives within the normative boundaries established by the legal system. The internal perspective is generally contrasted with approaches that view legal practice from the vantage point of an observer standing outside of it. In Maitland's case the example was history; for both Hart and Dworkin, the eschewed disciplines were sociology, economics, and political science.[3]

The issue identified by Maitland is central to the study of Talmud and halakhah, which like most legal systems consciously reads the texts of different generations and geographies together. In academic circles, however, the study of halakhah and rabbinic texts has been pursued overwhelmingly from the historical or external perspective. The central concerns have revolved around questions such as how the texts came about, who wrote them, and under what social and political conditions, how the texts were influenced by the surrounding culture, what they meant when written, and how their interpretation changed over time.

This external perspective leans towards what, to borrow a phrase from movie-making, we might call the "still-shot" approach to the study of halakhah. The assumption is that to understand any phrase in the Talmud, we must identify when it was written and interpret it in light of who wrote it and what was going on in the world at that time. Each moment, or camera shot, is frozen so as to fix the historical setting and to draw comparisons and contrasts to what came before and after. For a historian, one of the greatest sins is to read the texts of one era through the ideas and assumptions of another. In its more extreme forms, the external perspective insists on such a tight separation between each frame so as to deny that one can say anything meaningful about the concept of halakhah at all. At most, one can study what successive generations of halakhists (along with their supporters and detractors) understood as halakhah.

By contrast, lawyers and theorists working from the internal point of view assume that the texts of halakhah add up to system that can be engaged as a self-standing entity. This form of theorizing tends to view the tradition as a whole or, to extend the metaphor, analyzes the movie as a unit rather than as an aggregate of stills. This does not mean that the entirety of the law is an undifferentiated mass. Just as movies are divisible into acts and scenes, each with its own with mood, lighting, and score, so the legal corpus, or in this case the halakhah, can be divided into periods and movements governed by different assumptions. Still, where the historian aims to uncover in each period what *they* meant, "they" being the individual halakhist under consideration, the legal theorist aims to uncover what *it* means, "it" being the halakhah and the interpretive practices that construct it.[4]

My goal here is not so much to defend my method as to state it clearly. This book is largely an attempt to explain halakhah as experienced from within (or at least the view from within one room) the halakhic castle to an audience standing outside it. Thus, while knowledge of the historical and cultural background is at times central to the thesis, the goal is not to unearth the history of halakhah but to offer a constructive account of the interpretive and conceptual practices presented within it. In this way, this book departs from the dominant paradigm of academic writing on Talmud and halakhah, and follows the examples of works on general legal theory like Hart's *The Concept of Law* and Dworkin's *Law's Empire*, as well as Alasdaire MacIntyre's investigation of competing philosophical traditions in *Whose Justice? Which Rationality?*[5] Halakhah, no less than Western jurisprudence, deserves an informed articulation of its ambient theory.

PART I

The Nature of Halakhah

1

The Idea of Halakhah

Woe to you, teachers of the law and Pharisees, you hypocrites! You give
a tenth of your spices—mint, dill, and cumin. But you have neglected
the more important matters of the law—justice, mercy, and
faithfulness. You should have practiced the latter, without neglecting
the former.

—MATTHEW 23:23

Savory, hyssop, and thyme:
When they grow in the courtyard and are watched over,
they are deemed food and are obligated in the tithe.

—MISHNAH MA'ASROT 3:9

The Descent into Law: from the Bible to the Mishnah

To make sense of the idea of law cultivated by the talmudic rabbis, we
start by contrasting it to the view found in the Hebrew Bible.

Scripture places great emphasis on recognizing God as the creator of
the universe, that God chose the Jewish people from among the nations,
that God commanded them to live a life according to specific laws, and
worship only the one God of the Torah. The Bible is particularly concerned with the political consequences of God's choice of the Jewish
people, and its commandments focus on the nation and its institutions.
Though it contains some legal minutiae, legal dialogue and analysis
are conspicuously absent from the biblical verse. Instead, we see a few

central themes repeated again and again: worshipping one God, avoiding idolatry, honoring Shabbat, preserving sexual morality, and taking care of the less fortunate. The Bible's religious consciousness—the categories it uses to understand God's message—center on national/ political institutions such as the Temple, priesthood, prophecy, and the monarchy. In the Bible's ideal world, Jews live as a nation that follows the divine word.

The rabbis of the Talmud, too, held that God is the Creator and had chosen the Jewish people. For the rabbis, however, living God's will requires considerably more detailed knowledge of what the law mandates than a plain reading of the Bible lets on. To observe Shabbat one must know precisely when it begins, when it ends, and what "observing" entails. Similarly, refraining from idol worship requires a refined understanding of what acts constitute worship and which belief systems are deemed idolatrous. The talmudic sages held the laws of the Bible cannot be practiced until they are translated into more particular and detailed categories.

This, broadly speaking, is the project of the Mishnah, a code-like document compiled in the land of Israel in the second and third centuries C.E., which constitutes the foundation of rabbinic halakhah.

A critical difference between the worldviews of the Bible and the rabbis comes to light when examining the term *"mitzvah."* In the Bible, both the singular and plural forms of this term refer to the overall content of God's teachings and commandments. Throughout Deuteronomy, the people are implored "to follow the mitzvah which God has commanded"—that is, the whole of God's instructions. In the hands of the rabbis, however, the term gains a more concrete meaning: a mitzvah is a particular instance of halakhic-legal obligation. The rabbis held that the Torah is comprised of 613 individual *mitzvot*, each a foundational source of law. The Mishnah's goal is to articulate the scope of the mitzvot along with the rabbinic laws and enactments designed to expand and fortify them.

A second difference lies in the terminology used to talk about mitzvot. The Bible presents them within a series of grand theological and national narratives: the exodus from Egypt, the revelation at Sinai, the conquest of the land of Israel, and so forth. The Mishnah, however, analyzes the mitzvot in terms of their legal parameters. The Bible asks whether the Jewish nation is living in accordance with God's commandments. The Mishnah asks more specifically whether an individual is liable (*ḥayav*) or exempt (*patur*); whether certain foodstuffs are prohibited (*assur*) or permitted (*mutar*); and whether someone has discharged the obligation (*yatzah*) or failed to discharge it (*lo yatzah*).

Developing a Halakhic Consciousness

We can see the rabbis' halakhic consciousness at work in their analysis of the Torah's first mitzvah. The opening chapter in Genesis records, "God blessed [Adam and Eve] and said to them 'Be fruitful and multiply, fill the earth and subdue it.'" (1:28) On its face, this instruction does not explain what (if any) specific action is called for. Indeed, it has been reasonably interpreted as a poetic description of things to come, or a charge or blessing to humankind generally. The rabbis, however, understand it as a specific mitzvah that generates a legal duty incumbent every individual (male) Jew. To satisfy the legal requirement, the Mishnah rules that each male must sire at least two children. The Mishnah then presents a debate: in one view (held by students of the first-century mishnaic sage, Shammai), two male children are required; in the other (held by students of Shammai's frequent interlocutor, Hillel), the requirement is for one male and one female (m.Yevamot 6:6).

This snippet of Mishnah highlights two foundations of rabbinic law echoed in the narrative about the Academy of Heaven encountered in the introduction. First, it articulates specific directives: compare the Bible's "be fruitful and multiply" with the Mishnah's "have two children." Second, law is an object of analysis and debate. While the general framework (two children) is offered without any reservation, different views arise in considering the particulars. Finally, by preserving that debate, the Mishnah suggests that something is at stake here—the rule is *worth* debating.

Having assumed a legal framework, the Talmud—an elaborate commentary on the Mishnah compiled in the centuries following the

Mishnah's dissemination—investigates numerous derivative questions. What happens if the children themselves cannot reproduce—do they "count" toward fulfilling the halakhic obligation? What if the children die—must the father have more? If the deceased children lived long enough to have had children of their own, do these grandchildren count in lieu of the deceased parents (b.Yevamot 63a)?

Following the Talmud's lead, later generations of rabbinic scholars pushed these issues even farther. What if the child is the product of an illicit relationship (e.g., incest or adultery)? What if the children develop reproductive deficiencies?

Halakhic consciousness is defined by precisely these sorts of questions. Since the goal is to live in accord with the divine will, a person must know—with exacting precision—what is required for that purpose. Early halakhic texts establish the basic framework, while subsequent layers analyze, debate, and expand its details and applications.

Another example: though the biblical text prohibits *melakhah*—typically translated as "work" or "labor"—on Shabbat, it provides limited guidance as to what exactly this phrase means. The Mishnah, for its part, presents thirty-nine base categories of prohibited activities, one of which is writing (m.Shabbat 12:1–6). Here we learn that while a person who writes only one letter is exempt, one who writes two letters is liable for violating Shabbat. Use of ink, dye, or permanent liquids generates liability; while colored water or etchings in the dirt do not. Writing with the hand is a problem; writing with the foot, mouth, or elbow is not. Cases even more unusual than these are also taken under consideration, for example writing one letter on the ceiling and another on the floor, or two single letters on separate pieces of paper that are later put together. In the modern era, halakhists discussed whether it is permitted to piece together a puzzle on Shabbat (potentially problematic since it creates an intelligible picture) or to play Scrabble (generally okay, but in the Deluxe Edition the board's grooves hold the letters in place more permanently and may thereby produce a "writing").[1]

Legalized specification of this kind is carried out through thousands of rules contained in the nearly 4,000 compact paragraphs of the Mishnah. Some instances are prosaic: laws about the hiring of workers, buying foodstuffs, dealing with nosy neighbors (found in tractates Bava Metzia and Bava Batra). Some are intensely personal: the intricacies of how women diagnose the onset and completion of their menstrual cycles (tractate Nidda). Some are obscure: an entire tractate of the Mishnah discusses how to proceed when birds designated for one Temple offering become commingled with birds intended for a different offering (tractate Kinim). And some are positively bizarre: several paragraphs of Mishnah discuss groups of men wandering around taking bets—in the form of whether they will be obligated in nazarite vows—based on the identity of different animals and persons that cross their paths (m.Nazir 5:5).

Over the vast range of its topics, the Mishnah's common thread is the centrality of its legally structured categories.

The Kingdom of Halakhah

For all its complexity, the Mishnah is but the ground floor of the halakhic edifice. Over the period of the Talmud, and then in later rabbinic literature, the halakhic consciousness thickens, encompassing an even larger range of intellectual and spiritual topics investigated through the lens of law. There are times when it seems that the Talmud knows nothing but law.

An example is the retelling of the biblical narrative surrounding David and Saul. The relationship between these two figures is, to put it mildly, complicated. David is a young war hero and prominent army officer who becomes Saul's prophetic muse, the best friend of his son Jonathan, the object of his daughter's love, and eventually his son-in-law. David was also Saul's primary political rival, the focus of several failed assassination attempts initiated by Saul, and eventually the successor to—or, as Saul might have said, the usurper of—the royal throne.

David first comes to Saul's attention when the mighty Goliath, the celebrated champion of the Philistines, taunts the Israelite camp for lacking the courage to confront him. In want of better options, Saul promises "great wealth and his daughter in marriage" to whoever shall slay the formidable heathen warrior (1 Sam. 17:25). David takes up the challenge. His success in killing Goliath launches his meteoric rise and rapid displacement of Saul as the nation's beloved. Saul, always one to hold a grudge, first reneges on the promise of his first daughter and then offers the hand of another daughter, Michal, for the price of 100 Philistine foreskins, not-so-subtly assuming David would die in his effort to procure them. When David returns with not 100, but 200 enemy foreskins in hand, Saul hastens to give Michal in marriage to another man (1 Sam. 25:44). Later, when he assumes the throne after Saul's demise in battle, David demands "my wife Michal, for whom I paid the bride-price of 100 Philistine foreskins" from the deceased king's household (2 Sam. 3:14).

This is a story about power plays and palace intrigue; about family, passion, and jealousy; about alliances formed and allegiances broken. Its purpose is to demonstrate why David, and not Saul, is worthy of establishing the royal dynasty. The Talmud, however, re-reads it through a thoroughly halakhic lens (t.Sotah 11:9; b.Sanhedrin 19b). Ignored are the drama, the emotion, the egoism, and all the juicy details of human life that course through the biblical saga. Instead, the Talmud focuses on a legal conundrum: if David was halakhically betrothed to Michal, how could Saul give her in marriage to someone else? And if they were not legally bound, how could David (who, as God's chosen king, would never utter an extra-halakhic statement) demand "my wife" from Saul's household? In the talmudic view, David and Saul clashed not with swords, but with refined arguments, engaging in what the sages intentionally called "the battle of Torah." (More on this in chapter 5.) Per talmudic law, when a man gives a woman (or her father) an item bearing at least nominal value, she becomes formally committed to marry him. This betrothed status, known as *kiddushin,* cannot be created "through a loan", a category that includes forgiveness of a debt that the woman (or her father) owes the prospective groom. A debate arises, however, when someone seeks *kiddushin* through both forgiveness of a debt *and* the provision of an item of (at least) nominal value. Does the offer to forgive the debt invalidate the entire *kiddushin,* or is the *kiddushin* still formed through receipt of the item of value?

This, as the Talmud sees it, this was the real point at issue between David and Saul. David's proposal of *kiddushin* rested both on his forgiving of the "great reward" promised to Goliath's slayer (i.e., the debt owed him by Saul), *and* on the king's receipt of the nominally valuable Philistine foreskins. Since this was an effective *kiddushin*, Michal had become his lawful wife—or so he thought. Saul, however, held differently: the *kiddushin* was halakhically ineffective due to David forgiving Saul's debt/promise, leaving Michal free to marry another.

Underlying the talmudic discussion is, obviously (!), the assumption that David and Saul were not only fully committed to halakhah but conversant in its nuanced detail—details the talmudic rabbis were still debating thousands of years later. It's hard to know how seriously this should be taken. Did the talmudic rabbis really think David and Saul were arguing over the legal technicalities of *kiddushin*, or, did the biblical narrative simply offer a familiar reference point on which to sharpen their students' skills in halakhic reasoning?

Either way, the discussion offers a window into the rabbinic mindset. Since, halakhah is the framework through which reality can be interpreted, no detail is too small, no distinction too fine, and no case too remote to escape analysis and regulation.

Jesus's Critique of Halakhah

A nascent version of the legalism at work in the passage we've just examined is likely what prompted the critiques ascribed to Jesus against the Pharisees, the forebears of the Mishnah's authors. Throughout the Christian Gospels, Jesus claims the Pharisees' exclusive focus on the precise details of religious practice led them to mistake the legal trees for the spiritual forest. Jesus charges the Pharisees with hypocrisy for worrying about legal trifles like tithing "mint, dill, and cumin" while "neglecting the weightier matters of the law—justice, mercy, and faith" (Matthew 23:23). The same line of attack recurs in many of the arguments between Jesus and the Pharisees over the laws of, among other topics, Shabbat, kashrut, and ritual purity.[2]

This trend becomes more extreme in the writings of the apostle Paul (who had been a Pharisee himself). Paul encapsulates the difference between what he saw as the law-obsessed Pharisees and the God-focused early Christians in his famous phrase "for while the letter [of the law] kills, the Spirit gives life" (2 Corinthians 3:6). The same notes can be heard in writings of early church fathers.[3]

In many ways, these charges preceeded Jesus and Paul by several centuries. The biblical prophets Isaiah and Jeremiah chastised the people for focusing on Temple rituals rather than interpersonal conduct and the need for social justice. (For example, Isaiah 1:10–17; Jeremiah chapter 7.) But whereas the earlier prophets criticized the Temple rituals generally, Jesus zeroed in on the technical distinctions that, though rare in the Bible, are typical of rabbinic thought. In time, Jesus would be joined by a long line of critics—medieval and modern, Jewish and non-Jewish, polemic and apologetic, sympathetic and avowedly anti-Semitic.[4] The details would change, but the core criticism remained: by emphasizing the legal particular, halakhah inevitably blinds itself to the more relevant ethical, philosophical, and theological dimensions of God's revelation.

Was Jesus Right?

It might seem strange—perhaps a bit blasphemous—to introduce Jesus, of all people, at such an early point in our story. But precisely because his critique has framed both Jewish and non-Jewish understandings for centuries, it is worth taking seriously right at the outset.

A quick glance at the Mishnah reveals that Jesus was not wholly off base. He chastises the Pharisees for fussing over questions like the tithing of herbs—and it is true, the Mishnah does not find these questions the least bit trivial. As Mishnah Ma'aserot(3:9) explains, if "savory, hyssop, and thyme" are deemed foods, they require tithing; if they are merely plants, they will be exempt. Jesus also ridicules the Pharisees for focusing on the syntax of an oath rather than its substance—and yes, the very syntactical variations he disparages matter a great deal in the Talmud (b.Nedarim 10b–11a). In short, Jesus correctly diagnosed that the Mishnah and the rabbinic tradition that grew out of it tend to refract the human experience through legal-analytical prism.

Like all disciplines, the legal perspective illuminates some facets while crowding out others. Law is particularly useful for establishing and regulating the standards of compliance. When the Torah mandates that persons purify themselves via immersion in a pool of water (*mikveh*), the Mishnah offers ten chapters on what is meant by *immerse*, what qualifies as a *pool*, what defines *in*, and what halakhah deems *water*. And yes, these discrete legal rules are less suited for thinking about the ritual's broader goals and purposes, what Jesus calls the "the weightier matters," such that scarcely a word of the Mishnah's discussion of *mikveh* is devoted to articulating the spiritual transformation immersion is held to accomplish.

Quite the contrary: the halakhic consciousness first expressed in the Mishnah becomes even thicker in later sources. For example, the Mishnah presents a case of one who immerses in a *mikveh* later found to have lacked the minimum amount of water required (m.Mikvaot 2:2). In the mishnaic text, the focus is local and case-specific; it asks only whether immersion is valid. The Talmud, however, uses the ruling to elaborate more wide-ranging legal concepts, understanding this particular mishnah as establishing a presumption to be employed in any case when the exact moment of a legally significant event is unknown (b.Kiddushin 79a). These include: when *exactly* are barrels of wine deemed to have turned to vinegar (relevant to the laws of tithing)? When does a young woman approaching the age of maturity formally cross the line from minor to adult (relevant if competing marriage proposals are accepted at or around the transition point)? If a terminally ill person recovers from illness, at what *exact* moment does this transition from moribund to viability occur (relevant if transactions were conducted in the interim)? Though the conceptual-legal analysis is sophisticated, the Talmud pays scant attention to the theological or philosophical significance of *mikveh* immersion and its rules.

True, here and there, the talmudic sages offer statements regarding the meaning or purpose of a given mitzvah. In both the Talmud and in later sources, they speak not only in the language of law but also in the more evocative language of *aggadah*—(rabbinic narratives and storytelling), and function not only as lawyers but as inspirational preachers, social critics, moralizers, spiritual counselors, storytellers, and scriptural exegetes. Yet these discussions rarely coalesce into sustained analytical investigations, and generally lack the thoroughness and acuity of the Talmud's legal project. Though aggadah plays an important role, the overall thrust of the Mishnah and Talmud is undeniably legal.

While the differences between Jesus and the rabbis are rooted in the Christian Bible, they continue to resonate to this day. In the modern discourse, the motivation to do the right thing is expressed in terms of "values," "morals," or "ethical obligations." Contemporary Christians refer to their religious imperatives as stemming from "moral theology," "church doctrine," "religious teachings," "vocations" or the "Christian calling." For halakhic Jews, by contrast, religious commitments reside in a distinctly legal framework. Visiting the sick, honoring one's parents, giving charity (*tzedakah*), and returning lost objects may *also* be matters of morality, but they are first of all halakhic-legal obligations that carry defined properties and regulations.

For all the change over the past two millennia, the heirs of Jesus and the talmudic rabbis continue to argue over the proper role of legal thought in religious life. [5]

The Traditional Response—Law Is Not Everything

Jesus's complaints against halakhah have not gone unanswered. One form of response has been that this critique wrongly equates halakhah, or halakhism, with Judaism. In other words, Jesus and his latter followers failed to appreciate the different elements of the Jewish tradition that complement the law: the Bible, aggadah, the mystical tradition, midrashic exegesis, and so forth. When seen in its totality, Jewish religious thought is far more diverse than talmudic legalism.

A second type of response argues that, while the legal literature tells us much about the rabbis' aspirations for Judaism, it is much less informative about how Jews actually lived. In reality, according to this perspective, both commoners and educated dissenters maintained a far less legalistic conception of their religion than presented in the core halakhic texts; indeed, at many historical junctures, awareness of and adherence to halakhah were all but non-existent. Jews, in other words, have understood man's relationship to God in a variety of ways. There are more "Judaisms" than what is presented in the Talmud.[6]

There is much truth to both of these responses. Halakhah has never subsumed the entirety of rabbinic—much less Jewish—life. And we should not confuse the views of a rabbinic elite with those of the masses, nor assume that the image of halakhah found in one period is necessarily the same as earlier or later understandings.[7] Yet at their core, these responses concede the central claim: insofar as the subject is the corpus of halakhah, Jesus was correct. They differ only as to the relative importance of this corpus to Jewish life and to the intellectual and cultural traditions of the Jews.

A third response also effectively concedes Jesus's claim but celebrates it as a point of pride. Adherents of this approach argue that other religions are based on theological concepts that cannot be proven and fuzzy ideas of spirituality based on the subjective feelings of the individual believer. Because halakhah is armed with precise and legally rigorous categories mandated from the divine, it affords a religious experience that is God-given, rather than man-driven.[8]

If Law Is Everything, Everything Is Law

So where does this leave us? In this book, we will take our bearings from the premise that halakhah (a) is central to the identity and ideology of the rabbis, and (b) has played a significant role in creating and transmitting Jewish identity. But these premises are not incompatible with granting that Jesus and Paul were not wholly off-base in chastising early iterations of what would become halakhic thought for focusing on legal categories to the apparent exclusion of other religious and ethical issues. For in truth, prior to the modern period, rabbinic Judaism did not distinguish itself through its contributions to the humanities—whether in philosophy or ethics, arts, or sciences.

Jesus, however, missed a crucial point. Precisely because halakhah loomed so large in the rabbinic consciousness, it became the medium through which the rabbis did in fact engage the weightier matters of the law. This is true not only of halakhah—law in the narrowest sense of the term—but also the way the rabbis' project merges halakhic dialogue with storytelling, biblical exegesis, and theological reflection. Halakhah is both a body of regulation and the core element in the rabbis' culture and worldview.

As we saw in the introduction, the ability of halakhah to fulfill these multiple roles is enabled by two distinctive features: first, since at least as far back as the Mishnah, halakhah has never been the law of a state; and second, the ideals of *talmud Torah*. These factors set halakhah within a social and theological framework that inescapably blurs the lines between legal decision-making and the theoretical analysis of legal concepts; between rabbinic legislation and biblical interpretation, between operative rules and the stories, folklore, social criticism, and other material found in the Talmud's pages. It is the fluidity between halakhah-as-law and halakhah-as-Torah that enables it to assume its diverse roles.

We'll develop these points in the three chapters that follow.

2

Non-Applied Law

The [case of the] rebellious son never was, nor will it ever come to be.
Why then was it legislated?

    To say, study it and receive reward.

—TOSEFTA SANHEDRIN 11:2

The [case of the] rebellious city never was, nor will it ever come to be.
Why then was it legislated?

    To say, study it and receive reward.

—TOSEFTA SANHEDRIN 14:1

The [case of the] infested house never was, nor will it ever come to be.
Why then was it legislated?

    To say, study it and receive reward.

—TOSEFTA NEGAIM 6:1

TO UNDERSTAND THE WAYS in which halakhah is Jewish law *and* the ways in which it is not, we need a working definition of law. Debates over this concept have been ongoing for millennia and will not be resolved here. But most agree that law is a system that governs social behavior within a given political community. In the modern setting, the state is the most common form of political community.

In this thumbnail sketch, the state issues the laws that set the boundaries between the state and the individual and those which govern how citizens interact with each other. Law thus determines how the U.S. Congress passes a bill and how one establishes a corporation, as well as the scope of its powers and liabilities. Law decides whether the boundary line between two neighbors is the fence on the property or the deed tucked away in the county clerk's office, or whether an absentee father will be forced to pay child support. Law determines who owns what, who has rights to what, and how conflicts over these are resolved. Law, in short, tells us how to live together, and the state is charged with appointing the officers, judges, and bureaucrats authorized to interpret and apply it.

This state-centric account is not the only way to think about law. What, for instance, is the *source* of law? Some contend the ultimate source is human nature itself, which is then reflected in the laws of the state. For example, murder is not merely illegal because the state's law says so; rather, the state punishes murder because it is inherently evil. Others maintain that we don't need a state to have law, as law can emerge from the accumulated social practices of the underlying community. So when enough people start using online contracts, it becomes the law even before formal doctrines catch up and recognize this fact.

But regardless of whether law is the command of the state, an expression of values and ideas ingrained in human nature, or social convention, the definition of law coalesces around a central case: a system of governance residing in a political community where there is a reasonable possibility the law will be enforced.

It is this practical element of law—who is entitled to health care, who owns the oil reserves under the ocean floor, whether a CEO is personally liable when a factory owned by the corporation pollutes the drinking water—that makes it worth studying and knowing. Law is important because it governs. Law gets things done.

Halakhah, however, is not the law of any state. As classically understood, halakhah is part of the "oral Torah" that God revealed alongside the "written Torah" to Moses at Sinai. Whereas the latter became the cornerstone of the Bible, the former was transmitted from teacher to student down through the ages. Halakhah as we know it first became visible in the early centuries of the Common Era when rabbinic sages developed the teachings that eventually took form in the Mishnah and the *midrash halakhah*—the latter being a verse-by verse reading of the Torah that teases out its legal rules.

These sages, however, did not function within a politically autonomous society. Nor was this law developed to respond to the challenges of governance. For the most part, halakhah is a product of a theological condition known as *galut* (also pronounced *golus*). Literally translated as "exile," *galut* signified the understanding that, on account of their sins, Jews inhabited a compromised political, legal, and spiritual reality. Politically, *galut* meant Jews were subjugated to foreign rulers and no longer in possession of the central institutions of the biblical system: the monarchy, priesthood, prophecy, and the Temple. Legally, *galut* meant that halakhah had to function without the supreme legislative/judicial body known as the Sanhedrin, and therefore cannot adjudicate or enforce significant areas of halakhah. Spiritually, *galut* meant that the Temple lay in ruins, and the people were unworthy of the religious stature enjoyed by their forbearers. *Galut* is the spiritual account for why the lived reality of Judaism strayed so far from the ideals set forth in the Bible.

In many ways, the condition of *galut* began already in the biblical period, and was certainly in full force after the Babylonians destroyed the First Temple in 586 BCE. The current *galut* is generally associated with the destruction of the Second Temple in 70 CE by the Romans. From that time onward, as one noted scholar expresses it, Jewish religious and political life has been in a holding pattern, suspended between the ideal of the biblical past and the anticipated salvation of the messianic future.[1] It is in this context that halakhah as we know it developed.

Despite these sub-optimal conditions, halakhah thrived in *galut*. Virtually every work of halakhah—from the Mishnah, to the Jerusalem and Babylonian Talmuds, to the medieval commentaries of Rashi, Tosafot, and the twelfth-century code of Maimonides (*Mishneh Torah*), to the sixteenth-century *Shulḥan Arukh*, to the great works of scholarship issuing from the yeshivot of the nineteenth century—are all products of *galut*.

And yet, notwithstanding these monumental achievements, whose substance we will sample as we go along, the ideology of *galut* cast a long shadow over the entire halakhic enterprise. In its own self-image, halakhah stands as an inherently compromised legal regime, incapable of realizing its regulatory ideal.

The Law of the "As If"

While *galut* rendered Judaism's central institutions inoperable, one of halakhah's most astonishing features is that—at least some of the time—it has spoken ***as if*** it governs a broad array of public institutions. Perhaps the most famous example is the talmudic discussion regarding the law of capital punishment.

On the surface, little in the Mishnah's treatment of capital punishment reveals that by the time these texts were disseminated, these laws were no longer operative. Five of tractate Sanhedrin's eleven chapters are devoted to these laws—three to the underlying offenses, and two to the penal procedures themselves. And yet, in the rabbis' own recounting, the Sanhedrin—the High Court that sat in Jerusalem—ceded its capital jurisdiction forty years prior to the Temple's destruction in 70 CE (b.Sanhedrin 41a; b.Shabbat 15a; b.Avodah Zarah 8b), well before the Mishnah's publication. Further, by all accounts no such institution functioned after the fall of Jerusalem and the full assumption of Roman rule, and the Mishnah itself describes considerable hesitancy over administering capital punishment.

Despite the practical irrelevance of capital punishment, however, the Mishnah, and later the Talmud, developed an elaborate procedure detailing how it would be—or should be—administered. Further, when discussing the topic, the Mishnah does not speak of an idealized past, but rather in declarative tones of the governing present. For example, a mishnah in the first chapter of Sanhedrin unproblematically states that "capital cases are adjudicated in a court of twenty-three [judges]" (m. Sanhedrin 1:4). Later on, it describes the details of the procedure as follows (m.Sanhedrin 6:3):

> When the convict was four ells away from the place of
> stoning he would be undressed:

> A male is covered one part in front,
> and a woman—two parts in front and one in the rear.
> These are the words of Rabbi Yehuda.
>
> But the Sages say:
> a male is stoned naked,
> but a woman is not stoned naked.

The Mishnah does not think in terms of past or present. It simply declares what the halakhah *is*.[2] Locating when or where this halakhah applies in time or space is not part of the Mishnah's agenda.

Since few areas are more symbolic of the law's power to govern than its ability to kill those who violate its rules, the mismatch between the idealized halakhah of capital punishment and the facts on the ground creates one of the most striking illustrations of the halakhah of "as if." But the same holds true for the mishnaic halakhah relating to many public institutions: the practices of the Temple, the political system of kings, tribal leaders, prophets, and the procedures of the Sanhedrin itself—all told, constituting a significant portion of the mishnaic corpus. By the time the Mishnah came to be compiled, many of these institutions were distant memories, a fact freely noted in rabbinic literature. Yet, the Mishnah adopts an as-if jurisprudence; detailing regulations *as if* the Temple in Jerusalem stood in all its splendor; *as if* the Jewish people were sovereign in their land; *as if* the Sanhedrin exercised its powers; and *as if* Jewish criminal law was routinely enforced in accord with mishnaic doctrines.

But even if we assume that the Mishnah speaks of an era when the Sanhedrin enjoyed the full panoply of its powers, executing a criminal under talmudic law would still be all but impossible. Though many specific elements contribute to the legal nullification of talmudic capital punishment, none is more striking than the process by which the criminal had to consent verbally to his judicial execution, known as *hatra'ah* (literally, warning).

Writing in the twelfth century, Maimonides summarized the Talmud's thinking on this matter:

How would the witnesses warn the criminal? They instruct him to "cease" [the criminal act] or tell him "do not commit the crime, since it is a transgression and you are liable the death penalty or lashes for it." If he ceased, he is exempt. Similarly, if he was silent or nodded his head, he is exempt. Even if he said "I know," he is exempt—until he submits himself to be executed and says: "I am acting on the understanding [that I will be put to death]." In this case he is executed. Further, he needs to commit the crime within a moment of being warned. If he waited more than a moment, another warning is required. (MT, Laws of Sanhedrin 12:2)

A system requiring the criminal to verbally consent is unlikely to be very effective in punishing or deterring crime. So it's not surprising that the entire corpus of rabbinic literature records only a handful of incidents of capital punishment. And in each case, the Talmud explains why this was a unique situation that did not conform to the strict procedural requirements developed in the (later) halakhic sources.[3]

Nor is the requirement of hatra'ah limited to cases of capital punishment, which one hopes would be rare in any legal system. According to many commentators, the same rules apply to the (theoretically) more commonplace punishment of flogging or lashes, the standard sanction for mid-grade infractions of Jewish law.[4] As with capital punishment, nothing in the Talmud's presentation indicates these punishments were anything but routine. Listing more than sixty categories of offenses subject to lashes, the Mishnah discusses the finer points of the procedure like the size and thickness of the whip; the positioning of the flogger, the flogged, and the court crier; the verbal declarations assigned to each party; and the rather obscure requirement that the total number of lashes be divisible by three (m.Makkot 3:10–14). Yet, in applying hatra'ah to lashes, this lesser punishment becomes no more practicable than the death penalty.

Here too, we should not be surprised to find little evidence (either in or out of rabbinic literature) suggesting that someone was flogged in accordance with the procedures detailed in the Talmud. And because, other than fines, flogging and capital punishment represented the *only* judicially imposed criminal sanctions mandated by the Torah and recognized by the formal halakhah, we could legitimately conclude that much of halakhah—on its own account—was effectively unenforceable.

This leads to the most confusing aspect of all: neither the remoteness nor even impossibility of applying halakhah does anything to dampen the rabbis' ardor for legislating and debating its rules and procedures. Take, for example, the Mishnah's requirement that in the first stage of "stoning," the convict is pushed off a two-story ledge. Proceeding from this rule, the Talmud quotes Shmuel, a third century *amora* (rabbi of the talmudic era), who maintains that the prosecution's witnesses must take an active role in the execution, since the biblical verse intimates that the "hands" that witnessed the crime should be the ones that shove the criminal to his death (b.Sanhedrin 45a). Not satisfied with even this level of detail, the Talmud further elaborates that if one of the witnesses happens to have lost a hand in the period between observing the crime and the time of the execution, the convict cannot be executed. This position is later adopted as governing halakhah.[5] (The rule is different if the witness lost his hand *prior* to observing the criminal act!)

Leaving aside the substantive strangeness of this rule, it is worth retracing the gap between the talmudic discussion and what can be imagined as a governing reality. Standing alone, the elaborate warning requirements make capital punishment all but impossible. But even granting that we can locate a criminal who has verbally submitted himself to execution, the Talmud thinks it necessary to discuss how this law applies in the unlikely scenario that a witness' hand was cut off between having observed the crime and the execution—all based on the teachings of a sage born more than a century after the Sanhedrin could even theoretically execute anyone. And this rule, and many similar to it, would continue to occupy scholars in subsequent generations who gave scant attention to the reality or probability of putting these rulings into practice.

The Talmud contains hundreds, likely thousands, of details that relate to the intricacies of legal institutions far removed from the Babylonian context of the talmudic era. Nor is this tendency limited to areas of criminal or Temple-based ritual law. It is equally present in more commonplace examples like civil fines, which were beyond the jurisdictional authority of the Babylonian rabbis. More prevalent still are talmudic discussions of thousands of legal specifics whose likelihood is so infinitesimally small that it is hard to see why anyone would worry about them. Examples include the ritual status of a basket eaten and then excreted (whole) by an elephant, whether a farmer who attempts to plow his field with a goat and a fish violates the commandment against putting animals of different species together under a yoke, and, the perennial favorite, the legal fortunes of a man who fell off a roof and inseminated a woman. (Respectively, b.Bava Batra 22a; b.Bava Kamma 55a; and b.Bava Kamma 27a.)

Throughout Jewish history rabbis continued to study, debate, and produce halakhah on topics far removed from practical questions of governance with the same rigor given to issues of halakhah that formed the backbone of daily practice. At the same time, the most basic questions of legal and political theory remain unarticulated. Even the tradition's greatest scholars rarely discussed when, how, and to what effect this system could or can govern.

Historical Accident or Essential Feature?

Most of what we have said thus far is familiar to students of the Mishnah and Talmud. But the common reaction to it proceeds as follows: true, the talmudic rabbis continued to promulgate rules after the relevant institutions ceased to function, but their *initial* formulation reflected law in the more conventional sense. It was only later, once the Temple no longer stood and the Sanhedrin disbanded, when the circumstances of *galut* relegated these central institutions to historical memory, that the rabbis persisted in studying the rules as a way of memorializing the past. But even then it was because they believed the institutions would be re-established in the messianic future. Their goal, as such, was to preserve and develop the law in prayerful anticipation of its reapplication.

This claim can be strengthened by noting that the Mishnah and Talmud are keenly aware of their own *galut*-based status, and the Mishnah frequently registers shifts in halakhic practice traceable to the destruction of the Temple. That being so, one might argue that the rabbis themselves readily distinguished halakhic ideal from exilic reality. If we grant for the moment the historical accuracy of such a claim (itself subject to much debate), we could stipulate that many rules of the Talmud are mechanisms for articulating the aspirations for how Jewish society will be governed when the messiah arrives. We could also stipulate that these functions are critically important to a culture that sees its legal regime as suspended between the biblical past and messianic future.

Even so, we should note in passing that this is certainly a very different use of legal rules from the way in which law, particularly state law, is conventionally understood. But moreover, while this analysis provides a useful starting point, it fails to capture the complexity involved. First, in a number of cases the Mishnah records the halakhah applying to conditions that existed in the past but will not—by anyone's recounting—govern in the future. For example, it discusses the status under current circumstances of a leprous skin blemish that emerged prior to the giving of the Torah at Sinai (m.Negaim 7:1). Elsewhere, it speaks of someone who *designates* an animal for sacrifice during the historical era when offerings brought outside the Temple compound were permitted, but *offers* it in an era when such offerings are prohibited (and in the Mishnah's own view, will never be permitted again) (m.Zevaḥim 14:8–9). Likewise, the Mishnah discusses specific rules for a ceremony mandated by Moses and carried out by Joshua, 1,500 years prior to the Mishnah, and which is never to be repeated (m.Sotah 7:5). Notably, this never-to-be-applied-again halakhah is fully enmeshed within some of the most commonly practiced rituals described in the entire Mishnah, including the twice-daily recitation of the *Shema* and the thrice-daily recitation of the *Amidah*.

In these cases, the Mishnah is not preserving rules for future reapplication—they will never apply again. Rather, it is recasting biblical events into the language of law where they are analyzed alongside practices that apply in the present.

To this point we have largely been dealing with evidence drawn from the Talmudic corpus itself. But the questions become even stronger in light of modern historical scholarship which seriously questions whether capital executions were *ever* carried out according to the specific legal prescriptions of the Mishnah and Talmud, and indeed, whether the Sanhedrin *ever* functioned in the way these rabbinic texts describe. Although there is good evidence that an institution called the Sanhedrin functioned towards the end of the Second Temple era, few historians think it operated under the many nuanced halakhic strictures proscribed in rabbinic texts. For example, the first mishnah of tractate Sanhedrin posits not just that a Great Sanhedrin of seventy judges sat in Jerusalem, but that it exercised authority over an entire network of tribal Sanhedrins. Yet, as far back as the early Second Temple era, the tribes ceased to constitute a meaningful political entity, and most of the tribes no longer existed. Even earlier, in the biblical era, there is little evidence of a system of tribal courts subject to a "federal" bureaucracy centered in Jerusalem.[6]

In a similar vein, the Mishnah teaches that the Great Sanhedrin exercised halakhic jurisdiction over kings and high priests and over the decision to declare war. Though kings certainly went to war and high priests committed crimes, it is doubted whether leading officials of the late Second Commonwealth era saw themselves as subject to the jurisdiction of a halakhic court. In fact, the Talmud itself acknowledges at times that jurisdiction over the monarch was more aspirational than actual[7]—and that the Sanhedrin did not always adhere to the procedures detailed in the halakhic sources.[8]

Then, too, many of the Temple's laws may similarly be aspirational and theoretical. Although the historical record confirms that the Temple stood in Jerusalem, and sacrifices were offered on its altar, the Mishnah and Talmud divide and sub-divide sacrificial rituals into scores of classifications, each with its own set of reticulated procedures, triggering mechanisms, and disqualifying events. Did the Temple—at any point in its history—function in accordance with the exact specifications demanded by the Mishnah? And if so, did it incorporate the many further refinements established by the Babylonian amoraim and subsequent redactors of the Talmud? And what are we to make of all the detailed practices debated three centuries later and half a continent away?

Again, from a historical perspective, it is very difficult to answer such questions with a simple "yes."[9] While anecdotes about specific Temple rituals are sprinkled throughout the rabbinic corpus, rulings are more commonly posited with little indication as to whether they are assertions about historically existing practices, normative claims about what the law should be, or something only partially developed in-between.[10]

Thus while it is likely that at least *some* mishnaic law is the product of the era when the Temple and Sanhedrin functioned, by all accounts the process of detailing these laws continued seamlessly—and expands hundredfold—after these institution no longer functioned. It would be as if the repeal of the U.S. Constitution were followed by an explosion of legal analysis regarding the government's powers under the now-defunct constitution. Such a phenomenon could be possible only if the constitution had never been germane to legal exposition in the first place.

Numerous theories have been proposed to explain the emergence of the Mishnah during the centuries that followed the destruction of the Temple. Some scholars see the endeavor as a way of preserving the past, and others as an effort to imagine the messianic future, still others regard it as a reaction to the loss of autonomy and governance, as an educational tool and manual, or as an attempt to establish rabbinic authority through learning and lawmaking. Regardless of which explanation one may adopt, the central point is clear: many halakhot are most obviously *not* legislated for the purpose of governing.[11]

Laws Designed Not to Apply

And we are not yet done with the complexity of understanding halakhah. Not only do halakhic texts discuss laws that no longer apply, and not only do they detail laws that likely never applied, but in some cases, the rabbis interpret the laws so as *to ensure they will never apply*. Take, for example, tractate *Zavim*, which deals with the ritual implications of a genital disease called *zav*, typically translated as gonorrhea. The Mishnah cites R. Akiva's view, which makes it functionally impossible for someone to be declared a *zav* (m.Zavim 2:2). Sensing that R. Akiva's position would render a significant unit in the Torah (Leviticus 15:1–15 and Numbers 5) and an entire tractate of Mishnah dead letter, the Sages challenge it, stating that on R. Akiva's view there would never be a case of *zav*. Rather than defend himself from the charge, or try to drum up a case where the laws of *zav* would apply, R. Akiva simply demurs, stating: "you have no responsibility to ensure the application of the law of *zavim*." For R. Akiva at least, non-applicability of the law generates no concern.

In this particular case, the normative halakhah follows the Sages. Yet, the Talmud provides numerous cases where the rabbis read the law to have a considerably narrower range of application than a plain reading of the Torah would suggests. We have already considered the examples of capital and corporal punishment, but on other occasions the rabbis apply so many far-flung restrictions that in the three mentioned in the epigraph to this chapter—the rebellious teenager (*ben sorer u-moreh*), the rebellious city (*ir ha-nidahat*), and fungal infestation of the house (*tza'arat ha-bayit*)—the Tosefta states that the law "never was nor will it ever come to be." Faced with this assertion, the Tosefta wonders what could possibly be the point of such never-to-be-applied law. The answer is telling: "To say, study it, and receive reward [for the study.]" (t.Sanhedrin 11:2 and 14:1 and t.Negaim 6:1. See also b.Sanhedrin 71a).

Though this point is made explicitly in three cases, once we account for all the qualifications and exceptions presented in the Talmud, there is a considerably larger category of laws whose chances of application approaches nil, or that apply only under idealized settings far removed from the present situation. These include cases of conspiring witnesses (*eydim zomemim*), a suspected adulteress (*sotah*), a major infraction of sacrificial procedure (*pigul*), the practice of publicly hanging the bodies of persons subjected to capital punishment (*tliyat ha–met*), the ritual performed to atone for an unsolved murder (*eglah arufah*), the punishment for failing to submit to the authority of the court (*zaken mamre*), the case of the Sanhedrin that issued a mistaken ruling (*horayot*), the laws determining who gets drafted to war (*meshuah milhamah*), the laws commanding the obliteration of the Amalekite tribe (*meḥiyat amalek*), the prosecution of false prophets (*navi sheker*), the economic system envisioned by the laws of the jubilee year (*yovel*), and the requirement that one guilty of accidental homicide flee to a city of refuge (*ir miklat*).

So silent is rabbinic literature regarding its interpretive motivations that we can only speculate as to *why* the Sages adopted restrictive readings in so many areas. In some cases (capital punishment, the destruction of Amalek), the reasons may lie in a moral or political discomfort; in others, they may have to do with pre-existing interpretive commitments. Whatever the reason, the rabbis show little compunction when interpreting laws out of existence without explaining why they did so. Thus in varying degrees, the phenomenon of non-applied law recurs across the halakhic corpus.

Is Anyone Paying Attention?

Perhaps more surprising than all of these features put together is this: notwithstanding the near-fanatical devotion of generations of scholars to analyzing every jot and tittle of the Talmud, and notwithstanding the sheer number of unusual requirements found in halakhic criminal law, it took until the fourteenth century, roughly 1,200 years after the Mishnah, for anyone to step back and ask the most basic question: how is this system supposed to function?[12] Looking at the system as a whole, there is simply no way around the fact that the law did not work, the law does not work, and it's hard to see how the law could ever work. A legal system does not make much sense unless situated within a political and institutional context that allows for its application, yet why did no one bother to point this out?

The reason is that, however pressing this question may seem outside the web of halakhic argumentation and analysis, it is utterly unimportant within the halakhic tradition itself. That is why neither the Mishnah, nor the Talmud, nor most commentators show much concern over the impracticability of halakhah's rules. Despite the hundreds of thousands of pages of dense Talmudic commentary, with the lone exception of the one noted rabbi in the fourteenth century, it took until the nineteenth century for scholars to start querying the political context described in central halakhic texts, asking whether or how halakhah actually functioned as a system, or what Jewish society would look like if halakhah were to be restored in the messianic era.

This point is underscored by the mishnaic passage that, in serving as a coda to the discussion of the criminal law, comes closest to asking a "global" question of this kind (m.Makkot 1:10):

(A) A Sanhedrin that executes once every seven years is deemed destructive (חבלנית).

(B) R. Eliezer b. Azaria says: If it executes once every seventy years it is destructive.

(C) R. Tarfon and R. Akiva say: Had we sat on the Sanhedrin, no one would have ever been executed.

(D) R. Shimon b. Gamliel says: They too enable murderers to proliferate in Israel.

The Mishnah structures its argument along an escalating scale of abolitionist sentiment (A-C) followed by a dissent (D), yet the actual practices of the Sanhedrin are obscured. Instead of discussing how often the Sanhedrin *did* execute, it offers evaluative statements regarding how often it *should* have executed. Rabbis Tarfon and Akiva in particular make it clear that they speak of a halakhic ideal ("*had we sat on the Sanhedrin*") rather than a historical or political reality. Nor does the Mishnah discuss whether any adverse consequences followed the abolition of the death penalty, and if so, how crimes were actually deterred. Finally, even R. Shimon b. Gamliel's rather practical objection does not explain how the death penalty should or could be made more effective. All told, the Mishnah's final teaching on the subject reads more like a reflection on the theory of capital punishment than detailed legislation governing its operation.

Therefore, to the extent we want to understand halakhah as Jewish law, we must be willing to substantially expand our conceptualization of what "law" is and could be. In the next two chapters we will see that halakhic rules are not only about regulation but about expression. Rather than read non-applied law as relevant in only the most extraordinary circumstances, we would do better to understand the specifics of non-applied law, as well as many applied laws, as creating a web of interrelated concepts—or extended metaphors—that communicate social and religious meaning.

3

Halakhah and Governance

If a person receives lashes as a punishment for a sin, and then repeats
the sin, the court locks him in a dome where he is fed barley until his
stomach ruptures.

A person who murders another in the absence of witnesses to
convict him is placed in a dome and fed sparse bread and scant water.

—MISHNAH SANHEDRIN 9:5

IN THE PREVIOUS CHAPTER we saw how the mere fact that something
looks like law doesn't mean that it is designed to regulate. Still, a sub-
stantial body of halakhah indeed regulates in a more conventional fashion. The complexity lies in understanding how both applied and non-
applied types of halakhah exist on a single legal and theological
continuum. This chapter explores that issue.

Enforcement in the Court of Heaven

As we've seen, even while imposing certain judicial impediments to carrying out halakhah, the rabbis regarded it as much more than a system
of law enforced by human agents. The foundation of rabbinic theology
is that halakhah is God's word and ideally observed out of love for the
Creator. Since halahkah's ultimate enforcement lies in the tribunal of

heaven, the promise of eternal reward, or the threat of divine retribution, can be far more powerful motivators than any tools at the disposal of ordinary legal systems. Those committed to passionate fulfillment of God's word understand that halakhah governs, whether enforced by a public body or not.

Hundreds of stories throughout rabbinic literature illustrate the point. Some of the most dramatic incidents involve Rabbi Akiva, a second-century sage of the Mishnah. The Talmud recounts how even in prison, rather than drinking the allocated ration of water that would ensure his survival, R. Akiva made use of it to fulfill the rabbinic requirement of ritual handwashing. (b.Eruvin 21b). Elsewhere, we read of how, in the midst of being tortured to death by the Romans for the crime of teaching Torah, R. Akiva recited the *Shema*, a collection of biblical passages one is obligated to say twice daily, even as his soul departed. (b. Berakhot 61b). Such holy men required neither police officers nor court orders to inspire them to observe God's commandments.

The point is in fact driven home in the very first mishnah of the Talmud. Following the instructions of the Torah, the *Shema*, (Deuteronomy 6:7), is to be said "when you lie down and when you get up." The Mishnah discusses the earliest and latest time one is permitted to recite this prayer in the evening. Though it knows of no humanly initiated sanction for failing to perform this obligation, the Mishnah records that when Rabban Gamliel's sons returned home late one night from a wedding party, their father "reminded" them that the *Shema* is to be recited anytime till dawn. (m.Berakhot 1:1.) Surely in Rabban Gamliel's house, recitation of the *Shema* was a very real and practiced halakhah.

Conventional Enforcement

Further, even as many of halakhah's criminal laws provide far-fetched rules *preventing* enforcement, there are many examples in the Talmud where halakhah is applied through rather conventional means. In numerous cases, we find Babylonian amoraim adjudicating civil disputes on the clear assumption that their rulings will be implemented and enforced with little fanfare. Likewise, the Talmud frequently reports rabbis serving as judges or as issuing rulings in the realm of ritual halakhah, and these are common enough for the rabbinic editors to have developed a stock phrase (*ma'aseh* in tannaitic sources, *u'bda, atu lekamei* and *hahu gavra de* . . . in the Talmud) signaling the introduction of case law into the discussion.[1] The cases (and interpretation of them) vary in the degree to which the judgments were enforced by formal political authority, through communal persuasion and pressure, or merely via voluntary assent of the parties.

Though at times the Talmud is wholly unconcerned with the realities and practicality of its rules, in other instances it shows remarkable sensitivity to how commercial markets operate. In the context of determining when ownership of grain passes from seller to buyer, for instance, the Talmud considers which party has the greater incentive to bear the risk of potential loss (b.Bava Metzia 46b). Similarly, in analyzing whether employee or employer carries the burden of proof in a suit over unpaid wages, the Talmud asks whether labor is in greater need of capital or capital in greater need of labor, which side is more prone to error, whether special concessions should be made in light of the worker's weaker status, and the transaction costs of requiring highly formalized contracts (b.Bava Metzia 112b). And further, in the context of price-fraud laws, the Talmud discusses how a purchaser may seek to manipulate the legal rules by offering to pay more for an object so as to acquire the legal right to reverse the transaction in court, in effect obtaining an option contract for the good at below-market rates (b.Bava Metzia 51a). This form of strategic thinking is instantly recognizable to modern lawyers and policymakers who engage in similar discussions on a daily basis.

Sub-Halakhic Enforcement

The third method of enforcement might be called "sub-halakhah." For even as the Talmud goes to great lengths to ensure that the *official* punishments for heresy, desecrating Shabbat, committing adultery, or even theft are functionally unenforceable, communities retained other means for enforcing law and order. The talmudic rabbis describe thus several practices designed to do what established halakhah could not. The Mishnah, for example, speaks of a parallel legal regime, known as *kippa*, where murderers who got off on halakhic technicalities were confined to a small cell and fed a diet designed to explode their stomachs (m.Sanhedrin 9:5). Likewise, mishnahic sources speak of "lashes of rebelliousness," that is, ad-hoc beatings not subject to the cumbersome procedural protections required for administering the "official lashes" mandated by Torah law (t.Makkot 4:17; m.Nazir 4:3). Another statement records that "a court may flog and punish in ways that do not accord with the law," to deal with recalcitrant offenders or to instill religious zeal in the populace (b.Sanhedrin 46a; b.Yevamot 90b). The Talmud also affirms that communities and their courts have inherent authority to mandate social and economic legislation (b.Bava Batra 9a), to set and establish market prices and practices (b.Bava Batra 89a), and in appropriate instances to redistribute property rights.[2] Finally, the Talmud establishes that courts have the power to excommunicate those who do not follow their orders (b.Moed Kattan 16a; b.Bava Kamma 112b; b.Shevuot 41a). In eras when Jews had few exit options from established communities, excommunication was an extraordinarily powerful deterrent.

In this connection, we may note that in the past, as today, there was likely a gap between the ideals of the rabbinic elite and the actual practices of the general Jewish public. Further, the Talmud says very little about how communities actually lived, the degree to which halakhah functioned as a regulatory system, or how those outside the rabbinic orbit saw it. The absence of historical evidence from sources other than those written by the rabbis themselves makes it hard to know how the talmudic rabbis fit within the larger social and religious sphere of the time.

On this basis, some have questioned the degree to which, in the absence of a formal judicial system, we can speak at all of applied halakhah in the mishnaic era .[3] The answer to this objection is that while it may be impossible to know how many people saw themselves as bound by the regulatory aspects of halakhah, virtually all the evidence suggests that *within* rabbinic circles, these aspects were regarded as binding. In contrast to the examples presented in the previous chapter, where the Talmud goes out of its way to qualify certain types of halakhah into oblivion, rabbis advocated that the practices of applied halakhah become widespread among the populace.

Hence the Talmud frequently praises those who recite the *Shema*, ritually wash their hands, say the prayers, and so on, and castigates those who fail to do so. While it might be difficult to pinpoint which halakhot were seen as binding on which sub-groups during which era, the conceptual point remains valid: the Mishnah has no qualms weaving both regulatory and non-applied rules into a seamless web of halakhah.

Halakhah's Eternal Present

The interconnectedness between real and ideal halakhah is central to the rabbis' project. This is evident in the Mishnah's opening paragraphs about the obligation to recite the *Shema,* a classic example of applied halakhah that is encased in a presentation of non-applied laws. The passage from Mishnah Berakhot 1:1 reads as follows:

(A) From what time is the evening *Shema* recited?
From the time that the *kohanim* [priests] enter to eat their consecrated food [*terumah*],[4]
until the end of the first watch.
These are the words of Rabbi Eliezer.
But the sages say: until midnight.
Rabban Gamliel says: until the dawn rises.

(B) It once happened:
that Rabban Gamliel's sons came home [late] from a wedding party.
They said to him: "We have not recited the evening *Shema*."
He said to them: "If the dawn has not yet risen, you are required to recite the evening *Shema*."

(C) And not only that,

>but in all cases where the sages said that the time is "until
>midnight,"
>it is proper to perform the mitzvah until the dawn rises.
>The burning of the fats and limbs [on the Temple's altar
>which must generally be concluded by midnight]—
>The mitzvah extends until the dawn rises.
>Similarly, for all sacrifices that may only be eaten for one day,
>[and which must generally be consumed before
>midnight]—
>the mitzvah extends until the dawn rises.
>If so, why did the sages rule in these cases "until midnight?"
>In order to distance a person from sin.

This mishnah exemplifies the frustration in trying to separate halakhah into non-applied laws pertinent to the Temple era of the past and
applied laws of the later *galut*. It seems to open in the governing present:
what is the earliest time to recite the Shema? But the answer, *from the time
that the kohanim enter to eat their consecrated food,* harks back to the purity
rituals of Temple period. The anecdote in section B clearly shifts to post-
Temple times (we know when R. Gamliel lived), only to return, in section C, to a world where the Temple stands such that the "fats and limbs"
are being burned at night. Finally, in its concluding lines, the mishnah
presents a category of *mitzvot* that can "really" be performed until dawn,
but as a precaution, must be completed before midnight. Even within
this final grouping however, two rulings relate to the operation of the
Temple while the laws of the *Shema* continue to the present.

This mixture naturally raises the question of when and how this
mishnah came together. Was it originally taught when the priestly rituals reflected a lived reality, or did it emerge in a latter period as the rabbis
sought to connect their present-day rituals to days of yore?[5] Moreover,
some scholars argue that these are the wrong questions to ask, as the
mishnah should be assessed through literary and artistic criteria rather
than historical standards. To take one example, Berakhot, the Mishnah's

first tractate, both opens and closes with conspicuous discussions of the *Shema* and Temple practices that employ similar linguistic forms. This fact has led some to conclude that the Mishnah's structure may be designed to impart theological messages rather than to confirm historical practice.[6] Literary analysis of the Mishnah has recently come into vogue and the matter is still up for debate.

In any case, we know that by the time the Mishnah was organized, disseminated, and studied, the Temple and its ritual clock were meaningful less as concrete referents than as symbols in the network of halakhic rules. Yet the Talmud, which pores over every word of the Mishnah's rulings on the recitation of the *Shema*, never asks the most obvious questions: Why are we still talking in "Temple time" if it is not a meaningful marker? What is the purpose of grouping the *Shema* within the same conceptual timeframe as rituals that have not been practiced (from the Talmud's vantage point) in the last few centuries? In a post-Temple reality, what does it mean to rule that the "fats and limbs" on the no longer existing altar can be burned until dawn?

We will return to answer some of these questions in chapter 7. For now, and in light of the Mishnah's opening discussion, it is enough to appreciate how hard it is to maintain a clear line between applied and non-applied halakhah. The *Shema* may be the prototypically applied law, yet the Mishnah goes out of its way to structure it through analogies to non-applied rules and concepts. Throughout the Mishnah and Talmud, practiced halakhot are nestled within non-applied law, yet theoretical laws may in turn influence practical application. Hence, the time to burn fats on the altar is no less real than the time to recite the *Shema*; and when "the *kohanim* enter to eat their consecrated food" is as clear a reference point as midnight or dawn.

The intermixing of the real and ideal pervades the entire corpus of the Mishnah. There are few textual or analytical clues to distinguish the mishnah in Berakhot teaching laws of the *Shema* (likely describing rabbinic practice) from the mishnah in Sanhedrin describing the procedures for stoning the aforementioned rebellious son (which "never was nor will it ever come to be"), from the mishnah in Zevaḥim discussing sacrifices (wherein third-century rabbis legislate what the Temple law was or should have been), from the mishnah in Bava Metzia that regulates commercial law (whose relationship to the actual commercial practices of the second- third centuries is contested by historians),[7] from the mishnah in *Zavim*, which debates whether the law it describes is practicable.

Notwithstanding their different functions, however, these texts more-or-less reside within the same conceptual space and exhibit similar structure, style, and terminology. And that same interconnectedness is reinforced a hundredfold in the Talmud which constantly compares, contrasts, borrows, and distinguishes different areas of the Mishnah while showing scant awareness of the diverse social and regulatory functions assumed by each text.

Thus, from early on, scholars of the Mishnah have been arguing how to best understand it. As a legal code? A collection of sources for study? A textbook for beginning students of halakhah? Lecture notes of its credited compiler, R. Yehuda HaNasi? A work of philosophy?[8] But however maddening this combination may be to lawyers and historians standing outside the system, for the rabbis it is standard operating procedure. For them, halakhah exists in what Gershom Scholem, the great scholar of Kabbalah, called the "eternal present."[9]

Addressing an Important Counterargument

In the academic study of rabbinics, the claims we have pursued this far are often challenged on the following grounds: though we have been analyzing the idea of law represented in the works known as the Mishnah and Talmud, these texts were not written by a single person or even during a single generation. The Mishnah contains materials spanning at least two centuries, and the Talmud was produced over an even longer period of time and more diffuse geographic area. Both compilations may therefore bear the influence not only of different halakhic thinkers and ideologies but different social and political circumstances. Some of the Mishnah dates from close to when the Temple stood, while other parts are clearly of later date; some sections were assembled when rabbinic and halakhic influence was on the rise, others when its influence waned.

For these reasons, perhaps we are merely observing an amalgamation of different legal regimes later packaged together in works called "Mishnah" and "Talmud" that form a cohesive unit only in hindsight. How, then, can we derive anything approaching a "rabbinic idea of law"?

This global question bedevils almost every study of the Mishnah and Talmud, and in one form or another is frequently discussed among both rabbinic and academic scholars.[10] For our part, we can engage it from the perspective of a small slice of *Tosefta* that deals with the laws of the rebellious city encountered above. (t.Sanhedrin 14:1)

(A) The rebellious city never was and never will be.
So why is it written?
To say, study it, and receive reward.

(B) We do not declare three cities rebellious in the Land of Israel
lest the land become desolate.
But we can declare one or two cities rebellious.
Rabbi Shimon says:
even two should not be declared.
Rather, no more than one in Judah [i.e., south)
and one in the Galilee [north].

(C) Near the border, however, not even one city is declared rebellious—
for fear that the gentile [armies] will breach and destroy the land of Israel.

At first blush, this Tosefta appears to be sheer legal fantasy. Note that it *opens* the discussion of the laws of the rebellious city by announcing that they never did and never will apply (section A), and then, in sections B and C proceeds to examine exceptions motivated by fear of *practical consequences* of this wholly theoretical law.

Judged by the argument we have been pursuing in this chapter however, the Tosefta perfectly embodies the fluidity between halakhah-
as-regulation and halakhah-as-Torah. For just as the Mishnah records
a debate about whether the Sanhedrin should execute anyone, so
too, the practical effects of an imagined body of law are fair game for
discussion.

Objectors may protest that this Tosefta text is the product not of a
single editorial mind but of several independent strands that were
later layered together. It is possible, therefore, that section A reflects
a tradition in which the rebellious city is a fully theoretical or expressive law, while sections B and C reflect competing traditions that place
fewer restrictions on the laws of the rebellious city and are more concerned with their practical implementation. Alternatively, perhaps
what began as concern over practical consequences (sections B and
C) later morphed into an approach seeking to nullify the entire subject matter. Either way, these speculations suppose that we have here
nothing so grandiose as an "idea of law" but simply texts emerging out
of different contexts that are later (perhaps inelegantly) stuck
together.

Indeed, it is possible to support such a view from within the rabbinc
corpus itself. As it happens, not all talmudic rabbis agreed with the
"never was and never will be" view set forth in the Tosefta. The Talmud
records a Rabbi Jonathan who claimed to not only have seen a rebellious
city, but to "have sat atop the rubble heap" where it once stood. R. Jonathan enters similar testimony about the rebellious son and the leprosy-
infested house, the other two supposedly "never was and never will be"
laws (b.Sanhedrin 71a). In brief, one could maintain that the Tosefta
simply records conflicting opinions on whether certain laws were or
were not applied.

The point, however, is that even in disagreement, the competing
opinions together form a single idea of law. The debates over whether
the Sanhedrin did or should ever execute anyone, or whether the rebellious city does or does not exist, are plainly *not* about the historical
record but about the nature of halakhah itself. Specifically, must

halakhah be understood as a system that (at least in theory) relates to governance, or can it (or at least parts of it) exist solely in the realm of discussion and deliberation?

What needs to be understood is that these core questions of halakhic theory are themselves addressed through technical halakhic rules. The Talmud thus connects the narrow rule that even a single *mezuzah* (a small parchment containing the paragraphs of the *Shema*) on a single doorpost disqualifies an entire town from being deemed "rebellious," with the broad jurisprudential claim that the rebellious town will never come into being (b.Sanhedrin 71a). (The assumption is that any Jewish town will have at least one *mezuzah* in it.) For the rabbis, even the theoretical argument over whether a given halakhah can be purely theoretical is cast as a question over a narrow halakhic detail.

It is impossible to know how the text of the Tosefta cited above originally developed, though it appears in substantially the same form in the available manuscripts. What we do know however, is that it eventually became absorbed into a web of halakhic thought that does not fret over the conceptual chasm which stands at its core; in fact, the Talmud seems to celebrate it. This near-seamless reception is possible only because the rabbis' understanding of halakhah leaves room to account for both options.

Interim Summary: Halakhah and Governance

As far back as the Mishnah, halakhah incorporates legal regimes that are both highly imaginative and eminently practicable. Some halakhot are understood to demand strict enforcement in accordance with their terms, while others stand as ideals that in practice are replaced by rules more conducive to governance. On the one hand, simply knowing a rule of halakhah serves as no guarantee that it governs in practice; on the other, rules that govern in practice may not achieve the state of formal halakhah.

Further, these categories are themselves not static. Regulatory rules can be interpreted into obscurity, and standards developed in a non-practiced area of halakhah may be brought to bear on concrete cases. To give but one example: when the Talmud seeks to clarify who is deemed a town resident for purposes of taxation—arguably the most real world law imaginable—it draws on the residency standards developed for the laws of the rebellious city, the textbook example of non-applied law (b.Bava Batra 8a). In this way, even non-applied halakhah remains normative, and as we shall see in the following chapter, but a step away from re-emerging in the realm of practice.

In sum, and to repeat, the different types of halakhah exist along a continuum. At one end (the non-applied pole) we find halakhot that rabbinic sources claim never did and never would apply, laws like the rebellious son and the rebellious city (b.Sanhedrin 71a). Nearby are laws that may have once regulated but are no longer of any practical relevance, like the halakhot discussing the language used in the covenantal ceremony on Mount Grizim (m.Sotah 7:5), or the sacrificial procedures that applied only to the period before Solomon built the Temple (m. Zevaḥim 14:8; m.Megillah 1:11). At the opposite end, (the applied pole), we find laws like the specifics of Shabbat observance, the recitation of the *Shema*, kashrut, and so forth, laws which have been fairly consistently applied by members of the rabbinic caste and those who follow their rulings.

In the vast middle are laws regulating the Temple and Sanhedrin that may have (in part) applied and may apply again in the messianic future; laws that do not apply, yet influence how others are applied; laws that applied in one form and were then reinterpreted to apply in other forms; and laws that apply in broad strokes but whose specific procedures seem more aspirational than actual. Trying to pin down where a specific halakhah sits at a given point in time requires close analysis of the historical record. Which law? Which era? Which community? One must also establish criteria for what separates halakhah from sub-halakhah; and both of these from norms based on communal practices or familial suasion.

Conceptually, however, the rabbis' idea of law means that movement between the poles is not only possible but common. The Mishnah and Talmud do not tell us whether a given body of law describes an imagined legal reality, daily practice, rabbinic aspiration, or some combination thereof. On the contrary, by constantly mixing, matching, and moving among halakhah's meanings, the Talmud signals that, from its perspective, these distinctions are not very significant. This is one of the central insights of the rabbinic idea of law.

4

Halakhah as Torah

R. Akiva said: I once followed R. Joshua into the latrine.
Observing him, I learned three things . . .
Hearing this Ben Azzai asked: How did you act so impudently towards
your teacher?
R. Akiva replied: This too is Torah, and I must study it.

R. Kahana went and hid under Rav's bed. He heard Rav converse and
laugh with his wife and then have intercourse.
R. Kahana said: [Rav's] mouth is like that of one who has never tasted
food.
Upon which Rav exclaimed: Kahana, are you here? Get out! It is not
proper!
R. Kahana replied: This too is Torah, and I must study it.

—TALMUD BERAKHOT 62A

WE HAVE BEEN EXPLORING the different ways in which halakhah is
and is not applied as law. In this chapter we'll see how halakhah is best
understood as a central component of Torah—that is, as God's instruction or teaching.

What Exactly Is Torah?

In the narrowest sense, Torah means the first five books of the Bible. In
rabbinic parlance, the term usually refers to the "oral Torah." This incor-

porates not only the legal discussions of halakhah but many other passages found in the Mishnah, Talmud, and midrash that cannot possibly be characterized as law. These include creative readings and interpretations of the Bible, theological investigations, mysticism, stories about the rabbis themselves, rabbinic and popular aphorisms, cultural commentary, moral lessons, inspirational tales, and sermonic admonishments. All of this typically goes under the heading of *aggadah*. Though aggadah is classically contrasted with halakhah, in the talmudic period it constituted an integrated element of what the rabbis understood as the oral Torah—or simply Torah, period.

The quintessential embodiment of this conception of Torah is the Talmud. Not only does the Talmud contain almost every sub-species of halakhah and aggadah, it often weaves them together into single units of discussion known as *sugyot* (singular: *sugya*). In addition to being the source for adjudicating questions of Jewish law, the Talmud became the central repository of rabbinic thought on virtually every subject of inquiry. Consequently, anything in the Talmud, and any later work commenting or building on it, is also part of Torah.

But Torah is more than a series of texts. It is the sum total of God's revelation and the rabbis' interpretation and expansion of that revelation. Particularly in the diaspora—in the absence of a common land, language, or political and religious institutions—Torah became the Jews' "portable homeland" (in the coinage of the German Jewish poet Heinrich Heine). Torah is a source of identity that requires neither land, army, wealth, nor institutions, but simply the commitment of the faithful.

That commitment is powerfully captured in prayers recited at the crescendo of the Yom Kippur service. Bemoaning the loss of the Temple, land, prophets, and polity, the liturgist described how Jews have been sent scattered and tattered through the unending exile while God's face remains hidden. But none of this matters, "for all that remains is this our Torah." Jews endure because the Torah survives.

Finally, Torah is also a way of knowing. It provides the concepts and images through which the rabbis structured their lives, thought their thoughts, and interpreted their world. In effect, anything they knew—

and pretty much anything they deemed worth knowing—is part of Torah. The rabbis went so far as to claim that the universe's physical and metaphysical structure was embedded in Torah; as the midrash has it, the Torah serves as the blueprint of the universe (Genesis Rabbah 1:1). On a less cosmic scale, whenever a talmudic rabbi had something important to say, whether an ethical teaching, a political discourse, a theological investigation, or philosophical speculation, it was framed as Torah.

In praising one of the leading rabbis of the mishnaic era, the Talmud notes that he was conversant in "Scripture, Mishnah, Talmud, halakhah, aggadah, grammar, scribal traditions, deductive logic, linguistic connections, astronomical calculations, numerology, the conversations of angels, conversations of demons, conversations of palm trees, proverbs of washwomen, proverbs of foxes," as well as the workings of the Heavenly Chariot and the intricacies of talmudic analysis; presumably, all sub-departments of Torah (b.Sukkah 28a). Elsewhere in the Talmud, even breaches of student-rabbi protocol as attested in the epigraphs to this chapter are successfully defended with the statement: "This too is Torah, and I must study it." Much later on, in seeking to incorporate Aristotelian concepts into his law and theology, Maimonides would argue (though not without pushback from others) that manifestations of Greek wisdom were also part of Torah.

Torah, in sum, is the all-encompassing religious worldview through which the rabbis, bereft of political and other institutions, built and transmitted their culture.

The Legal Infrastructure of Torah

Although "Torah" encompasses a wide range of *topics*, it most commonly assumes a legal *framing*. When presented in the Talmud, material that we might classify as philosophical, political, or theological, tends to look and feel like law, at least initially. The results can be seen in two distinct features. First, a sugya in the Talmud will often begin in a narrow halakhic key, but then expand the analysis outwards to other, non-halakhic issues. Second, the line between regulatory commands and explorations of enduring religious and human questions is permeable and at times nonexistent. A conversation about one easily morphs into the other.

Let's look at a few examples. In chapter 2, we cited the Mishnah's discussion of whether a criminal sentenced to stoning is executed dressed or undressed. By way of reminder, here's the relevant text from Mishnah Sanhedrin 6:3.

> When the convict was four ells away from the place of stoning he would be undressed:
>
> A male is covered one part in front,
> and a woman, two parts in front and one in back—
> these are the words of Rabbi Yehuda.
>
> But the sages say:
> A male is stoned naked,
> but a woman is not stoned naked.

Reading this mishnah as law, we inevitably return to the questions asked two chapters ago: was the Sanhedrin operative? Was this punishment ever enacted? How was execution administered historically? And so forth. But reading this mishnah as Torah, we now ask not what it regulates, but what it teaches.

Tellingly, the Talmud itself inquires as to the source of this debate, and reframes it in a highly didactic manner. Operating under the assumption that the convict's clothing serves as a protective layer which prolongs death, it reasons as follows: The sages who hold that a (female) subject remains clothed maintain that preserving a woman's dignity can justify an increase in physical pain. R. Yehudah, by contrast, is willing to trade the disgrace of near-nakedness in order to lessen the physical pain of the death. Hence the subject is stoned undressed (b.Sanhedrin 45a).

In this brief exchange, what began as a technical debate over the procedures of an imaginary system of capital punishment turns into a discussion about the relative weights of physical and psychological pain. This presentation takes the focus away from speculating whether the

Sanhedrin actually administered the stoning punishment. Rather, the Talmud is staking out an important claim: technical halakhic rules reflect on core questions of human nature.

Indeed, later halakhists brought this same discussion to bear on the issue of whether funds set aside for poverty relief should be allocated towards the provision of food (to alleviate physical pain), or the provision of clothing (to alleviate emotional and psychological pain of nakedness).[1] Today, contemporary discussions of welfare policy, as well as medical and battlefield ethics, continue to dwell on the relative weighting of these two forms of human degradation.

Measuring Man

Another example emerges from chapter 21 of Deuteronomy: the case where a murdered victim is found outside a town while the killer remains unknown. In such an event, the elders of the town are called to claim responsibility by assembling in a barren riverbed, where they ceremonially hack a calf's neck and wash their hands in water as a symbolic gesture of atonement. To determine which town is obligated to perform this ceremony, the Torah instructs the elders to measure from the victim's body to the nearest locale.

For its part, the Mishnah becomes inordinately preoccupied with the specific formalities of this measurement. In what might be seen as a parody of halakhic legalism, the Mishnah (Sotah 9:4) asks:

> From which part of the corpse do they measure?
> Rabbi Eliezer says: from his navel.
> Rabbi Akiva says: from his nostrils.

Talmudic debates like this one may well be what prompted the early Christian sources to mock the Pharisees as myopically legalistic. If we look at the matter more closely, however, it becomes less obvious that this mishnah is about "law" in the sense of regulation. First, for the hacked-calf ceremony to be triggered, a number of rather detailed specifications must be met.[2] Second, on the mishnah's own account, the ritual had been abolished altogether before the destruction of the

Temple—well before the time Rabbis Akiva and Eliezer squared off in this mishnah. Finally, for this mishnah to be relevant in practice, one would have to assume that in addition to all the other conditions, the corpse was found perfectly equidistant between two towns save for the trifling distance between the navel and the nose. (Where you measure a town from is not even discussed.)

So if this mishnah is not about regulation, what is it about? The Babylonian Talmud (Sotah 45b) offers an intriguing answer by inquiring as to the source of the debate between the two rabbis:

> One master [R. Akiva] holds:
> the primary element of life is in his nostrils.
> And one master [R. Eliezer] holds:
> the primary element of life is in his navel.

The Jerusalem Talmud (Sotah 9:3) presents a related idea this way:

> Rabbi Eliezer says:
> from his navel—
> from the place that the fetus is created.
> Rabbi Akiva says:
> from his nostrils—
> the place where the face is recognized.

In both variants, the issue is not how we measure a man's corpse but how we measure the human essence. Both turn a superficially trifling legal question into a broadly philosophical one: is man a primarily physical being—created from the navel on out? Or fundamentally a spiritual being—measured from the breathing passages?[3]

The halakhic context is no less significant, as the ceremony of the hacked calf is specifically designed to draw attention to the uniqueness of the human being. When an animal carcass is found at the side of the road, halakhah offers no response. But when a human is killed, the entire body politic is engaged. (The Talmud records a view that even the king and the Great Sanhedrin were involved in the procedure (b.Sotah 44b)). What makes a human corpse different? This is the very issue discussed by Rabbis Akiva and Eliezer.

In Christianity, questions about the nature of humanity are assessed in the context of the theological disciplines; in the modern academic setting, they are discussed in the humanities, the social sciences, biology, or neuropsychology. For the rabbis, the relevant context is halakhah—and this is why the Mishnah matters, and matters crucially, even if its rules will not be implicated in practice.

Halakhah as Metaphor

A third example shows how rabbinic ideas can be formed through the very activity of studying Torah. The Talmudic tractate Menaḥot deals with grain-based offerings presented in the Temple. One such offering, known as the showbread or Bread of Presence, was placed on a ceremonial table inside the Temple each Shabbat where it resided for an entire week, as outlined in Exodus chapter 25 and Leviticus chapter 24. According to Exodus 25:30 this bread, "shall be in My [God's] presence *at all times* [תמיד]." The Mishnah reads this verse as indicating that the Bread of Presence must remain on the table at literally every moment—including the moment it is being replaced with a fresh offering. The Mishnah (Menaḥot 11:7) describes the process as follows:

> Four *kohanim* (priests) would enter . . .
> Those bringing in the new bread would stand to the north facing south,
> and those removing the old bread would stand to the south facing the north.
> One group pulling out the old as another group replaces it with the new
> such that the space left open was immediately covered—
> as Scripture states: "in My presence *at all times*."

The mishnah goes on to record the view of R. Yose, who allows for a more relaxed procedure: so long as the new bread is installed the same day as the old is removed, the requirement of "at all times" has been satisfied.

But whereas the mishnah is focused on the small technicalities of Temple procedure, the Talmud (Menaḥot 99b) quickly transitions from bread to theology:

> From the words of R. Yose we learn:
> That even if a person studied only one chapter in the morning, and one in the evening,
> he has fulfilled the obligation [derived from Joshua 1:8]
> *This Torah shall not depart from your mouth.*

The Talmud transforms the Temple into a template for life, a legal metaphor for exploring the foundational religious question of how one lives in the presence of God "at all times." What matters is not the physical existence of the Temple but how the rabbis conceptualize the halakhic infrastructure of its rituals. The priests and the bread may be long gone, but the *halakhah of the bread* serves as a reference point for life's most important decisions.

We'll return to this text in the next chapter, but we can pause to take stock.

When seen as elements of Torah, questions of whether the Sanhedrin ever stoned anyone, or whether a court ever measured from a victim's body to the nearest town, or whether the priests in the Temple followed the opinion of R. Yose, hardly form the most pressing issue. Instead, by presenting, preserving, and contrasting these opinions *as halakhah*, the Mishnah establishes them as authoritative reference points for future halakhic discussion. Halakhah applies not only when carried out as law, but when standing as a normative idea in a system that continuously analyzes and cross-references its foundational concepts.

This sense of "apply" is possible precisely because the rabbis do not view their law only as a collection of bureaucratic commands imposed by an external agent (even if that agent is God), but as a language of wisdom that explores values, shapes thought, and guides behavior through legal instruction. Halakhah may be law, but it is also the analogue of a classical liberal-arts education, offering a set of concepts for understanding and interpreting the world and making decisions within it. The question is not what halakhah regulates, but what it teaches through the process of regulating.

The Study of Torah

The Talmud brims with encomiums to the study of Torah. Its heroes are scholars who demonstrate diligence, humility, and aptitude in the quest for mastery. Torah is described as the elixir of life, the tree of life, and the life-giving force of water. Virtually every available simile is applied to Torah, up to and including the erotic: "Just as a female deer has a narrow birth canal and is thus desirable to her mate each time as much as the first time, so too, the words of Torah are desirable to those who study them each time as much as the first" (b.Eruvin 54b). Torah is both the content of what the rabbis think about and how they think about it. As the Talmud sees it, through the study of Torah man comes to understand his God, himself, and his world.

The halakhic-legal framing of Torah, however, places considerable burdens on its students. As beginners painfully learn, the entry barriers into talmudic literacy are high. In many ways one needs to already have learned Torah in order to make sense of it. Hence the rabbis' most important contribution to law is not found in any particular rule but in the centrality accorded to its study—to *talmud Torah*. By legislating Torah study, halakhah calls on a Jew not only to obey the *mitzvot*, but to follow the rabbis in constructing his worldview; to be not merely the subject of the law's regulation but the addressee of its internal dialogue. No wonder, the rabbis held Torah study equal to all other commandments.

Over time, the nature and purpose of Torah study came to be understood in different ways by different communities. We will explore these distinctions further in chapter 9, but for now, I'll introduce a cluster of three related ideas:

(i) *Torah lishmah*: Torah for its own sake. The study of Torah has intrinsic value, and therefore one studies it not only to become a more proficient practitioner of halakhah but to fulfill the obligation towards *talmud Torah*. According to some, Torah study is the supreme act of religious devotion, and understanding Torah brings the human mind and soul closer to its Creator. In this perspective, study often centers not only on applied and non-applied elements of halakhah, but also extends to extra-halakhic material.

(ii) *Talmud Torah k'neged kulam*: the study of Torah is a devotional and religious activity on a par with the performance of all other obligations. A talmudic passage recited in the daily prayer service states that Torah study is equal to honoring parents, performing acts of kindness, visiting the sick, providing for a bride, burying the dead, engaging in prayer, and resolving disputes between people (b.Shabbat 127a). Another source teaches that when a person appears before the Heavenly Court, one of the first questions asked is whether he "set aside time for learning Torah" (b.Shabbat 31a). Yet a third source debates whether the study of Torah or the observance of mitzvot is greater, concluding, somewhat paradoxically, that "study is greater for it leads to practice" (b.Kiddushin 40b).

(iii) *Mitzvat talmud Torah*: the *mitzvah* of Torah study. There is a lifelong obligation for each male to engage in Torah study. So encompassing is this obligation that the Talmud finds it necessary to reconcile two apparently divergent biblical imperatives: one calling on the farmer to "harvest your grain in its season" (Deuteronomy 11:14), and the other, mandating that "this Torah shall not [ever] depart from your mouth" (Joshua 1:8) One view holds that the call to Torah study must be tempered by competing obligations (like the grain harvest), while the other demurs, arguing that if one plows in the plowing season, sows in the sowing season, reaps in the reaping season, and so on, "What will become of Torah!?" While siding with the former view, the Talmud nevertheless holds that one should "make Torah his vocation and his work secondary" (b.Berakhot 35b). Maimonides took this to mean that the working man (but not the full-time scholar) should spend **three** hours a day at labor and **nine** (!) in Torah study (*MT, The Laws of Torah Study* 1:12).

Bittul Torah

Torah study is so important that the positive ideal of *talmud Torah* has a corollary in the sinful concept of *bittul Torah*, the abnegation of Torah. The talmudic rabbis imputed all manner of tragedies to shortfalls in Torah study, including the destruction of the Temple in Jerusalem, infant mortality, droughts, and famines (b.Shabbat 119b; b.Shabbat 32a and b.Taanit 7a, respectively). The Talmud also warns that one who forgets Torah is responsible for his own downfall, and one who forsakes Torah in favor of idle chatter should be force-fed red hot coals (m.Avot 3:8 and b.Avodah Zarah 3b, respectively). Other sources warn Jews not to visit the Greco-Roman stadiums, coliseums, and circuses lest they fall into *bittul Torah* (b.Avodah Zarah 18b).

Nor is the tension between Torah study and competing pursuits limited to the realms of idle chatter and popular culture. The Talmud records the question asked by a young man of his illustrious uncle R. Ishmael: "What about a person such as myself, who has studied the entire Torah? May I study the wisdom of the Greeks?" To which the esteemed rabbi answered: "Go and find a time that is neither day nor night, and then you can study the wisdom of the Greeks" (b.Menaḥot 99b). We will have more to say about this story as we go on, but the result of this sentiment is that even activities or recreations that may be otherwise halakhicaly neutral become problematic if they detract from Torah study.

In the sixteenth century, R. Moses Isserles' authoritative commentary on the *Shulḥan Arukh*, the work commonly referred to as the Code of Jewish Law, gave permission, if grudging and limited, to the study of non-Torah wisdom (Yoreh Deah § 246:4):

A person should only study the Torah, Mishnah, and Talmud and works derived therefrom, such that he will receive reward in this world and the next. This is not the case regarding to the study of other wisdoms. Nevertheless, it is permitted to study other wisdoms periodically (באקראי), so long as they are not works of heresy . . . But a person should not do so until he has filled himself with Torah: that is, to know what is permitted and what is prohibited and the laws of the *mitzvot*.[4]

Indeed, not every yeshiva student, let alone every layman, lived the ideals of *talmud Torah*. For many Jews, even reading the Bible was a daunting task, not to mention wending one's way through the talmudic circumlocutions. For their part, many great halakhists were versed in the surrounding culture, both high and low. But if the image of East European *shtetel* Jew dashing at every moment to the study house is a piece of false sentimentality, the ideals of *talmud Torah* that pervade rabbinic literature have inspired communities to show fidelity to Torah by valuing and practicing its study. Thus, a reputation as a Torah scholar has long been a source of cultural capital and an avenue to positions of communal leadership and authority.

Torah and Greek Wisdom

The post-talmudic history of this issue is complex and contested. The cosmopolitan rationalists of the tradition, epitomized by Maimonides and the Golden Age of Spain but also prominent in tenth century Iraq as well as in in Central Europe in the seventeenth to nineteenth centuries, tended to embrace Greek/Western modes of thought and sought to reconcile them with Torah. This strand effectively rendered the prohibition irrelevant by limiting the category of forbidden "Greek wisdom" to ancient Greek astrology and soothsaying.[5] By contrast, the more insular halakhists of northern Europe in the eleventh to thirteenth centuries, and Eastern Europe in the seventeenth to nineteenth centuries tended to understand Greek wisdom to include classical philosophy and most of Western thought. Adherents of this latter view were either uninterested in or theologically opposed to reconciling Jewish and Greek thought, claiming that a Jew's knowledge came from the Torah, not the wisdom of the heathens. A middle ground is reflected in R. Is-serlis' comments cited above, who reluctantly permits the study of Greek wisdom but only after insisting on its inferiority to Torah.

It is instructive to contrast halakhah's hesitancy in relation to Greek wisdom with the relatively warm embrace this wisdom receives in much of Christian thought. Like the talmudic rabbis, some early Church Fathers asked, in Tertullian's famous phrase, "What has Athens [i.e., philosophical reasoning] to do with Jerusalem [i.e., biblical revelation]?" Yet, Christian theologians from Augustine (354–430) to Aquinas (1225–1274) forged a detente between the two modes of knowing; by the medieval period, universities were closely associated with Church teachings and institutions. To be sure, much of this was contested during the Reformation, and the faith versus reason debate featured prominently in the Christian past and survives to the present. But certainly in the Catholic and some of the Protestant traditions, Aristotle's philosophy has not been seen as a threat to Church teaching. To the contrary, Aristotelian concepts are embedded in those teachings to a degree unimaginable in halakhic sources.

The tension between Athens and Jerusalem in halakhah extends to far more than philosophy in the narrow sense of the term. For whether by circumstance or design, in the Jewish mindset, the Talmud and its study displaced much of Western thought and culture. In the 800-year period that begins with the Mishnah and stretches well past the close of the Talmud, it is hard to find many lasting Jewish contributions to political or social theory, science, music, visual and dramatic arts, or general philosophy.

Furthermore, with a few notable exceptions (most prominently, Maimonides, whose books were burned for this very reason) creativity in these fields remained modest until Jews stepped out from behind the Talmud's shadow in the nineteenth century. Particularly in the European orbit, there was always a rivalry, if not downright hostility, between the arts, philosophy, and science (understood in one way or another as the wisdom of the Greeks) and the study of Torah.

At its most basic level, the conflict between Torah and philosophical inquiry is a conflict over knowledge and its source. But beyond this is another debate—over the means by which knowledge is processed and transmitted. The Western tradition values structure and systematic thinking. Its model for communicating ideas is a single individual positing a thesis supported by arguments that flow from premise to claims to conclusions. Though in the first century, before the mishnaic project got off the ground, pre-rabbinic Jews such as Josephus and Philo wrote this way, amazingly, *none* of these characteristics are true of the Mishnah, Tosefta, Babylonian Talmud, Jerusalem Talmud, midrash-halakhah, midrash-aggadah—or *any* classical text of Jewish law or thought. None is the work of a single individual. All were compiled by largely unknown editors (redactors) from statements made by numerous persons who in some instances lived centuries apart.[6]

Nor does the Talmud display a narrative or conceptual arc. Traditionally, the halakhic topography has been captured as in the phrase, "the Sea of the Talmud": very broad, potentially deep, and without fixed reference points—a realm where the uninitiated can be left gasping for breath. A more contemporary metaphor likens the Talmud to a network: a system where individual nodes can be arranged and rearranged in multiple configurations, but that has no true beginning, middle, or end.[7] Both metaphors underscore that at every point, the Mishnah and Talmud assume familiarity with the whole—a thought we shall return to in part II. An adage circulates in yeshivot that all the Talmudic tractates begin on page 2, because the elusive page 1 contains the background and presuppositions the student is already expected to know.

In addition, though it comes to us in written form, the Talmud remains a fundamentally oral text that feels unedited and unfinished. This is because it stacks together discussions of several generations, one on top of another, without clearly distinguishing among them. A saying that begins its life as an interpretation of an earlier text may quickly become the base-text that a later layer will build upon, in a process that can be repeated several times over.

This layered texture is the Talmud's most enticing yet frustrating feature: enticing, since the student-reader is invited into a multi-generational discussion that is constantly in the process of formation; frustrating, because the freewheeling discussion can be cacophonous.

Sudden shifts in subject matter, perpetual uncertainty as to the guiding direction, conversations that simply stop rather than conclude—all are well-known features of talmudic give-and-take.

Paralleling these structural peculiarities, the Talmud does not follow the reasoning methods associated with Greek philosophy. For all the focus on themes of justice, holiness, and faith, nowhere in the Talmud's two million words is there a sustained discussion on topics such as "What is justice?" or "What is holiness" or "What is faith?" In fact, the Talmud seems preternaturally suspicious of such philosophical abstractions. Moreover, generally foreign to the talmudic mind are such central legal, political, and scientific categories as logic, rhetoric, ethics, philosophy, theory, universalism, particularism and even theology.

Instead, the Talmud offers a profoundly different way of thinking. Its starting point is the mitzvah—God's call to action—and its core intellectual tool is interpretation, be it of the Bible, the Mishnah, or its own earlier material. As we have stressed, the Talmud develops its ideas through a guiding voice that shifts between halakhic and aggadic concerns, and pushes legal analysis outward to related concepts and upward to higher levels of abstraction. In doing so, the Talmud draws meaning not only from the law's content, but from its analogies, allusions, and arrangement; not only from what is said, but from what is left unsaid.

In the tenth century—well after the close of the talmudic period— rabbinic Jews would start to think and write in the Greek format. In the Talmud, however, the central questions of religious life may be approached through the discussion of obscure rituals like the treatment of showbread in the Temple; the nature of humanity may be explored via the technicalities of the calf-hacking ceremony; and essential issues in human psychology are debated in terms of the imagined judicial procedure of stoning.

What is beauty? What is truth? What is the best political ordering? The Talmud anchors such macro questions in the context of a specific mitzvah and its obligations. Thus, the issue of how many judges should sit on a panel is approached by considering whether the role of a court is to secure social peace or to determine legal truth (b.Sanhedrin 6b-7a). The central issue of legal theory—whether a court makes law or simply

declares pre-existing law—is hashed out through the details of an obscure sacrificial procedure (b.Horayot 2–4). Which books are deemed
part of the Bible is assessed through a discussion of which books are
rescued from a building burning on Shabbat, or which scrolls transmit
ritual impurity.[8] Whether truth is an absolute value, or subject to utili-
tarian calculus, is a question of how one should greet a bride on her
wedding day (b.Ketubot 17a). The legal strictures of the Yom Kippur
fast frame the question of the relative value of human life versus obedience to God's commandments (b.Yoma 84b). What we now call the life/
work balance is negotiated in the Talmud by weighing a worker's contractual obligations towards his employer versus his religious obligations of daily prayer (b.Berakhot 16a).

In brief, what the Greeks pursued through reflective and speculative
philosophy, the rabbis read into, out of, and through halakhah.

Between Talmud Torah and Law

The multiple understandings of Torah underscore why the phenomenon of halakhah cannot be explained outside the devotional, educational, and even artistic motivations of Torah study. There are many
reasons why halakhah is produced, and many incentives for rabbinic
scholars to devote their lives to its technical discussions. These include
a desire to know the rules and comprehend the laws, to become more
devout in one's religious practice, to fulfill the mitzvah of *talmud Torah*,
to absorb rabbinic wisdom, to develop theological and philosophical
insight, to absorb and communicate values, to develop a shared communal discourse, to accumulate cultural capital, and to assume leadership roles.

The reason these are accomplished specifically through Torah, however, owes to the rabbis' belief that the study of Torah is man's highest
calling. Historically speaking, of course, commitment to these ideals
within the general Jewish populace was almost certainly more aspirational than actual. Just as certainly, within the subset of scholars regarded as authoratative expositors of halakhah, the gap between the
ideal and real was considerably smaller.

We must therefore shift our expectations about both what it means to study Jewish law and how to do it. The most effective way to expose oneself to the full range of halakhah is to dive headfirst into the Talmud, to experience firsthand how legal rules, biblical verses, and aggadic meanderings merge into single analytical units that both regulate and educate. Part II now turns to do exactly this through a study of several talmudic sugyot.

PART II

Talmudic Readings

Introduction to Part II

In this section we'll examine a number of talmudic sugyot that demonstrate how the rabbis use the most inclusive definition of Torah to express their ideas. Just to be clear, I am not claiming that *every* legal text or detailed discussion in the Mishnah, Talmud, or later sources is pregnant with existential meaning. That claim goes much too far. Much of halakhah is best seen as law in the conventional sense. Moreover, while the readings below emphasize the layered dimensions of halakhah, many great halakhists engaged in learning, writing, and producing halakhah simply because God had commanded it. No further explanation or theory was needed.

But neither is the opposite claim true. The mere fact that a discussion looks impenetrably technical does not mean the only motivation behind it is to regulate conduct. In addition, as ideas and concepts shift over time, halakhic rules that began as simple commands, in the hands of later scholars, lend themselves to embodying multiple layers of meaning.

In sum, rather than consigning a piece of halakhah to either the regulatory or the expressive category, we are better advised to see a range of non-exclusive possibilities. With this in mind, we'll follow the rabbis' lead in the four chapters to come. Chapter 5 addresses questions of religious life and chapter 6 speaks to social and economic relations. In chapter 7, we'll consider these same themes in terms of the distinction between halakhah and aggadah. Finally, chapter 8 will assess the costs and benefits of encountering life's central questions through a legal prism.

5

Halakhah as Theology

Is Torah study greater or action [mitzvah observance] greater?
Rabbi Tarfon answered and said, "Action is greater."
Rabbi Akiva answered and said, "Study is greater."
The rest of the assembly answered and said:
"Study is greater, since study brings about action."

—TALMUD KIDDUSHIN 40B

"THE MEDIUM IS THE MESSAGE," quipped Marshall McLuhan.[1] For the rabbis, Torah is not only the message but also the medium through which the message is crafted and transmitted. We therefore cannot learn what the rabbis "think" apart from the process through which they come to understand the world.

In this chapter, we will see how halakhic details are the medium for addressing several foundational theological questions: how do mortal humans live in God's presence? What constitutes manliness? What are the ends of mankind? And, why do we pray, and what do we pray for?

Living in the Presence of God

In chapter 4 we introduced a talmudic passage examining man's relationship with God in the context of the ritual of the showbread in the

Temple. The bread is to be stationed on the ceremonial table "before God at all times." The Mishnah's dominant view, as we saw, is that "at all times" must be taken literally. R. Yose, however, offers a looser interpretation, holding that so long as the new bread is presented on the same day as the old is withdrawn, the requirement of "at all times" has been satisfied.

We now enter the Talmud's (Menaḥot 99b) discussion of this mishnah with a statement by R. Ami that transitions the inquiry from the Temple in Jerusalem to the temple of the heart:[2]

(A-1) R. Ami said:
         From the words of R. Yose we learn:
         Even if a person studied only one chapter in the morning,
         and one in the evening.
         He has fulfilled the obligation, derived from Scripture,
         This Torah shall not depart from your mouth. (Joshua 1:8)

These are the opening lines in the sugya. Still adhering to halakhic language, the rabbis embark upon an intricate analysis of the God-conscious life:

(A-2) R. Yoḥanan reported in the name of R. Shimon b. Yoḥai:
         Even if a person does no more than recites the *Shema* at
         night and in the morning
         He has fulfilled the requirement derived from Scripture,
         [This Torah] shall not depart your mouth,
         and you shall meditate on it day and night. (Joshua 1:8)

(A-3) But it is forbidden to teach this in the presence of the
         unlearned.
         But Rava stated:
         It is a commandment to teach this to the unlearned.

The opening passage (A-1) draws an analogy between the method by which the Temple bread is placed "before the presence of God" and how humans are called to do the same in daily life.[3] Equating the two, however, is a tall order, as few can realistically live with the religious punctiliousness demanded in the Temple's sanctum. The Talmudic discussion thus atypically begins with R. Yose's lenient, minority opinion in the Mishnah regarding the showbread. This serves as the basis for R. Ami's reworking the requirement that Torah not depart from a person day or night to mean that each day should be framed with Torah—a bit in the morning and a bit in the evening, but not necessarily more.[4]

Passage A-2 pushes one step further, holding that even recitation of the *Shema* (mandated as part of the prayer service) can do double duty and "count" toward the obligation of Torah study. From this perspective, the lofty idea of standing before God can be reduced to a bare legal minimum, one that does not even require much extra effort.

Passage A-3 records the Talmud's hesitation with this bare-bones approach: should the minimal standard be made public, thereby reminding people how easily they can live in the presence of God? Or, does this view lower the bar to the point of encouraging laziness? The Talmud presents two contrasting opinions, but leaves the matter unresolved.

If the above passages present a case for religious minimalism, the maximalist extreme is on offer in the Talmud's next lines which discuss the legitimacy of studying Greek Wisdom—another topic encountered in chapter 4. To remind:

(B) ben Dama, the nephew of R. Ishmael, asked his uncle:
    What about a person such as myself
    who has studied the entire Torah—
    may I study Greek wisdom?
    In response, R. Ishmael read him the Scripture,
    This Torah shall not depart from your lips,
    and you shall meditate on it day and night. (Joshua 1:8)
    Go and find a time that is neither day nor night,
    and then you can study Greek wisdom.

Here the encounter with God is seen as all-consuming, to the point where even one who has mastered the entire Torah may not divert from it for even a moment. Torah is not about acquiring information, but about standing in awe of the divine presence; a primary intellectual and spiritual activity that may not be "departed from," whatever the allure of the wisdom of the Greeks.

This second extreme is then challenged by a third view that contests both its textual and its philosophical premises. Textually, the Talmud creates a what we now refer to as a hyperlink connecting the relatively obscure term "*depart*" (ימוש), found in the book of Joshua (cited in passages A and B) with yet another appearance of this term in Exodus 33:11. In the latter source it is employed to emphasize Joshua's wholehearted devotion to the Torah, noting that Joshua would "not depart from the tent" where God's presence resides. In its various conjugations, this term appears only twenty times in the entire Bible, and the fact that two of these appearances relate to Joshua—the only person associated with this term—creates a linguistic and thematic link between them. The Talmud continues as follows:

> (C) But [R. Ishmael's view] argues with R. Shmuel b. Naḥmani.
>> As R. Shmuel b. Naḥmani stated in the name of R. Jonathan
>> This verse [Joshua 1:8] is neither an obligation nor a mitzvah,
>> but rather a blessing:
>> God saw that the words of Torah were very dear to Joshua,
>> As the Scripture states:
>> *And [Moses's] servant Joshua ben Nun, a youth, did not depart*
>> *from the tent [of Torah study].* (Ex. 33:11)
>> God said to Joshua:
>> "Joshua, the words of Torah are so dear to you?
>> [I bless you that]
>> *The words of Torah shall not depart* (ימוש) *from your mouth, and*
>> *you shall meditate on it day and night.* (Joshua 1:8)

R. Shmuel b. Naḥmani's point instructs us that that to understand Joshua (the person) as well as the opening chapter of the book bearing his name, we must read the character holistically. True, from the text of the first chapter alone, one may get the impression that God is *warning* the newly installed leader not to forsake God's Torah as he embarks on an ambitious military and political career—a danger that entrapped more than a few of Israel's latter kings and leaders. R. Shmuel reminds us however, that the book of Exodus already teaches that whatever role Joshua may come to inhabit, at his core Joshua is one who does "not depart" from the godly tent. His approach to Torah is dominated not by a legal command booming down from heaven, but by the opportunity to ennoble his soul in the divine presence. Therefore, the best reading of chapter 1 of Joshua is not—as R. Ishmael in passage B would have it—to understand God as admonishing Joshua, but as reassuring him. Though Joshua is about to leave the tent of Torah for the turmoil of politics and warfare, God offers the blessing and opportunity that Joshua will "meditate on [Torah] day and night."

But is this the full scope of R. Shmuel's argument with R. Ishmael? Does he merely offer a different reading of a key passage, or is he advancing an alternate conception of living in God's presence? In its concluding lines, the Talmud subtly proposes the latter:

(D) It was taught in the academy of R. Ishmael:
The words of Torah should not be an obligation upon you,
But neither are you free to release yourself from them.

When one approaches Torah as a regulatory burden, one of two extremes will likely emerge. The first is reductive and looks for the easiest method of discharging the obligation, typified by the one-chapter-in-the-morning, one-chapter-at-night approach described in passage A. At the other extreme is the totalizing encounter with God that leaves no room for human thought or accomplishment, embodied here in the prohibition against learning Greek wisdom, the Talmud's stand-in for human accomplishment. Taken together, passages C and D suggest this is a false dichotomy. A true student of Joshua understands that, contrary to passage B, Torah is not an all-encompassing or stifling "obligation." Rather, Torah is a liberating opportunity to engage the intellect in the study of God's Torah with love and devotion. All the same, however, Torah is not a purely voluntary activity, one is not "free to release" themselves from it. A Jew finds liberating expression through Torah precisely because it is God's wisdom and command.[5]

As is often true in the Talmud, the debate remains unresolved. Yet just below the surface, the Talmud offers some clues as to where its sympathies lie. The first clue is structural: passages A and B represent extremes; passage C reflects the golden mean.

The second clue resides in the Talmud's phrasing in passage C. There, R. Shmuel b. Naḥmani, a third-fourth century talmudic scholar (*amora*), is presented as retrospectively debating with R. Ishmael, a mishnaic scholar (*tanna*) of an earlier era. Notably, the passage begins with a technical term indicating that "this view conflicts" (ופליגי)—an innocent-sounding phrase that in context is quite revealing. Usually the Talmud assumes the view of an earlier *tanna* trumps that of a later *amora*; one would therefore expect the Talmud to introduce R. Shmuel b. Naḥmani's view using a different stock phrase, one that signals a challenge based on a higher source of authority (מיתבי). Instead, by using the neutral term "it conflicts," the Talmud quietly upgrades the later view, presenting it as formally equal to the earlier.[6]

Finally, when the Talmud, in passage D, wants to support the view of the *amora* R. Shmuel (passage C), it cites a teaching from, of all places, the academy of the selfsame *tanna* R. Ishmael. This signals that perhaps even R. Ishmael would agree to the moderated approach of passage C, and that his sharply worded barb to his nephew, "go and find a time that is neither day nor night," is best heard rhetorically.[7]

We might strengthen this point by focusing on the character of ben Dama, R. Ishmael's nephew, who claims to have "studied the entire Torah." This statement is as audacious as it is unusual: no first-rank rabbi is recorded as saying, I have mastered the Torah, now let me move on. Nor does it seem that ben Dama's assessment of his own talents was widely shared. No teachings are attributed to his name, and his only other significant appearance in the rabbinic canon concerns an argument with his uncle over the permissibility of employing a magical (perhaps Christian) healer. There too, ben Dama is attracted to a form of extra-rabbinic knowledge deemed taboo by his uncle.[8]

Indeed, this passage offers a contrast between the personality of ben Dama and that of the biblical Joshua. To the arrogant ben Dama who approaches Torah as a body of information to be mastered, Torah must be presented as an all-consuming obligation, and Greek wisdom remains off-limits. Not so for Joshua. Having matured in God's tent, he is trusted to balance commanded obligation with human aspiration.

These four passages neatly draw out what it means to view halakhah through the lens of Torah study. To begin with, we have seen how halakhah operates on different levels, with a discussion about Temple ritual transitioning into a discussion of how to lead a Godly life. Thus, when studied as part of Torah no halakhah is truly irrelevant: even non-applied Temple procedures are recast as meaningful guideposts to life's difficult questions.

But that is not all. The Talmud itself emerges as a product of Torah study. The sugya makes its case by means of the Talmud's narrating voice, which studies Torah by stringing these otherwise unrelated passages (labeled A-D) into a coherent discussion. In form as well as in substance, then, the sugya speaks to the centrality of Torah and its study.

Additionally, though framing its discussion in legal terms, the Talmud teaches even as it legislates. Though it seems to encourage R. Shmuel's integrative approach, several other perspectives are left open as possibilities. And that, too, is a lesson: how a mortal can possibly stand "at all times" before the Creator is an existential question whose answer cannot be reduced to a one-size-fits-all formula of a legal rule.

In a similar fashion, the structure of the talmudic passage invites further study and analysis. What constitutes the wisdom of the Greeks? Should the minimalist position be taught to the masses? Which reading of Joshua is correct? Is R. Ishmael dressing down his arrogant nephew or issuing a statement of social policy? How should this text be assimilated with passages that pull in other directions? These are but some of the central questions the Talmud's later commentators would return to address.

Finally, notwithstanding its open-endedness, the sugya conveys a clear message: Torah study is at the center of religious experience. The specifics—including such enduringly controverted issues as the tension between Torah and Greek wisdom, and between religious minimalism and maximalism—are debated, yet the common ground is reinforced throughout: people should aspire to live in the constant presence of the divine.

Manliness and Mankind's Destiny

So far, we have looked at cases of non-applied halakhah where a later source (the Talmud) draws expressive meaning out of an earlier source (the Mishnah). This may lead to two false impressions: first, that the Mishnah presents flat legal rulings alone, into which expressive content is later read back; second, that only non-applied law functions as expressive halakhah, but that applied halakhah for its part, serves exclusively as conventional law.

That then brings us to our next example, in which the Mishnah itself pursues strikingly expressive ideas through legal rules—in this case, the thoroughly applicable laws of Shabbat.[9]

The halakhic background is as follows: in general, one is prohibited from carrying objects in the public domain on Shabbat. Since the Mishnah distinguishes *wearing* from *carrying*, clothing and certain adornments—what we might call fashion accessories—are permitted. The question is what counts as an adornment that can be worn, as opposed to an item that is merely carried. The Mishnah (Shabbat 6:4) states:

> A man should not go out on Shabbat:
> Not with a sword, nor a bow, nor a shield, nor a lance, nor a spear.
> And if he did, he is liable for a sin offering.
>
> R. Eliezer says:
> They are an adornment for him.

Typically for the Mishnah, in this statement we find agreement on the general rule coupled with debate over a smaller detail. At least at the outset, the anonymous voice in the mishnah holds that since military gear is carried rather than worn, it is off-limits. R. Eliezer, for his part, permits them as accessories. But then comes the response of the mishnaic sages, which changes the stakes of the debate entirely.

> But the sages say:
> They [tools of war] are but a disgrace.
> As Scripture states:
> *They will beat their swords into plowshares*
> *and their spears into pruning hooks.*
> *Nation will not take up sword against nation,*
> *neither will they train for war anymore.* (Isaiah 2:4)

The obvious question is: what do Isaiah's end-of-days prophecies of world peace have to do with the technical rules of Shabbat regulation? What makes the sages "go messianic" on R. Eliezer?

Let's begin with him. In arguing that a sword is "an adornment," R. Eliezer makes it clear that he is talking not about a weapon carried for defense but about an accessory that projects an image of power.[10] Indeed, military regalia have long adorned the ceremonial garb of kings and princes as tokens of physical strength, military prowess, and sovereign power. In a culture that deploys weapons symbolically ("an adornment"), R. Eliezer holds they become part of the dress uniform, and therefore permitted on Shabbat.

Other sages then disagree. Designating a sword as ceremonial signals that the decorated warrior is a valid image for a Jewish man to portray. The symbolic sword is not used to fight, but to demonstrate that fighting is valorized. The sages counter R. Eliezer's cultural ideal with another. Theirs is not militaristic but messianic, invoking a time when wearing a sword will have all the logic of carrying "a lamp in broad daylight," as the Talmud phrases it. True, in the compromised present, a war hero offers a respectable image of manhood. But in the long view of human history, symbols of warfare are not ceremonial adornments but reminders of human disgrace.

It's also possible that the sages are hinting at an idea found elsewhere in the Talmud and emphasized later by the ḥasidic masters—namely, that Shabbat is an aspirational time that peers into the messianic era.[11]

The sword belongs to the six days of Creation, a reflection of the less-than-ideal present. Shabbat, by contrast, embodies an anticipated domain in which symbols of war are wholly out of place.

The Talmud then raises the stakes even higher, shifting the discussion from what items can be carried on Shabbat to what are the ends of human history (b.Shabbat 63a). In other words, just what will the messiah bring about?

According to the sages, Isaiah's prophecy that "Nation will not take up sword against nation," implies the messiah will usher in an era of human perfection where swords are obsolete. R. Eliezer is less upbeat about what the messiah will bring about. He cites Deuteronomy 15:11, which states that "the poor will *never cease* to be in the land" to imply that poverty will *always* be with us—even come the messiah. Poverty is inconsistent with perfection because when there is poverty, discord and war are sure to follow. R. Eliezer therefore posits a muted conception of the messiah. True, the messiah will bring about an era of Jewish political restoration, but any broader hopes of world peace or human perfection will remain elusive. Since, messiah or not, poverty and strife are inevitably parts of the human condition, the sword retains its symbolic function.

The Talmud next offers another and even more foundational explanation of R. Eliezer's dispute with the sages. Here, both sides assume the messiah will usher in the era of human perfection, but the debate has moved to what human perfection entails. Based on Isaiah's "swords into plowshares" prophecy, the sages assume it will mean the end of war and the reign of peace. R. Eliezer, by contrast, follows the imagery of the Psalmist (45:4) who praises the king, whom the rabbis understand as referring to the messiah, stating, "Gird your sword on your side, you mighty one, clothe yourself with splendor and majesty."[12] Far from being either a disgrace or a mere symbol of power, even in ideal messianic times the sword is associated with splendor and majesty. The armed warrior then, represents the ideal on mankind.

Not, evidently, for the Talmud. The Psalmist may valorize the messiah's military power, but talmudic men distinguish themselves not in armed combat but by jousting in halakhic argument, what the rabbis call "the battle of Torah." To the rabbinic mind, even a militaristic verse from Psalms cannot but speak of the battles of Torah, that is, metaphorically. The ideal man is not a physical warrior, but a scholar who, in the words of the eleventh-century commentator Rashi, bears sharp arguments that are ready for deployment on halakhic battlefield. True, the Talmud stipulates, "a verse is never devoid of its plain meaning" [אין מקרא יוצא מידי פשוטו], but metaphors are compelling only when the comparison rings true.

In this sugya, a small detail in the halakhah of Shabbat initiates a discussion over the ideals of manhood; intellectual versus physical prowess; the relationship between poverty and politics; the possibilities of human perfection; and the true end of human history. The seamless transition between the technicalities of Shabbat law and the ends of messianic time illustrates how hard it is to distinguish between regulatory and expressive halakhah. Indeed, even as this sugya remained the basis of longstanding Shabbat observance, it simultaneously serves as a forum of ongoing theological and eschatological speculation.[13]

What Does Prayer Accomplish?

Prayer plays a role in almost every religion. People pray for health, wealth, salvation, and scores of other material and spiritual benefits. The practice, however, raises many questions: Does God need our prayers? Does prayer work? Can we change God's mind?

The rabbis' approach develops from the laws of prayer—or more precisely from the rules about how *not* to pray. Hence the Mishnah teaches that one who "cries out" over an event that has already occurred "utters a prayer in vain" (Berakhot 9:3). It offers the following example:

> If a man's wife is pregnant, and he declares:
> "[God], May it be Your will that my wife bear a male child."
> This is a prayer in vain.

In the Mishnah's theology, though it is legitimate to pray about events in the future, asking God to undo what has already been done is improper. God responds to prayer, but does not retroactively intervene in the laws of nature.

For a system premised on belief in an all-powerful God, this is a surprising view—which is indeed challenged in the Talmud (b.Berakhot 60a). The question comes in the form of a midrashic interpretation of the verse in Genesis (30:21) about the birth of a daughter named Dinah to the matriarch Leah. In that reading, Leah, who previously had borne six sons, prayed for the sex of this seventh infant to be changed from male to female. This however, contradicts the Mishnah's view that such a prayer is in vain. The issue is resolved by the Talmud's answer that Leah's case was exceptional, and we do not conduct our lives based on miracles performed for biblical heroes.

Significantly, this story about Leah's prayer does not occur in the text of the Torah itself. It is a rabbinic aggadah, likely triggered by the contrast between the Torah's explanation of the names given to Jacob's twelve sons and its total silence regarding the intention behind the name Dinah, which derives from the Hebrew word *din*, meaning judgment. The aggadah explains that in praying for a daughter, Leah "judged" herself—presumably as the birth of another male offspring would have imposed additional stress on her relationship with Rachel, her until-now barren sister and co-wife. (Indeed the tension between the sisters is the dominant theme in this chapter of Genesis.) Taken alone, this aggadic exploration does not appear to stake out a position on a contested matter of halakhah.[14] But as part of the canon of Torah, even an aggadic story may enter and impact the legal conversation.

To return to the laws of prayer: Moshe Halbertal notes that in this sugya the Talmud touches on an issue that has long occupied theologians. How does an all-powerful God interact with the natural order?[15] The Talmud's theology suggests that the petitioner must take the world as it is known. One prays that a tumor will shrink, not that an amputee will grow back a leg; that the sick will heal, not that the individual deceased will return to life. Given the theological implications of this position, however, we should hardly be surprised it is disputed.

In its discussion of this same mishnah, the Jerusalem Talmud (Berakhot 9:3) and the midrash Genesis Rabbah (va-Yetze §72:6) cite Jeremiah 18:6 (made popular by the Yom Kippur liturgy) which analogizes humans to "clay in the hands of the divine potter." Just as a potter has free range with his clay, God can fashion human beings at will. Based on this reading, two further opinions are recorded: one may pray for the desired sex either until the onset of labor, or even, once labor has begun.

The variance in views rests on divergent understandings of how God interacts with the world. All agree that God *can* intervene, but they differ as to the legitimacy of asking, particularly once a given reality has been decided. And this touches on the understanding of prayer more generally. Is prayer a plea for God to intercede in the natural order, as suggested by the Jerusalem Talmud and Genesis Rabbah? Is it a request for insight to cope with a given set of circumstances, as reflected in the Mishnah's view that one must "bless God over calamities just as one blesses God over good fortunes," or is it a range of points in between? Whatever the answer, the talmudic rabbis see the theology of prayer as inseparable from the laws that govern its implementation.

Each of the laws in this chapter already assumes a specific theology: none makes sense outside of the assumptions that God chose the Jewish people, answers their prayers, and commands them to study Torah and observe Shabbat. Yet halakhah is also the forum for defining and refining these same axioms. The laws of prayer reflect on the meaning of prayer; the meaning of Shabbat is derived from the laws that constitute it. In short, halakhah both constructs and is constructed by the underlying theology.

What does this tell us? On the one hand, rummaging through passages like these in search of a systematic Jewish theology will surely lead to disappointment. Although the Talmud speaks to central questions of Jewish thought—standing before God, Torah and secular wisdom, the messianic era, the efficacy of prayer—these big ideas are rarely the direct subject of the Talmud's discussion. On the other hand, to read these passages simply as regulation very much misses the point. The Talmud's claim is subtle but significant: the Torah's ideas do not stand apart from the regulations that give rise to them.

6

Halakhah as Education

Law as Torah is pedagogic. It requires both the discipline of study and the projection of understanding onto the future that is interpretation. Obedience is correlative to understanding. Discourse is initiatory, celebratory, expressive, and performative, rather than critical and analytic.

—ROBERT COVER[1]

TO THIS POINT, we have stressed how halakhah encompasses legal regulation as well as cultural and religious education. But while these roles often reinforce each other, their goals and methods are not fully aligned. This chapter will focus on how the two aspects interact in the context of halakhah's overall project of education. In doing so, we will also shift our attention from laws about human relations with God, to laws about relations with other persons.

Symbolic Law and Moral Education

In the seventh chapter of tractate Bava Metzia, the opening mishnah addresses default terms in a contract—that is rules that apply unless the parties explicitly state otherwise.[2] The mishnah's example has to do with the food an employer is obliged to provide for his worker in cases where the amount has not been specified in advance. In mishnaic times, food was no trifling matter. Indeed, it was an important part of a worker's wages. The Talmud even discusses cases of people working for food alone (b.Bava Metzia 92a).

The Mishnah relates:

(A) In a place where it is customary to feed the workers,
    The employer must feed them.
    To supply them with dip,
    The employer must provide.
    All is in accordance with the local custom.

(B) It once happened
    That R. Yoḥanan b. Matya said to his son,
    "Go out and hire workers for us."
    The son went and contracted to provide food for the workers.
    When the son returned to his father, his father told him:
    "My son, even if you prepare for them a feast like Solomon's at the height of his grandeur,
    you would have not fulfilled your obligation toward them.
    For they are the descendants of Abraham, Isaac, and Jacob!
    Rather, before they begin work, go and tell them:
    '[You are employed] on condition that you have no claim other than for bread and beans exclusively.'"

(C) Rabban Shimon b. Gamliel says:
    It was not necessary for him to say all this.
    Rather, everything is in accord with local custom.

In this mishnah, the rules in sections A and C strike us as quite reasonable. Section A posits in a straightforward manner that, unless agreed otherwise, the employer is required to provide the amount of food customary in the locale. Section C reiterates that local practice governs if the specific term "food" is otherwise undefined.

But if these two sections are precise, concise, and legal, section B is an outlier, being expressive (it tells a story), expansive ("the children of

Abraham, Isaac, and Jacob"), and exaggerative ("even if you prepare a feast like Solomon's"). Nor is it clear that section B proposes a legal standard: all we know is that *even* a feast of Solomonic proportions would not have sufficed. At the same time, however, R. Yoḥanan does not think the employer *should actually* provide an elaborate banquet. Rather, the problem seems to lie in the son's failure to specify the amount of food and contract around the overly generous default rule. To repair the deficiency, the father calls on him to restructure the contract and promise the workers no more than a basic meal.

As regulation, R. Yoḥanan's rule is hard to understand. Why should an employer provide a royal feast simply because he failed to say what should be obvious all along: in the context of a day-laborer's employment, "food" means a basic meal? Not surprisingly, R. Yoḥanan counseled his own son against it, and no later halakhists deemed an employer so obligated.[3] Notwithstanding the mishnah's legal context, R. Yoḥanan is best read as using hyperbole for emphasis. But this should not be confused with regulation.

Here we see the Mishnah operating on both the legal and educational levels. As a contract law directed to courts, the rule of sections A and C surely prevail. A Solomonic feast cannot be imposed by law—if it were, no worker would ever be hired. But the Mishnah also functions as a source of religious wisdom. From this perspective, the remark that *even* a Solomonic feast would be insufficient reminds employers that lowly day-laborers are nevertheless "sons of Abraham, Isaac, and Jacob" who deserve more than the market can bear.[4] As law, the Mishnah regulates contract terms. But as Torah, it influences how an employer—himself obligated in the study of Mishnah—should interact with those in his employ. Depending on time and place, the second aspect may exert greater influence than the first.

Though the decided halakhah rules against R. Yoḥanan, its educational message resonates with later scholars. For example, the thirteenth-century Provençal scholar, Meiri, connects R. Yoḥanan's view with talmudic teachings that call on wealthy householders to provide their hired staff with food of the same quality as that eaten by their masters and allow them a taste from each such dish.[5] Likewise, the nineteenth-century codifier R. Yeḥiel M. Epstein concludes his analysis of employment contracts by noting that, whatever local custom may be, it is a "mark of piety" for a master to allow his servants to taste from every dish.[6]

In sum, while both elements of the mishnah regulate, they do so in different ways. The rule that "everything is in accord with local custom" is halakhah in the sense that parallels civil law. It binds both parties to a transaction and establishes the baseline for how a rabbinic judge would resolve a dispute. By contrast, the literary regulation of section B functions as an ethical argument and moral teaching—closer to how a documentary movie on deleterious working conditions of farm laborers is designed to spur legal and political action towards improving those conditions. Though different in purpose and scope, both forms of regulation accord with established meanings of halakhah.

The Educational Approach of the Talmud

So far we have focused primarily on the Mishnah. To understand the Talmud's educational and expressive messages more fully, however, we must take a closer look at some classic sugyot of the Babylonian Talmud. In these structured units of analysis, the Talmud's narrating voice displays its distinctive method of studying and teaching Torah. While far fewer than half of the Talmud's words adhere to this developed form, it exerts a strong influence on how later scholars came to understand and practice *talmud Torah*. To this day, many regard it the essence of the Babylonian Talmud.

Topics vary widely. Some are tightly focused on technical questions of precise halakhic detail. Others touch on more general matters: whether priority should be given to how a biblical text is written or to how it has been traditionally read (b.Sanhedrin 4a-b); which statistical assumptions can be used to decide questions of civil law (b.Bava Batra 92–93); the degree to which an act that contravenes a halakhah is nevertheless effective (b.Temurah 4–6); which takes precedence if a given action both fulfills a positive commandment while at the same time violating a negative one (b.Yevamot 3–8), and many others.

The Talmud's classic sugyot tend to follow a predictable pattern. The presumed goal is either to uncover the core element of a given halakhah or to investigate the authority for a specific ruling. The narrating voice then examines several tannaitic or amoraic statements or rulings that serve as prooftexts, to determine whether these affirm or contradict the sugya's central premise. In general, each prooftext is subjected to a two-stage process. The narrating voice begins with an "initial assumption" (stage 1) that reads the prooftext as supporting one side of the sugya's basic question. Following some give-and-take, the initial reading is then rejected, such that in the "conclusion" (stage 2) the Talmud re-interprets the prooftext as either neutral or as supportive of the opposing side. A typical sugya works through several stage 1/stage 2 cycles before either reaching a final conclusion or simply moving on to another topic.

One of the more curious aspects is that the Talmud can be rather obstinate about accepting or rejecting proffered proofs. Sometimes the stage 1 assumption seems deeply implausible while the stage 2 conclusion obvious. This raises the question: what was the Talmud thinking in the first place? In other cases, the opening assumption is straightforward while the stage 2 reading seems tortured and improbable. Why is the Talmud so adamant to reject the natural reading of the predecent source? Though rabbis and academic scholars have long debated these issues, the questions remain better than the answers.[7]

Nor are the goals of the Talmud's sugyot always fully transparent. Many are oriented toward determining the accepted position of halakhah by clarifying and ordering different positions and reconciling conflicting authority. These moves mark the sugya as the first step toward establishing a halakhic code. But other sugyot run in the opposite direction. The Talmud is notorious for investigating views that are known to be rejected, and for transforming straightforward rules into complex and impractical abstractions. And either way, many sugyot simply end without resolving the question under review.

This leaves us to ask: what are the sugya's goals? If it is elucidating the halakhah, why is that task so often left incomplete? Or, perhaps it is to further answer a practical legal question, to engage halakhah's underlying principles, to delve into God's law, or to speculate on matters of social and religious thought. But what is the relationship between these various goals?

To investigate these recurring questions, we will look at two examples. In line with the talmudic structure, we'll examine the relevant mishnah first and then see how it is analyzed by the Talmud's narrating voice.

The Worker's Eating Rights

Earlier in this chapter we discussed the Mishnah's presentation of a worker's *contractual* rights. Following that topic, the Mishnah moves to consider rights granted to the worker under Torah law. The source of these rights lies in the rabbis' understanding of Deuteronomy 23:25–26, which permits workers to eat produce in the fields while in the process of harvesting. The Mishnah (Bava Metzia 7:5) addresses the scope of this "eating right" as follows:

(A) A worker may eat cucumbers even if they are worth a dinar [a large amount of money], and dates even if they are worth a dinar.

(B) Rabbi Eleazar Hisma says: a worker should not consume more than his wages.

(C) But the sages permit this. Nevertheless, a person should be taught not to be a glutton and block the entrance before him. [That is, workers who develop a reputation for abusing their rights will not be rehired.]

This mishnah presents three views. Section A begins at one extreme, holding that a worker may eat without regard to the monetary value of the food consumed. Section B takes the opposite view, limiting the right to the value of wages due under contract. Literarily, the mishnah's aim is to draw the reader toward the middle approach adopted in section C. This stresses that while, strictly speaking, the eating right may be unlimited (section A), consideration also needs to be given to the position of section B. Section C performs the educative function of reminding us that while Torah law can grant an entitlement, it cannot force employers to hire workers who game the system. In teaching workers to self-moderate, the mishnah encourages them to become desirable employees. As expected, section C becomes the normative halakhah.

The Talmud (b.Bava Metzia 92a), however, wants to probe deeper into the conceptual underpinnings of the eating right. What is the nature of this right? What are its properties, source, and scope? The sugya sets up the issue as follows:

> They queried:
> When a worker eats in accordance with his eating right,
> does he partake of his own food?
> Or does he partake of food granted by heaven?
>
> What is the difference?
> Take a case where the worker said, "Give the food to my wife or child."
> If you say the worker partakes of his own food,
> then we [allow him to transfter the property right and] give it to them.
> But if you say the worker partakes of food granted by heaven,
> the Torah only granted the right to the worker,
> but not to his wife or children.
> What is the law?

This opening frame neatly captures the ambiguity embedded in many classical sugyot. The evocative phrase, "food granted by heaven," uses symbolic language to point to the underlying theory of halakhah: should we think of the worker's eating right as a matter of contract law (that is, an implied term between employer and worker) or as a ritual obligation (that is, a gift bestowed by God that the employer is required to transmit to the worker)? This can be seen as a particular application of a question regarding the Torah's civil laws more generally: are they social and commercial conventions that become formalized through a halakhic imprimatur, or are they religious obligations applied to commercial settings?

And yet, despite this theoretical staging, the question is also presented in concrete legal terms: can the worker assign his rights to his wife and children? Though the two ways of describing the question are related, they are not the same. Indeed, reconciling the two axes of this sugya became the topic of considerable discussion among later commentators.[8]

Over the course of the sugya, the Talmud works through nine different prooftext cycles before concluding that the rabbis of the mishnaic era were themselves split on the "his food" versus "heaven's food" issue. To get a better sense of how the Talmud operates, we will zero in on a particular prooftext cycle nestled within the sugya's nine attempts. The discussion is admittedly technical, but it allows us to understand why the process of drawing conclusions from the Talmud can be so contested and difficult.

The sugya's second prooftext offers up the debate between sections B and C recorded in the mishnah above. On its face, the mishnah deals with a technical question regarding the amount of produce a worker is permitted to eat as he toils in the field. The sugya, however, assumes the Mishnah's rules are not only commands but repositories of legal ideas. The sugya therefore, mines the Mishnah for information about the structure of the halakhah in question.

Confronting the Mishnah, the initial (stage 1) assumption is that the debate between Rabbi Eliezer and the sages exactly parallels the two sides of the Talmud's query. In this construct, Rabbi Eliezer—who limits the worker's eating right to the contract price—holds the right is contractual in nature: since the worker "partakes of his own food," the right is correspondingly limited. The sages, however, see the eating right as a heavenly gift, and therefore the correlated eating right is unlimited. (Recall the sages limit the eating right due to practical concerns, but hold that fundamentally, the eating right allows the worker unlimited consumption.) Since the sages are the presumptive majority, the halakhah generally follows their view, and in this way the Talmud's reading of the mishnah supports the "heaven's food" perspective.

Stage 1 can be diagramed as follows:
The Mishnah states:

Prooftext (Mishnah)	Mishnah's holding
Rabbi Eliezer:	worker should not consume more than his wages.
Sages:	worker has unlimited legal right to eat.

The Talmud reasons:

Talmud Stage 1	Rationale for Mishnah's holding
Rabbi Eliezer:	since worker partakes "of his own food," the right is limited to the contract wages that give rise to it.
Sages:	since worker partakes "of heaven's food," the heavenly gift provides unlimited eating right.

Though plausible, stage 1 is then rejected by stage 2, which offers a different framework for the mishnah. In this interpretation, the debate between Rabbi Eliezer and the sages is not related to the "his food versus heaven's food" issue but speaks to another topic entirely, in this case a textual disagreement surrounding an enigmatic phrase found in the verse that gives rise to the eating right. Deuteronomy 23:25 states: "when you come into the field of your fellow you may eat grapes *as is your desire*, to be satisfied." For reasons we need not get into, both Rabbi Eliezer and the sages understand the phrase "as is your desire" to *limit* the scope of the worker's biblically-mandated eating rights. In stage 2, the debate of the Mishnah revolves around the type of limitation indicated by that phrase.[9]

According to Rabbi Eliezer, "as is your desire" limits the eating rights of the worker. The sages, however, apply the limitation not to the rights of the worker but to the extent of the employer's liability. The import of "as is your desire" is that, somewhat counterintuitively, the employer **cannot** be held liable should he prevent his workers from exercising their eating rights. However, because the limiting term applies to the employer's liability, the sages find no basis for restricting the amount of food the worker may eat while harvesting. Hence their view in the Mishnah: the worker can eat as much as he desires.

Continuing the diagram, the Mishnah again held:

Prooftext (Mishnah)	Mishnah's holding
Rabbi Eliezer:	worker should not consume more than his wages.
Sages:	worker has unlimited legal right to eat.

In stage 2, the Talmud understands that the Mishnah's argument is not related to the issue of his own food versus heaven's food. Instead, it turns on how each side interprets the biblical phrase "as is your desire," as follows:

Talmud Stage 2	Rationale for Mishnah's holding
Rabbi Eliezer:	"As is your desire" limits the worker's eating rights to the value of contracted-for wages.
Sages:	"As is your desire" limits the employer's liability for restricting eating rights. However, the eating right itself is not limited.

In stage 2, the Talmud associates the sages with the view that the employer faces no liability for restricting his worker's eating rights. This is a somewhat anomalous view of the law, as the overall thrust of the sugya is that the employer would indeed be liable for violating this biblical prohibition. Nevertheless, since accepted halakhah tends to follow the sages, and since this view appears elsewhere in the Talmud, the view attains normative status.[10]

And here we come upon one of the central difficulties in interpreting the Talmud. When the Talmud rejects the second of its nine precedent texts in stage 2, is it *necessarily* adopting the view that exempts the employer from liability, or does it merely wave aside the hypothesis offered in stage 1 by showing that a different reading of the mishnah is *possible*? In other words, is the association generated by stage 2 the Talmud's reasoned conclusion, or simply a waystation in the sugya's overall progression?

Questions of this sort abound in the Talmud and frequently cause debates among later commentators.[11] The source of this tension, however, is the ambiguity inherent in the nature of the sugya itself. A perspective that understands the sugya as constructed for answering a specific question is more likely to assume that each stage reflects a precise and necessary link in the chain of legal analysis. By contrast, the more we see the sugya as an academic discussion akin to a Socratic dialogue or law-school classroom, the more we might conclude that some arguments are placeholders, and that statements may be made rhetorically to emphasize a point.[12] Fittingly, the opening lines of the sugya of the workers' eating rights offer support for each approach.

Seen from this perspective, an interim stage 2 conclusion, offered in the context of a larger sugya, may not be a definitive articulation of the law but simply as a way of moving the discussion forward. In this vein, the Talmud's medieval commentators claimed that some of the "forced answers" found in the Talmud do not carry normative weight, but that these statements are proffered as the "ebb and flow of the talmudic discussion" and can be disregarded as a matter of practiced halakhah.[13]

Reverse-Engineering Halakhic Ideas

Another notable feature of the talmudic sugya is its practice of "reverse-engineering" broader halakhic ideas from specific regulations. We can see an example of this trend in the sugya discussing animal welfare (b. Bava Metzia 32–33).

Exodus 23:5 requires a bystander to aid the owner of an animal that has collapsed on the roadside under the weight of its burden. The Mishnah divides this duty into two separate mitzvot. The first involves *un*loading the burden from the collapsed animal; the second requires *re*loading the animal to help the owner continue on his way. These obligations are referred to as the mitzvot of "unloading" and "reloading," respectively. There is, however, a crucial difference between the two obligations. Whereas unloading must be done for free, the bystander is permitted to demand payment for reloading services.

The leading theory explaining this difference is as follows: since unloading aids both the human owner *and* the animal (by literally taking the load off its back), the terms for it should logically have been deduced from those for reloading, which aids the human owner alone. Having stipulated the reloading obligation, by specifically commanding unloading, the Torah must be adding some additional teaching—that this service must be performed free of charge. Moreover, because unloading (which aids the animal) takes precedence over reloading (which does not), the Talmud finds that halakhah must be concerned for the animal's pain and welfare.

The sugya then moves to consider the degree to which animal welfare is indeed a significant halakhic concern. This is framed as a debate over whether animal welfare is a major, "Torah-level" concern, or a less significant "rabbinic-level" concern. The Talmud then cycles through nearly ten prooftexts in its efforts to answer this question. Employing a somewhat loose translation, let's examine one of them more closely.

Attempting to show that animal welfare is only a minor (rabbinic) concern, the Talmud cites the following proof. (b.Bava Metzia 32b):

> Though *un*loading usually takes precedence over *re*loading:
> As between unloading a friend's ox and reloading an enemy's ox the order is reversed.
>
> This is to countermand the natural inclination to aid one's friend and shun one's enemy.
> Thus, one should first help an enemy to reload and only then aid a friend to unload.

The stage 1 reasons as follows: if the demands of moral education take precedence over animal welfare, then animal welfare must be only a minor, rabbinic concern. Otherwise, how could the law circumvent a major biblical principle for the sake of moral education? Stage 2, however, rejects this either/or assumption. It holds that even if animal welfare is of biblical concern, in a case where it conflicts with the moral education of a human, the former gives way to the latter. In other words, animal welfare may be of biblical importance, yet other values may nevertheless overrule it.

Our brief tour of this sugya nicely captures how the Talmud views the relationship between bottom-end legal rules and abstract concepts. Here the entry point is not the idea of animal welfare in the abstract, but technical rulings addressing the scope of the respective obligations to unload and reload a faltering beast of burden. By working through these technicalities, the Talmud sees that a concern for animal welfare is indeed implied in the halakhic structure. While the concept is initially derived from specific rulings, once recognized, it becomes an independent factor in the halakhic landscape. (e.g., b.Shabbat 128b and 154b).

The sugya also sheds light on how the Talmud reworks specific halakhic requirements. As a self-standing regulation, the rule about aiding a friend versus an enemy is relevant only in the most unlikely scenario where, at exactly the same moment, a person encounters his best friend and his sworn enemy stranded on the roadside. (Otherwise, all agree that the person seen first would take precedence.) This may seem like legislation by sophistry. But by shifting the focus from the specific case to its underlying concept, the sugya transforms an obscure ruling into a value-laden claim about the relative position of animals and humans in the halakhic ecology. Underwriting this method is the ongoing assumption that halakhah is multidimensional—and that the sugya's own performance of Torah study brings these different dimensions to the fore.

7

Halakhah as Aggadah

A living and vital halakhah is an aggadah that was or that will be.
And the same is true in reverse. In their beginning and end, the two
are conjoined.

—ḤAYYIM NAḤMAN BIALIK[1]

THE DIVIDE BETWEEN HALAKHAH (the domain of binding law) and
aggadah (the loosely structured collection of narrative, thought, and
ethics) has endured through generations of talmudic commentary and
analysis. In large part, this is because the core of each is generally so
distinctive. Indeed, ancient and modern scholars alike have found it
difficult to understand how the rabbis who operate with such precision
in halakhah become so uninhibited and expansive in aggadah.

As the Talmud came to be seen as a proto-law code, the prominence
of this distinction expanded. The process of transforming the massive
body of Talmud into applied legal rules required excising a great deal of
material. And from this perspective, the most obvious candidates for
exclusion were the fantastical readings of the Bible, exotic stories, and
ruminations that constitute the bulk of aggadah.

More recently, however, and in line with the argument we've been
pursuing, scholars have argued that this split is overdetermined.[2] In an
earlier chapter, we already saw how the aggadah about the prayer of the
matriarch Leah for a sex change in her fetus influenced the Talmud's

understanding of the halakhah of prayer. Likewise, our emerging idea that halakhah regulates at different levels can be restated as suggesting that halakhah can also function as aggadah. In a sense, the Talmud not only encompasses halakhah and aggadah but to a degree claims that they are one and the same.

In this chapter we'll develop these claims in the context of two sugyot that display a less defined structure than the classic sugyot described in the previous chapter. The first explores the opening lines of the entire Talmud, showing how the halakhic debate over the time at which to recite the *Shema* prayer relates to the meaning of the ritual itself. The second shows that while aggadic texts are initially introduced in service of a halakhic argument, the halakhic discussion in turn spawns a philosophical inquiry into the Torah's legal theory. Finally, prefiguring Part III of this book, we will peer ahead to see how later interpreters confronted these elements of the sugya.

The Talmud's Opening Scene
To Teach in a Roundabout Manner

In chapter 3, we encountered the first mishnah in the opening tractate of Berakhot. Discussing the nighttime *Shema*, it states as follows:

> From what time is the evening *Shema* recited?
> From the time that the kohanim [priests] enter to eat their consecrated food,
> until the end of the first watch period—
> These are the words of Rabbi Eliezer.
> But the sages say, until midnight.
> Rabban Gamliel says until the dawn rises.

As its initial line of inquiry, the Talmud questions the structure of the entire first chapter of the Mishnah. The issue is this: while the chapter opens discussing the nighttime *Shema*, subsequent paragraphs move on to the laws of daytime *Shema*, only to return to the nighttime *Shema* at the end of the chapter. Why not group all the laws of nighttime *Shema* together?

The Talmud answers its own question noting that the Mishnah is organized in accordance with a literary device found in both biblical and rabbinic texts known as a chiastic structure. The chapter both begins and ends with the laws of the nighttime *Shema*; these enclose and act as bookends to the "interior" laws of the daytime *Shema*. The exchange is compact, yet significant. The Talmud's starting premise assumes a legal universe organized conceptually by topic. The response, however, is that the Mishnah is not only law, structured for clarity, but literature, which communicates through structure and form.[3]

A similar line is pursued in the Talmud's second inquiry. The Mishnah's opening clause holds that the *Shema* should be recited "from when the kohanim enter to eat their consecrated food." This statement functions less as an indicator of time than as a hyperlink that takes us from the familiar laws of the *Shema* to the obscure laws of ritual purity. Unless we assume that the general public was deeply learned in laws relevant only to a small priestly subset, the Mishnah here offers little guidance to the actual time for reciting the *Shema*. This is in sharp contrast with the more intuitive references to natural phenomena like "until midnight" or "until the dawn rises." The Talmud assumes that the kohanim enter to eat their *terumah* when the stars become visible (starlight), and thus wonders: why hasn't the Mishnah simply cut out the priestly business and state the law directly: the *Shema* can be recited from starlight?

Its answer is telling: the Mishnah has faced a choice and made a deliberate decision. The choice is whether to pursue the legislative ideal of stating the law in clear and unambiguous terms, or to adopt a more complex phrasing that will teach something in a roundabout manner. As the Talmud sees it, the Mishnah willingly sacrifices clarity to shed light on the seemingly unrelated purity laws. Though we needn't delve into the specifics, the central claim is clear. On its very first page, the Talmud shows how the imminently practicable laws of the *Shema* and the obscure laws of priestly purity are interconnected through the web of Torah study.

A similar approach is found in the Talmud's third inquiry of the Mishnah. Here it investigates R. Eliezer's view that the *Shema* may be recited "until the end of the first watch." Questioning the opaque term "watch," the Talmud again answers that the intention is to add aother dimension. This time, however, the addition is not technical or legal but broadly cosmological. R. Eliezer's term conveys that "just as there are watch periods on earth, there are watch periods in heaven." Elaborating, the Talmud goes on to state that the transition period between these heavenly watches are marked by "roars" emerging from the divine throne, as God bemoans the destruction of the Temple and the exile of the Jewish people.

From this starting point, the Talmud embarks on a lengthy aggadic discussion of the phenomenology of night, focusing on themes of exile, destruction, fear, and demons, while noting that the *Shema* and the study of Torah can hold these forces at bay (b.Berakhot 3a-4a). For us, the point is clear: when forced to choose between regulatory clarity and developing a religious phenomenology (in this case, of night), the Talmud reads the Mishnah to value the latter over the former.

Is it mere accident that the Talmud's first three inquiries into the Mishnah draw attention to the difference between reading that work as law and reading it as literature? Some modern scholars contend that the opening sections of talmudic tractates are a late product: one of the last layers in the lengthy editing process. According to this theory, the Talmud's final composers sought to introduce the tractate (or maybe the Talmud as a whole) by presenting its major themes and preoccupations in condensed form; but these claims remain inherently speculative.[4] Be that as it may, our review reveals that on three separate occasions the Talmud begins with the assumption that the Mishnah should speak with legal precision and in each case concludes that the goal of expanding and teaching Torah takes precedence.

The Teaching Function of Halakhic Regulations

According to the Talmud, the mishnah's phrase, "from the time that the kohanim enter to eat their consecrated food," is enigmatic as it relates to the *Shema* but is nevertheless helpful since it clears up an ambiguity in the purity laws. This answer, however, is only partial, since in the very next lines the Talmud cites seven additional views regarding timing of the nighttime *Shema* that follow a similar pattern. The order of the eight views is as follows:

1. From when the priests *enter* to eat their consecrated food. (mishnah)
2. From when a poor person *enters* to eat his bread with salt.
3. From when people *enter* to eat their bread on Shabbat eve.
4. From when the priests are entitled to eat their consecrated food; a marker for this time being starlight.
5. From when one sanctifies the day on Shabbat eve.[5]
6. From when the priests become purified to eat their consecrated food.
7. From when the priests immerse to eat their consecrated food.
8. From when most people *enter* to sit and eat their meal.

Viewed together, the eight opinions show a concerted effort to avoid natural markers like sundown, darkness, or starlight. Thus, it is not only the mishnah, but *all the competing views* cited in the Talmud work hard to tie the recitation of the *Shema* to different religious or social phenomena.[6] Further, some are so minutely distinguishable (immersion to eat versus purification to eat versus entering to eat versus entitled to eat) as to be unintelligible to all but the most scholarly astute. Indeed, the Talmud understands that at least some of these descriptors are simply different ways of describing the same moment. The difference among them is less a matter of time as measured on a clock than which categories are employed to observe time.[7]

The exact meaning conveyed by these time-referents is open to interpretation.[8] On the whole, they reflect how different layers of society effect the transition from public daytime activities to the private sphere of the home-based evening meal (a theme emphasized by recurring use of the term "enter," connoting a move from the public domain to a private arena). Beyond this, as the table below indicates, the eight views can be divided into two basic categories: four discuss the priestly preparations before a ritualized dinner of consecrated foods, and four relate to the evening schedule of ordinary folk.

Priestly Schedule	Ordinary Life Schedule
From when the kohanim **enter** to eat their consecrated food.	From when the poor person **enters** to eat his bread with salt.
From when the kohanim are **entitled** to eat their consecrated food.	From when people **enter** to eat their bread on Shabbat eve.
From when the kohanim become **purified** to eat their consecrated food.	From when one **sanctifies** the day on Shabbat eve (*kidesh hayom*).
From when the kohanim **immerse** to eat their consecrated food.	From when most people **enter** to sit and eat their meal.

The two columns spotlight how the sugya grapples not only with *when* to recite the *Shema* but also which conception of time is most appropriate for *understanding* the recital of the *Shema*. Is it the priestly schedule that sees daily life in a ritual frame? Or a workday cycle that centers on a social view of people coming home in the evening? The former concerns a regimented meal dominated by the requirements of time (after starlight), ritual status (purity), and social status (this form of consecrated food may be eaten only by priests and their households). The latter, less institutionalized view, tracks how different social groups conclude their day. Centuries later, rabbinic scholars of the eighteenth and nineteenth centuries would put the question this way: is the mitzvah of the *Shema* tied to ritual parameters of how halakhah defines night, or to a more socially grounded understanding of the Torah's phrase, "as you retire."[9]

Seen in these terms, the sugya presents an ongoing dilemma not only about the nature of the *Shema* but perhaps about religious life more broadly. Does it stand "outside life"—what theologians call the transcendent—or is it a "within-life" affair—what theologians call the immanent? The issue is relevant to the *Shema* because the rabbis saw this prayer as the central affirmation of God's dominion, recited twice each day, in accord with the Torah's instructions, "as you retire and as you arise." The sugya is simultaneously interested in both the timing of ritual performance as well as its mindset: how the central act of faith is inserted into the daily schedule, and how it ought to construct the daily routine.[10]

This perspective on the talmudic deliberations may be reinforced by examining a related debate in the same chapter of Berakhot (m.1:3) between the the disciples of Shammai and Hillel. Though the issue here is not timing, but physical positioning, similar concerns emerge:

> The house of Shammai say:
> in the evening all persons should lie down and recite the *Shema*,
> while in the morning they should stand and recite the *Shema*.
> As Scripture says, *as you retire and as you arise*.
> But the house of Hillel say:
> Each person recites it as is the custom.

Scholars have noted that the degree of positional formality is related to the experiential dimension of reciting the *Shema*.[11] The Hillelites, who claim that halakhah does not mandate a specific position ("as is his custom"), point to a "within-life" understanding. The Shammaites, by contrast, who insist on a specific ritualistic posture, argue that the *Shema* requires pulling "out" of the daily routine. The Mishnah's normative assessment is made clear in its concluding lines:

> R. Tarfon said:
> I was once traveling,
> and I lay down [at night] to recite the *Shema* as per the house of Shammai,
> and I endangered myself on account of highway bandits.
> They said to him:
> "You put yourself in danger for going against the words of the house of Hillel."

In the ordinary course of life, there may not be much difference between the views of Hillel and Shammai; it may even be common to recite the evening *Shema* in a natural state of repose. R. Tarfon, however, deliberately pulled himself "out" of the traveler's natural position (presumably walking or riding on an animal) to assume a position that has no logic other than as a ritualized obligation. Transforming the recitation of the *Shema* from an "in life" to "ritual" affair put R. Tarfon in the in the company of the rejected Shammaites, such that the Mishnah finds the punishment well-deserved.

Tracing the Sugya over Time

The Talmud does not decide between the various opinions regarding the earliest start-time for the *Shema*. Nevertheless, pursuant to the general rules of halakhic decision-making, the halakhah should follow the view expressed in the Mishnah, here understood as starlight.

In this case however, the matter turns out to be more complex. As far back as the ninth century, some of the earliest post-talmudic authorities noted that the *Shema* was routinely recited considerably before starlight.[12] The issue came to a head in the writings of the Franco-German authorities in the twelfth and thirteenth centuries, when the long evenings of the northern European summer exposed the rift between the astrological (and thus ritual) cycle of time, in which starlight does not occur until as late as 11:00 pm, and social time, whereby people retire considerably earlier. Moreover, because the Talmud commends recitation of the *Shema* prior to the evening meal, many communities adopted the practice of reciting the *Shema* and then eating dinner several hours before stars became visible in the summer night's sky.[13]

The issue plays on both the legal and experiential elements of our sugya. R. Isaac b. Samuel of Dampierre (d. circa 1184) defends the early recitation of the *Shema,* arguing that in this case the halakhah does not follow the Mishnah but accords with the fifth view presented above.[14] In a similar vein, R. Eliezer ben Nathan of Mainz (d. 1170) holds that since the biblical verse ties the *Shema* to when people retire, the obligation tracks the human rather than the halakhic clock.[15] Others held that although it would be ideal to recite the *Shema* after starlight, halakhah does not require those who have already made the transition into home life to reemerge late at night for evening prayer.[16]

Shades of this debate continue to the present day. In communities that consist mainly of laymen, the afternoon (*minḥah*) prayers are rolled together with the evening prayers (*ma'ariv*) and recited around dusk. Though this results in reciting the *Shema* slightly before starlight, the obligation can be accomplished before people retire to their private spheres for the night. By contrast, in certain communities there is a much stronger insistence on coming out for communal prayer, even after having entered one's home for the evening. Again, the issue touches on the central question of our sugya: does the obligation of the *Shema* track the pattern of daily life, or should daily life be constructed around the obligation?

In its opening sugya, the Talmud mixes halakhah and aggadah into the same unit of analysis. The mandated time for the nightly *Shema* undeniably functions as law. Yet in linking its regulation to the phenomenology of "night" and the theology of what it means to "accept God's dominion," the Talmud uses the halakhic data to convey the inner content of the commanded act itself. As subsequent scholars came to formulate halakhic practice under different social and geographical conditions, they returned to consult both the technical and the experiential dimensions of this first sugya.

Halakhic Arguments in Aggadic Form

Our second example is drawn from the laws describing a legal procedure known as *p'sharah,* or alternatively *bitzua,* a term best translated as "compromise." This process is similar to what American lawyers know as Alternative Dispute Resolution (ADR). The goal is to bring the parties to a compromise that will end the dispute outside the formalized rules of halakhah, or what the Talmud calls *din*—the law.

The rabbis' foundational assumption, however, is that God gave the Jewish people the law on Mount Sinai, and thus the questions arises: In a legal system whose specific rules are divinely ordained, how is this even an option? Can a terrestrial judge deviate from the divine law to resolve a case based on an ad-hoc compromise?

The Talmud engages this question by analyzing an extensive corpus of text from the Tosefta, which discusses the halakhic permissibility of adjudication via compromise (b.Sanhedrin 6b).[17] As is often the case, the Talmud's theoretical arguments must be teased out from both the form and substance of the text under consideration.

The passage is built around four basic views. Sections A and D subscribe to the moderate view that a compromise is permitted. Section B holds that it is prohibited. Section C, going to the opposite extreme, maintains it is required. The textual presentation of the views can be diagrammed as follows:

(A)   Compromise is permitted until the case is completed.
　(B)　It is prohibited to enact a compromise.
　(C)　It is a commandment (mitzvah) to enact a compromise.
(D)　Compromise is permitted until the judge has formed an opinion on the merits of the case.

A quick glance shows that the text encompasses two different modes of conversation. The outer, or enveloping, opinions (A and D) engage in a lawyerly analysis of judicial process. Both assume that deviating from the law for the sake of compromise is permitted, the issue being the point at which the judge may no longer switch from one track to the other. By contrast, the inner sections (B and C) engage in a more foundational argument: is adjudication-by- compromise a religious *commandment* (mitzvah) or a religious *prohibition*?

In addition, while the outer sections generally stick to a presentation of their legal rules with relatively few embellishments, the structure of the inner sections is considerably more complex. Below, we'll examine how sections B and C employ several aggadic readings of biblical verses to link the technical question about legal procedure with the philosophical question about the nature of justice. For ease of presentation, I have edited out small portions of this text.

Compromise Is Forbidden

In Hebrew, the compromise procedure under discussion is alternatively called *p'sharah* or *bitzua*. The latter term, *bitzua*, means something akin to splitting, making it an apt term for the method under discussion. While words such as splitting and compromise may have neutral or even positive connotations, in the Bible the Hebrew root of the latter word, *b.tz.a* (ב-צ-ע), carries more sinister inflections. Depending on the context, it can mean something along the lines of "greedy," "covetous," "breaking," or "tearing apart." Interestingly, there is a clear parallel to this ambivalence in English. The term "compromise" can refer either to the praiseworthy act of reaching consensus ("Congressional leaders reached a compromise on important legislation") or, in a more negative light, the place where truth, integrity, and values go to die. ("Senator Smith was found in a compromising position, and then further compromised his integrity in the cover-up.")

Section B argues, in effect: do not be fooled, a compromise is not a peaceful and equitable resolution, but a perversion of justice. It states:

> (B) R. Eliezer the son of R. Yossi says:
>   It is forbidden to perform a compromise (*bitzua*).

The Talmud then supports this halakhic ruling by citing a somewhat enigmatic verse from the Book of Psalms (10:3) that contains the same root term for splitting/compromise (*b.tz.a*). The neutral translation of these verses is, "[The wicked person] blesses the greedy (*b.tz.a*) and reviles the Lord." As poetry, however, the verse leaves much open to interpretation, and the Talmud responds with three different options labeled B-1, B-2, and B-3.

B-1 argues against allowing a judge to sidestep the law and effectuate a compromise.

> (B-1) And anyone who performs a compromise (*bitzua*) is
>   deemed a sinner.
>   And anyone who praises someone who performs a
>   compromise (*bitzua*) reviles God.
>   As Scripture states:
>   *He who blesses the compromiser reviles the Lord.* (Ps. 10:3)
>
>   Rather, let the law pierce through the mountain,
>   As Scripture states:
>   *For judgment belongs to the Lord.* (Deut. 1:17)
>
>   Thus Moses would say, "let the law pierce through the
>   mountain."

But Aaron, loved peace and pursued peace,
and made peace between people,
As Scripture states:
True rulings were in his mouth,
and nothing perverse was on his lips;
He served Me with in peace and uprightness
And turned back many from iniquity. (Malakhi 2:6)

The overall legal theory is reflected in the verse, "*For judgment belongs to the Lord,*" and the correspondingly evocative image, "let the law pierce through the mountain"—a phrase that appears nowhere else in the Talmud or prior Jewish literature. God is the author of the law and the true arbiter of justice. Thus, section B requires a judge to defer to the law's piercing authority, shutting out arguments based on the parties' economic or social standing. Any compromise more concerned with social factors than God's law is wholly prohibited. Moreover, since God's law defines what is just and unjust, it is nothing short of blasphemy to replace this law with an ad-hoc compromise. Using English equivalents, B-1 can be summarized as follows: compromise inevitably compromises justice, thus when one tears (*b.tz.a*) adjudication away from the law, the results are unjust.

The contrast between Moses and Aaron adds an important qualification to this position. As the consummate judge and legal authority, Moses maintains the law must reign supreme. But as the high priest, Aaron occupies a different religious position. The Torah characterizes Aaron's priesthood as a "covenant of peace" (Numbers 25: 12–13), and the cited verse from the second chapter of the prophet Malakhi elaborate on this theme. Further, the description of Aaron here tracks the language of the Mishnah in Avot (1: 12) which states that Aaron "loved and pursued peace and thereby brought people closer to Torah."

The implication is that even according to the anti-compromise stance of section B, not every social dispute must be brought resolved via a formal adjudicative process. It is entirely proper, and even laudable, to follow

Aaron's model of bringing people together outside the law. The problem with *p'sharah* is not that it seeks peace, but that, once the parties have invoked the divine law by looking to Moses rather than Aaron, *"judgement belongs to the Lord."* The law must pierce the mountain.

From here, the Talmud moves to its second reading of the Pslamist's verse, now playing on a different understanding of *b.tz.a*, which as mentioned can also mean "break" or "split" and is the standard rabbinic term for "breaking bread" (בציעת הפת):

(B-2) Rabbi Eliezer says:
> The verse refers to one who stole a quantity of grain,
> Whereupon he ground it, baked it, and separated a gift to the kohen from it (*ḥallah*).
> When he comes to ask: "What blessing should be made?"
> He does not bless, rather he reviles!
> As the Scripture states:
> *He who recites a blessing over the breaking* (root. *b.tz.a*) *of stolen bread, reviles the Lord.* (Ps. 10:3)

The argument is as follows: ordinarily, one who breaks (eats) bread is required to bless God, and is commended for doing so. Yet the Psalm alludes to a case where reciting a blessing while breaking (*b.t.z*) bread is sinful. The implied question is: why is this particular blessing deemed blasphemous? Because the person stole the wheat, processed it, refined it, and then attempted to legitimize his actions by offering the priestly gift from it. When the wheat is obtained by theft, the false piety of asking, "What blessing should be made?" is nothing short of blasphemy.

In the final reading, B-3, offers yet another interpretation of the same verse. It reads as follows:

(B-3) Rabbi Meir says:
> The profiteer (*b.tz.a*) discussed in the verse refers to Judah.
> As Scripture states:
> *Judah said to his brothers,*

"What will we profit (root b.tz.a) if we kill our brother and
cover up his blood?" (Gen. 37.26)
And anyone who praises Judah reviles,
As Scripture states:
He who blesses the profiteer (b.tz.a) reviles the Lord. (Ps. 10.3)

This passage recalls the appearance of the term *"b.tz.a"* in the book of Genesis when Judah tries to convince his brothers to sell Joseph into slavery. To recap, when Joseph sought his brothers out in the fields, they conspired to kill him. Though Reuben, the eldest of the brothers, tried to thwart the plot, he failed. Judah, however, appealed to his brothers, saying: *"What will we profit (b.tz.a) by killing our brother?"* and thus, rather than murder Joseph, the brothers sold him into slavery for a tidy profit. Though the text of Genesis never condemns Judah for his actions, through the verbal echo of the word *b.tz.a,* the Talmud understands Psalm 10 to call Judah to task. Some might celebrate Judah for saving his brother, but in B-3 he is held accountable for Joseph's enslavement.

Taken as a whole, section B's argument against compromise is headlined by the image "the law must pierce through the mountain." But while B-1 is clearly relevant since it casts the compromiser as reviling God, the relevance of B-2 (stolen wheat) and B-3 (Judah as profiteer) to the discussion of compromise is not so clear. In fact, both traditional and modern readings of this passage assume they are substantively unrelated to the topic at hand, and merely cited as alternative explanations of a difficult verse. A closer investigation however, reveals how these seemingly independent aggadic passages work to buttress section B's overall argument.

B-2 claims that when a tribunal takes assets that legally belong to one party and transfers them to another, the judge/compromiser is nothing short of a glorified thief. This form of theft is particularly pernicious since it garbs itself in the righteous cloak of the law. But whereas the common criminal is shunned, the successful compromiser is held up as a hero and communal role model. B-2's argument is that in actuality such a person is a thief who has attempted to shield his crimes through various purifying processes (grinding, baking, tithing—or, in our day, money laundering, accounting tricks, shell corporations, or philanthropy). But just as no amount of physical change can hide the underlying theft, no amount of legal process can compensate for the flawed mode of adjudication.

The theme continues in B-3. In linking the poetic phrasing of Psalm 10 to Judah's use of the term "profit" (*b.tz.a*) in Genesis, the Talmud recalls Judah's "compromise" between the brothers who wanted to kill Joseph, and Reuben who sought to spare him. B-3 declares that since "*judgment belongs to the Lord,*"—a worldview that assumes just and unjust answers—disputes cannot be solved by merely settling on an arbitrary midpoint between the contending parties. Moreover, whereas Judah thought himself a hero, and others are inclined to praise Judah for saving Joseph (according to Gen 29:35 the name Judah means grateful praise), the truth is that he compromised his integrity by consigning Joseph to slavery.

This reading has the further advantage of explaining why the critique is directed not only at the judge/compromiser who enacts the settlement but also at the onlookers who "bless the compromiser." Amicable settlement appeals not only to courts and feuding parties but also to the broader community that wants to end infighting and litigation. By reading Psalm 10 to mean that those who support compromise are also blasphemers, section B chastises the polity that sacrifices the idea that "*judgment belongs to the Lord*" for the sake of social harmony.

Compromise Is a Mitzvah

The intensity with which section B argues that compromise is prohibited is matched only by the insistence of section C that, on the contrary, it is a mitzvah, commanded. In contrast to the unyielding image of "let the law pierce through the mountain," section C sees adjudication as a balancing act between formal justice on the one hand, harmony and charity on the other. The ideal legal outcome is a mediated compromise that locates the common ground between the parties.[18]

The bulk of section C develops contrasting images of how King David structured his government. The Talmud's starting point is the Book of Samuel: "*David reigned over all of Israel, administering justice and tzedakah* [righteousness or charity] *for all his people*" (2 Sam. 8:15). For the Talmud, the Bible's description of the archetypal Jewish king offers the perfect vehicle to debate the ideal system of law and government. The issue is presented in terms of the tension already hinted at in the verse, namely that David managed to administer both strict, formal justice and "*tzedakah,*" which the Talmud, at least initially, understands as something close to charity, or even mercy.

The juxtaposition of these two terms prompts the timeless question of statecraft: how could King David commit to both? Aren't justice and charity in a perpetual state of conflict? Three competing resolutions are explored; we'll label them C-1, C-2, and C-3.

> (C-1) Rabbi Joshua b. Korḥa says:
> It is a commandment [mitzvah] to enact a compromise.
> . . .
>
> Regarding David, Scripture states:
> *So David reigned over all Israel,*
> *administering justice and charity to all his people.* (2 Sam. 8:15)
> But how is this possible?
> For wherever there is strict justice there is no charity,
> and wherever there is charity there is no strict justice!
>
> Rather, what is the case of justice that contains charity?
> I say, this is a compromise.

This first reading supports the overall theme of section C that sees compromise as the ideal solution to a legal dispute. David understood that legal process requires balancing the hard rules of justice with the call to charity. He therefore focused on forging a compromise between the parties, rather than determining the legally correct position.

The next reading, however, offers a different interpretation:

(C-2)   When David adjudicated a case,
   he would find the innocent party not liable, and the guilty
   party liable.
   Neverthless if he saw that an indigent person was liable,
   David would pay the claim from his own funds.
   Thereby accomplishing [strict] justice for one party and
   charity for the other:
   Justice for the claimant—by returning his money,
   and charity for the defendant—that the claim was paid
   from David's own funds.

According to C-2, the law must be true—not simply expedient. As such, it is inconceivable that David would have sacrificed justice for the sake of social harmony, and surely his court ruled according to the strict letter of the law. Yet if a poor defendant became obligated to pay a rich claimant, in an act of charity, David would pay the claim out of his own coffers.

For its part, C-3 claims that even this view is untenable, since David would never have favored one segment of society over another. Thus:

(C-3)   Rabbi [Judah] raised the following objection:
   Scripture states *he administered tzedakah,* (here rendered
   as righteousness) *to **all** his people.*
   Yet, according to the interpretation [of C-2],
   Scripture should have said *he rendered charity to the poor*!
   Rather, though David never paid claims from his own
   accounts,
   But nevertheless satisfied both justice and righteousness.
   Justice to the claimant—by returning his money.
   And righteousness to the defendant—by ensuring he
   would not retain stolen property.

Harking back to the meaning of the word *tzedakah* that is more prevalent in the Bible, C-3 denies that there is any tension that needs mediating. *Tzedakah* does not refer to the extralegal concept of charity but to righteousness, an idea with strong parallels to a strict understanding of justice. On this reading, David neither altered justice for the sake of social harmony nor gave preferential treatment to the poor. Rather, the charge of his court was to pursue righteousness, where each party receives what it deserves, but no more. Righteousness requires that even poor man return what is not lawfully his, and public funds cannot excuse him from this obligation. In a righteous society, no one retains property that does not—under a strict measure of justice—belong to him.

As recent scholarship has noted, in these three readings, the Talmud offers an aggadic meditation on the age-old discussion of the nature of justice. C-3's claim that social positioning should play no role in the judge's decision correlates with what Aristotle calls corrective justice. A judge is only authorized to reverse the harm that A caused B; the broader issues of economic equality and distribution of wealth lie beyond the grasp of corrective justice. By contrast, C-2 hints at what Aristotle terms distributive justice, advocating practical measures to redress wealth disparities. C-1 goes yet farther, arguing that justice requires a judge to factor into his decision both the consequences of that decision and the relative economic standing of the parties.

The Talmud eventually rules in accord with section C (compromise is a mitzvah), though this view is substantially modified in the process. Per the Talmud's conclusion, the judge must offer the parties the *option* of compromise, even though there is no *requirement* for the case to be resolved on that basis. In sum, compromise is preferred, though not required.

The Sugya's Multiple Functions

Our discussion of compromise offers an excellent example of how the Talmud works both as a legal text that establishes rules of practice and as a literary text that reflects on the nature of God's law. Nevertheless, these functions pull in different directions. Law calls out for decisive conclusion, while literature resists it. Though this tension is already felt in the Talmud, it resurfaced in later rabbinic literature. Because while the Talmud clearly rules that compromise is the favored procedure, other than a terse statement in the Jerusalem Talmud noting that "*p'sharah* requires sound discretion" (הכרע הדעת) (Sanhedrin 1:1), halakhic sources offer surprisingly little guidance as to what standards a judge should use in reaching a decision.

Writing in early-eighteenth-century Bavaria, Rabbi Jacob Reischer held that ordinarily when a judge proceeds with to craft a *p'sharah* he should simply declare a fifty-fifty split between the two sides. However, if the parties specifically request the court to institute a compromise that takes halakhic standards into account, the judge should rule two to one (sixty-six to thirty-three percent) in favor of the legally correct party.[19]

Nearly two centuries later, Rabbi Malkiel Tannenbaum who lived in the eastern Polish town of Lomza sharply criticized this view. He began by asking a rhetorical question: if A robs B in broad daylight, and then claims that B owes him three times the amount, should A be permitted to keep the stolen funds simply by insisting on a judicially managed compromise with B?

R. Tannenbaum thought the answer was obviously no and supported his view with reference to the literary structure of a passage quoted above. Why was the seemingly unrelated teaching about Judah selling Joseph (B-3) cited in the course of the Talmud's discussion of judicial procedure? R. Tannenbaum's response tracks our suggestion: The Talmud criticizes Judah because, instead of assessing the legitimacy of each side's claim, he simply averaged them together. In other words, Judah ignored the fact that the brothers' plan for Joseph was nothing short of murder, and that no compromise involving murder is possible. Based on his literary analysis, R. Tannenbaum ruled that before a judge searches for a midpoint between the parties' claims, he must ensure that each side meets some minimal standard of legal validity. Not every claim warrants compromise.[20]

The debate between Rabbis Reischer and Tannenbaum touches on the different roles assumed by the Talmud. There is no disagreement that the Talmud's ruling in favor of promoting compromise (section C) is normative halakhah. For R. Reischer, once this decision is reached, the anti-compromise theory promoted in section B is of no further relevance, as law requires a conclusion. R. Tannenbaum's view is otherwise. Though the practiced halakhah accords with section C, the ideas embedded in the talmudic sugya are not exhausted by this legal determination. The sugya continues to remain "in play." That being the case, R. Tannenbaum draws on the teaching that seems to support the position of section B to refine how section C is administered and applied.

A related example can be found in the works of the twentieth-century halakhist and philosopher, Rabbi Joseph B. Soloveitchik (whom we will encounter again in chapter 12). R. Soloveitchik reads the Talmud as requiring a therapeutic view of the legal process:

> In *p'sharah,* social harmony is the primary concern of the *dayyan* (judge). The fine points of the law and the determination of precise facts are of secondary importance. The goal is not to be juridically astute but to be socially healing. The psychology of the contenders, their socio-economic status and values, as well as the general temper of society, are the primary ingredients employed in the *p'sharah* process. These considerations are evaluated within the broad halakhic parameters of the *Hoshen Mishpat* [Code of Civil Law], and the final resolution of the conflict is a delicate and sensitive blending of both objective legal norms and subjective humanistic goals. For this reason, *p'sharah* is the preferred alternative.[21]

Like R. Tannenbaum's analysis, this passage is premised on the interplay between the Talmud's different modes of communication. R. Soloveitchik assumes that when the Talmud rules in favor of section C, it adopts not only its legal rule (compromise is a mitzvah), but the entire ideological superstructure that supports it. Hence the judge's "responsibility is primarily to enlighten, rather than render decisions on points of law"; to "persuade both sides to retreat from their presumed points of advantage"; and to "preach ... the corrosive personal and social effects of sustained rancor." This radical portrait of judging is found neither in the Talmud nor in the medieval halakhic literature. Rather, it is based on R. Soloveitchik's analysis of the Talmud's aggadic discussion, which he assumes as a normative source of authority.

Two final points in this connection. First, notwithstanding the aggadic overlay, since the issue is grounded in halakhah, R. Soloveitchik's therapeutic account of the judicial role is understood as what halakhah *requires*. Second, in a nod back to the sugya itself, R. Soloveitchik's discussion is not presented in an opinion of halakhic practice, provision of a halakhic code, or even a work of talmudic commentary—writings typically classified as halakhah. To the contrary, his comments were presented in an aggadic lecture focused on the theological aspects of God's judgment on Yom Kippur. Yet, because the theological message arises out of the halakhic details, an aggadic homily can, in turn, influence the real-time practices of rabbinic courts.

In R. Soloveitchik's hands, the Talmud's rehearsal of the necessary balance between halakhah and aggadah comes full circle.

8

Thinking Legally

The main business of a lawyer is to take the romance, the mystery, the irony, the ambiguity out of everything he touches.

—ANTONIN SCALIA[1]

OUR READING OF THE TALMUD'S SUGYOT has emphasized three core principles. First, halakhic rules form the basis of discussions about a range of issues whether legal, social, or theological. Second, the Talmud's analysis of these rules establishes both the legal and the metaphorical context that gives them meaning. Finally, when constructed as Torah that one is obliged to study, otherwise marginalized questions of social and theological significance can move to the center of rabbinic thinking.

The import of Torah study also means that halakhah cannot be fully actualized through practice alone. This is not only for the technical reason that no single person is obligated in the entirety of halakhah. (Some rules apply only to men, only to women, only to priests, etc.) Nor is this even because halakhah contains non-applied or rarely applied laws to which access is gained primarily through Torah study. Rather, it is because halakhah's regulations entail *meanings* that can be accessed only through detailed study.

Thus, as we saw in the previous chapter, the recitation of the *Shema* at its proper time constitutes not only the fulfillment of the mitzvah but a performance of the idea represented by the given time-marker. Likewise, when a judge enacts a compromise, he is not only following the normative rule of halakhah but (as R. Soloveitchik stresses) affirms the conception of justice reflected in the pro-compromise talmudic passage. Through Torah study, these actions are transformed from flat regulations into three-dimensional expressions of rabbinic thought and values.

This view of halakhah represents a partial response to the critique of religious legalism epitomized by Jesus. Early on, Jesus scoffed at the Pharisees' legal obsessions, arguing that their edifice of technicalities inevitably distracts the believer from the "weightier matters of the law." From the rabbinic perspective, however, what this fails to understand is that those same technicalities are the prism through which the weightier matters obtain religious significance.

To be clear, I am hardly claiming that the Talmud brims with legal detail simply because each is a cipher for more universal or philosophically illuminating discussion, or that idea-centric readings offer the best explanation for large swaths of the talmudic text. The proliferation of halakhic material both within and beyond the Talmud is motivated by the need to clarify and follow the halakhic rules, as well as by the desire to acquire the spiritual and cultural capital that accrues from Torah study. Nor can we discount the impact of "path-dependency," the desire of later generations to follow trails charted by their forebears, a tendency especially strong in a culture conscious of its traditions and its continuity. Finally, causation likely runs in the opposite direction as well; since the rabbis themselves were the recipients of a tradition of holy, yet not always relevant, legal materials, they drew out additional layers of meaning to ensure the law's ongoing relevance. The more halakhah came to be seen as the authoritative avenue of expression, the more it came to host theological and cultural discussions.

Therefore, a modest response to Jesus's challenge would acknowledge that all legal systems—halakhah included—have the potential to become overrun by technical minutiae that can drown out the law's overarching goals and principles. The rabbis' idea of halakhah, however, suggests that the opposite may also be true. Whether by design, effect, or some combination thereof, halakhah became the forum to explore and develop the most weighty matters of the law.

Law and Thought: Diverging Styles and Goals

According to a school of legal thought championed by the late U.S. Supreme Court justice Antonin Scalia, the ideal legal text displays no ambiguity and has but one meaning that can be applied with little controversy or discretion. This enables the statutory text to set forth rules that allow people to know their rights and predict when the law's enforcement powers might be brought against them. For Scalia, this was the central idea behind the "rule of law."

What Scalia held desirable about legal texts are exactly opposite to the qualities that allow a text to sustain and inspire vitality in a culture. Literary and artistic works frequently employ irony, ambiguity, humor, metaphor, symbolism, and allusion to create layers of overlapping and conflicting meaning. Philosophers, for their part, are known to articulate extreme positions, not because they are sincerely held but because the exercise can reveal unstated assumptions that stand behind mainstream ideas. Whereas law seeks to close options and strive for unambiguous conclusions, literature and philosophy are designed to open discussion and enable further reflection.

To this point in our consideration of halakhah, we have generally celebrated the mixing of regulatory and expressive modes of thought into a single discourse. But, since the goals of law and literature are so different, this mixing inevitably raises some tensions. Below, we'll explore three complications that result from entwining texts that regulate with those that educate.

Big Ideas and Small Details

The conceptual relationship between technical halakhic rules and upper-level ideas is a theme we've encountered in previous chapters. In chapter 5, for example, we focused on the sugya that frames the prohibition against carrying a sword on Shabbat in terms of competing views of the messianic era. But what exactly is the relationship between these two very different subjects? Do the technical details of Shabbat generate the theology of the messianic age? Does the theology generate the legal rules? Or does each build on the other? We also saw how the Talmud's codifiers ruled that practiced halakhah should follow the view of the sages. But does this mean that the sages' view of the messianic era also attains the status of binding law? And is this even an issue that can be decided legally, or is that taking the Talmud's suggestive analogy a step too far?

In this particular case, halakhah's decision-making apparatus did little to quell the debate in Judaism over how the end of days would play out.[2] But other cases differ. Recall, for example, the connection drawn by the Talmud between the laws of the Bread of the Presence, which can be resolved via standard halakhic argumentation, and questions of religious life more generally, which are by definition open-textured. The Talmud's linkage of the two made it all but inevitable that some would assume that resolving the laws of Temple procedure would yield a definitive ruling on a very different type of issue.[3]

The same problem looms in sugyot that address other perennial tensions, such as those between psychological and physical pain, immanence and transcendence, justice and social harmony, and the physical and spiritual aspects of human beings. These sugyot ponder some of the core oppositional dilemmas of social and spiritual life. Yet the halakhic-legal framing may encourage the notion that they can be resolved with the finality of a legal verdict—thereby precluding, rather than encouraging, thoughtful reflection on the underlying questions.

Law's Formalizing Tendencies

A second complication is the impact of an approach to law that generally goes under the heading of "formalism." Positing that considerations not established as law are irrelevant to legal decision-making, formalism is suspicious of giving legal weight to morality, ethics, and other amorphous principles alleged to "stand behind" or "animate" the law. Since halakhah casts so many discussions in legal form, a strong commitment to formalism will likely rule out taking into consideration many important categories of thought on the grounds that they lie beyond the realm of valid halakhic argumentation.

To demonstrate, let's return to the Mishnah's discussion of the default terms in employment contracts presented in chapter 6. This mishnah, as we saw, speaks at two levels. From the perspective of judicial enforcement, R. Yoḥanan's call for giving a worker a meal of Solomonic proportions is rejected; an employer is obligated to provide no more than a basic meal. At the literary level, however, R. Yoḥanan's expansive view re-emerges. By stressing that day-laborers are also sons of the biblical patriarchs, who thus deserve more than even Solomon could have provided, the Mishnah aims to educate employers about the proper treatment of workers.

The codifying authorities are primarily interested in the judicial aspects of the Mishnah and thus ignore R. Yoḥanan's view. Proceeding from formalist assumptions, once the Codes have spoken, however, that view bears no further relevance on halakhic decision-making. Hazy notions of a mishnah's literary structure and educational message may serve as nice fodder for rabbinic sermonizing, but carry no weight in rigorous halakhic ruling.

Much the same can be said of the Talmud's theological reflections. In chapter 7, we read the Talmud's opening sugya as showing how the required timing and positioning for the recitation of the *Shema* both regulates prayer and molds its experience. The formalist view of law, however, finds little use for such soft and legally ambiguous concepts as the experience of prayer. Similarly, on our reading, the difference between when *"the kohanim enter to eat terumah"* and when *"ordinary people enter to eat dinner"* tracks a conceptual debate over what it means to be commanded by God. Seen solely from the perspective of the halakhic clock, however, the entire debate may concern no more than a few seconds in time.

Thus shorn of the layered meanings developed through the sugya, these rules can be reduced to a list of pedantic regulations, and halakhah to no more than an obstacle course of specific formal procedures. While some are inclined to view this tragically, to some formalistic theoriests of halakhah, these are the system's positive features, not bugs.

When Everything Is Law

A third issue relates to what lawyers know as the "rule of recognition," which in our context means determining which passages should be taken as binding and normative law. Because the massive "Sea of the Talmud" consistently mixes applied law with moral exhortation, sermonic admonition, cultural practice, aspirational ideals, non-applied law, and more, considerable uncertainty may arise about the status of any given statement.

A dramatic example is found in the Talmud's analysis of a story recorded in Genesis 38. There, Judah has sentenced his daughter-in-law Tamar to death on counts of prostitution and adultery. Tamar, however, is in possession of physical evidence proving it was none other than Judah himself who had solicited her sexual services. But rather than exonerating herself by displaying the evidence for all to see, Tamar delivers it to Judah discreetly, allowing him to decide how to proceed. The Talmud assumes Tamar's actions are exemplary, stating "better that a person be thrown into a furnace of fire rather than embarrass another in public" (b.Sotah 10b).

Nevertheless, we must ask, in what sense is this statement intended to apply? One school of thought reads it as a moral or ethical teaching that one must endure considerable personal costs to avoid embarrassing someone else. This position is taken by the medieval scholar Menaḥem Meiri (to Sotah 10b), according to whom the Talmud is employing its rhetorical powers to promote ethical behavior. Meiri's approach draws textual support from the Talmud's phrase "*better* that a person be thrown into a furnace of fire . . ." (נח לו לאדם), which carries more of an aspirational flavor than the typical term "one is required/ obligated" (חייב), that tends to prevail in the Talmud.

The halakhic context, however, makes it all but inevitable that others will read this statement in a more explicitly legal framework. Variations of the view that one must martyr oneself rather than embarrass another are found not only in ethical treatises and works of talmudic commentary but even in commentaries surrounding classical halakhic codes and works of ostensibly practical responsa.[4] Though it is difficult to imagine a halakhic norm that would actually require jumping into a fire to stave off another's embarrassment, the divergence of views found in the post-talmudic literature accurately reflects the ambiguities intrinsic to the nature of halakhah.

The Costs of Thinking Legally

Despite everything we've said about the way halakhah combines several modes of thought, there is no gainsaying that its regulatory aspects dominate. The reasons are obvious. Legal thinking is almost inevitably drawn toward concrete rules, and legal directives are far easier to communicate than textured motifs constructed from the literary and legal subtleties of the Talmud's sugyot. Finally from a governance perspective, direct commands more effectively establish communal authority and control than reliance on open-ended renderings of difficult talmudic passages.

This creates a recurring danger of halakhah collapsing into a system of increasingly obsessive legal commands. For to the degree a legal rule can inspire a broad discussion of life's central questions, the converse will also be true: the rabbis' loftiest ideas may be reduced to no more than formalized legal rules.

To demonstrate, let's examine two sugyot that stand in the background of current debates over male/female relations in halakhically observant communities. In each case, the halakhah's legal framing can push interpretation away from the Talmud's literary, moral, and conceptual possibilities and towards specific and exacting regulation.

Moral Guidelines or Legal Rules?

Established halakhic principles prohibit men from seeing a woman's hair or hearing her voice in song. The primary source for this rule is the Talmud's discussion in Berakhot 24a, which states as follows:

> Shmuel said: A woman's voice is *ervah* [a sexual taboo],
> as Scripture states:
> *For your voice is pleasant and your appearance attractive.* (Song
> of Songs 2:4)
> R. Sheshet said: A woman's hair is *ervah*,
> as Scripture states:
> *Your hair is as a herd of goats.* (Song of Songs 4:1)

Leaving aside whether a modern (or ancient) woman would be flattered by comparison to a herd of goats, we can approach the Talmud's determination of female hair and voice as *ervah* from two opposing directions. Starting at the de-legalized end, we might say that since under certain circumstances, even a seemingly innocent glimpse of hair or sound of voice may be arousing and sinful. Therefore men who observe halakhah must honestly assess when interactions cross the line, even if they are not sexual in the strictest sense of the word. In support of this reading, one may note that Song of Songs contains some of the most erotic passages in the entire Bible. This alone might suggest that when a man and woman interact as the two lovers portrayed in that book, the result is *ervah*.

This perspective roughly corresponds with Jesus's admonition in the Sermon on the Mount: *whoever looks at a woman lustfully has already committed adultery with her in his heart.* (Matthew 5:28). Though few read Jesus to demand that anyone gazing at a woman be tried and convicted of adultery in a court of law, a common line of Christian interpretation understands that not only copulation, but even the mere arousal of desire, can be morally considered a form of adultery.

At the other extreme, one could read the Talmud as creating a formal syllogism. As a technical term, "*ervah*" not only signifies a tabooed union but also refers specifically to the genitalia. The Talmud could be claiming that *ervah* denotes a legal status, such that all strictures that apply to prohibited sexual unions, or to gazing at female sexual organs, apply with equal force to gazing at her hair or hearing her voice. Under this legalistic approach, any perceived disparity between a woman's voice or hair and her sexual organs is irrelevant. The Talmud creates a blanket rule of law that demands adherence.

Though every halakhic commentator understands the Talmud to mean something more law-like than the first approach, few have argued for the most rigorous application of the second one either. The Talmud (b.Berakhot 24a) suggests that seeing a woman's hair or hearing her voice is of particular concern during prayer—a limitation that makes little sense if hair and voice are fully equated to gazing at a woman's sexual organs (prohibited at all times). Similarly, other Talmudic sources suggest that hair may be uncovered inside the home or that a few inches may be revealed in public,[5] again, leniencies that do not apply to sexual organs.

Still, the Talmud's use of legal—rather than moral—terminology is highly consequential. Viewed from the perspective of prudence, morality, or ethics, there may well be relevant differences between everyday conversations and erotic vocals, or between braids and bonnets and highlights and hair extensions. Likewise, from a moral perspective it is not hard to see distinctions between a mother singing "Happy Birthday" at a three-year-old's party, campers belting out color-war cheers, or soft-pop music that plays in the background of the mall, from a diva's sultry performance at a smoky cabaret. If viewed as a strictly moral question, the subjective experience of the listener would seem to be a highly pertinent factor.

Yet the legal nature of halakhah makes it difficult to take these contextual factors into account. To be sure, traces of such distinctions are found in the literature, but advocates of more culturally attuned approaches face the uphill task of arguing for exceptions to a generally applicable legal rule.[6] By contrast, those opposed to such carve-outs require no special justification. The blanket nature of the Talmud's prohibition favors a reading that prohibits listening to a woman's voice or seeing her hair under all circumstances. Viewed as a legal rule, form, not substance, tends to dominate the conversation.

Law as Literature, Literature as Law

Our second example explores the potential costs incurred by the fluidity between law and literature in the Talmud, by way of a talmudic story about a man who becomes infatuated with a certain woman (b.Sanhedrin 75a):

> There was an incident with a man
> who set his eyes on a certain woman.
> He became infatuated with her [literally, his heart became full of black bile].
> When they asked the doctors how he could be healed, they replied:
> "he will not be healed unless she cohabits with him."
> When the matter came before the sages, they declared:
> "let him die rather than cohabit with her."
> They asked: "Shall she stand before him naked?"
> [The assumption is this would heal the man without resort to a sexual union.]
> The sages replied: "No. He should die rather than have her stand before him naked."
> They asked: "Shall she speak to him from behind a fence?"
> [The assumption is this would heal the man without resort to a sexual union or even seeing the woman.]
> The sages replied: "No. He should die rather than converse with her from behind a fence."

The Talmud then cites two rabbis who disagreed about the status of the aforesaid woman.

> One said she was married.
> Another said she was single.
>> According to the view she was married,
>> I understand [the sages' reasoning for prohibiting these contacts].
> But if she was single, why all these stringencies?

The Talmud offers two reasons. First, having the woman participate in the contrived encounter would impugn her dignity and that of her family. Second, there is a policy against using women as objects to relieve male desires. The Talmud then concludes:

> But assuming she was single, why did the man not just
> marry her?
> This would not have appeased his desire.
>
>> In accordance with R. Isaac, who said:
>> from the day the Temple was destroyed,
>> the enjoyment of intercourse was taken away [from those
>> who perform it lawfully]
>> and given to sinners.
>> As Scripture states:
>> *Stolen waters are the sweetest, and the bread of secrecy most*
>> *pleasant.* (Proverbs 9:17)

Let's begin by placing this story within its relevant talmudic context. It appears as the concluding lines of the eighth chapter of tractate Sanhedrin, which opens with the law of the rebellious son, the prototypical case of law designed not to apply. This figure is unique among the Talmud's miscreants because he is sentenced to death not for crimes he has committed, but out of concern for where his unchecked desires are likely to lead (b.Sanhedrin 72a). Thus, from a literary perspective, the talmudic chapter ends on the same note that it began: someone committed to death due to uncontrolled desires.

To turn to the more local context, this story follows a sugya that details cases where someone is required to die—that is, undergo martyrdom—rather than violate the Torah's commandments. Though the general rule is that all the commandments may be violated to preserve life, in the three exceptional cases of murder, foreign worship, and illicit sexual relations (known as "uncovering *ervah*"), even one coerced at sword's point must die rather than transgress. The sugya preceeding this story however, focuses on the specifics of the coerced act itself and does not consider whether the coerced party bears any responsibility for being in a situation where death is the only alternative to violating the Torah's cardinal rules.

As a literary coda to the discussion about martyrdom, the role of our story now becomes more understandable. The prior sugya analyzed coercion in the form of a sword-wielding foe who menacingly threatens, "Sin, or I will kill you." The case is dramatic enough to capture the legal theorists' imagination, but also relatively rare. Far more common are the daily battles within each person's soul—for what, after all, is sin if not acceding to internal compulsion? Seen in this light, infatuation to the point of insanity is not something that just "happens." The man in the story did not not venture out at the wrong place and time to be caught by a sadistic thug determined to test his religious resolve. Rather, as is common in romance novels, his lovesickness is the consequence of a long process for which he bears a great deal of responsibility.

The Talmud therefore emphasizes that one cannot work himself into a lustful delirium and hope the law or the rabbis will bail him out. The point is made explicitly in the sugya's closing line. When the Talmud asks, "if she was single, why not just marry her?" The answer is that this would not have helped. The man's "illness" was the unquenchable desire for an illicit encounter; for this, halakhah offers no cure.[7]

Here we once again encounter the tension between the Talmud as law and the Talmud as literature. This approach to the story understands the Talmud as moralizing literature. Read more legally however, the story potentially challenges several prevailing halakhic norms. Typically, actual intercourse, or at least something close to it, is required for a sexual sin to be deemed flagrant enough that one must die rather than transgress. Thus, while acts such as flirting, gazing, and touching that may lead up to intercourse are forbidden, they do not require the ultimate sacrifice of one's life. Yet, according to the story, the rabbis ruled the infatuated man should indeed die rather than gaze or even talk with the woman. Taken as a regulatory text, one may therefore conclude that talking to—or even looking at—a woman is not simply prohibited, but falls into the most severe category of sins for which one must die rather than transgress.

One contemporary scholar has argued that the struggle over how to approach this story is already evident in the text of the Talmud itself.[8] The initial lines of the story (before the marital status of the woman is investigated) constitute an independent literary unit. Then, beginning with the two rabbis who disagree about the woman's status, the Talmud seeks to integrate the story into the surrounding legal structure. This line of thought continues until the point where, having no good answer for why the man should be left to die instead of simply marrying the woman, the Talmud returns to an aggadic register. In the concluding lines, the Talmud thus concedes that the real issue is the spiritual and psychological state whereby the man could only be sexually satisfied through a forbidden encounter.

The tension found in the Talmud is replicated in how post-talmudic authorities analyzed this story. Most early medieval codifiers allow the story to play the quasi-legal, quasi-literary function assumed in the Talmud. Thus, the influential halakhists R. Isaac Alfasi and R. Asher ben Yeḥiel simply repeat the narrative verbatim, importing the ambiguities latent in the Talmud into their halakhic summaries. Maimonides' view is somewhat clearer, as he limits the relevance of the story to where someone has become lustfully infatuated to the point of delirium.[9] Still others follow a more rigorously legal approach, and see the story as legislating generally operative rules. The fifteenth-century Spanish halakhist R. Joseph ibn Habib argues that since the rabbis in the story ordered the man to die rather than speak or gaze at the woman, not just intercourse, but even the acts leading up to it, are such severe prohibitions that one must martyr himself rather than transgress the halakhah.[10]

Though this last position reflects a minority view, it became more mainstream when it was (apparently) adopted by R. Moses Isserles in his sixteenth-century halakhic codification.[11] Thereafter, some halakhists sought to limit its applicability only to licentious forms of hugging and kissing, while others argue for application even with respect to desexualized touching.[12]

The tug of war over this talmudic passage sheds light on how even non-erotic forms of touching or conversing may be conceptualized as prohibited to the degree that one must die rather than transgress. Since few males can, in good faith, assure that the sound or sight of an attractive female will not arouse even slight interest, there are non-trivial halakhic grounds for suggesting that daily life in a mixed-sex society implicates the most severe halakhic prohibitions. Leading rabbis of the twentieth century were asked in utmost sincerity whether there is halakhic justification for walking during the summer near a beach or on streets where it is common for women to expose parts of the body that halakhah requires must remain covered. Similar questions arose regarding whether one may ride on a crowded bus or subway where incidental contact can be all but inevitable.[13]

While no halakhist deems that such activities trigger the requirement of martyrdom, this talmudic story has clearly cast a long shadow over halakhic reasoning and policy formulation. This and similar texts have become the central grounds for arguing that halakhic society requires separate-sex schools, workplaces, buses, stores, and marketplaces. Even in cases where such strictures may not be mandated by the letter of halakhah, ritual logic results in the argument that since *even the possibility* of violating a commandment must be avoided at all costs, one is called upon to act stringently. After all, these cases might even require the ultimate personal sacrifice.[14]

Why Not Just Say It Directly?

At this point, we need to step back and address a matter that has been with us since chapter 1. Instead of employing halakhah to address a range of theological and social issues, why not just address the central questions of human existence directly? The question is even more poignant in light of the conceptual, political, and practical dangers detailed above. Would we not be better off leaving halakhic circumlocutions aside? Why frame everything in such a roundabout manner?

One basic answer doubts whether a conscious decision was ever made in favor of this style of writing. For the rabbis, Torah is God's wisdom, and thus the locus of intellectual and spiritual attention. This is captured in the famous statement about Torah: "Turn it and turn it, for all is in it (m.Avot 5:22)." Since God is the Creator of the universe and the Torah is God's direct communication with man, much (perhaps all) of what man needs to know is found within it.

This theological claim feeds into more sociological considerations. Every society maintains its preferred modes of discourse. In today's data-driven climate, arguments based on the quantifiable methods of economics, behavioral psychology, and neurobiology fare better than more traditional forms of philosophical investigation, theological reasoning, or psychoanalysis. These trends become reinforcing. Once a given way of talking becomes dominant, those who want to influence the culture have a clear incentive to adopt the favored discourse.

A similar dynamic may be at work in halakhah. Rabbinic theology places halakhah at the center of its intellectual universe. As the primacy of halakhah and its study grew, so did the incentives to channel artistic, literary, and political impulses towards halakhic debate and discussion. Indeed, in the rabbinic context, framing something as Torah grants it legitimacy and cachet that neither philosophy, literature, or science can match.

A historical approach would proceed accordingly to examine how this idea of law developed over time, how it responded to surrounding cultures, and what intellectual and material factors caused it to wax or wane in different settings and periods. No doubt this line of inquiry would yield important insights. Our focus here, however, is somewhat different. Rather than asking how or why the rabbis' idea of law developed as it did, we are pursuing the phenomenological question: what is the *effect* of this multi-dimensional understanding of halakhah? In doing so, we can usefully contrast two ways of communicating ideas. One is the abstract method of analytical philosophy; the other is the embedded method of literature.

The goal of analytical inquiry is to approach a subject in the purest and most abstract form possible, free of any distracting contingencies. A philosopher confronting the question, "Is Amy honest?" will look to distinguish between the essential matter of defining honesty, and the more contingent issue of Amy's character traits. Further, in assessing "honesty," the philosopher works through reason alone, downplaying reliance on the specific traditions, laws, or histories of a given society.

Literature starts from the opposite perspective. To understand a work of literature, one must inhabit the plot, characters, symbols, and universe the writer presents. The more one tries to overcome specifics of a novel and speak abstractly, the less illuminating the analysis. The claims that *Anna Karenina* is about jealousy and desire, *The Catcher in the Rye* about teen angst and alienation, or HBO's *The Wire* about institutional decay and corruption, are likely correct. But a novel is valuable precisely because it explores these ideas indirectly, dwelling on nuances and details that cannot be captured through direct prose. To ignore the novel's detailed settings and to read it like a philosophical essay is to rob literature of its most valuable asset. So while the philosopher wants to get at the heart of the matter by stripping away all contingencies, the interpretive literary method denies there are any contingencies to begin with. Any detail, an alliterative word choice, a character's name, or what she is wearing, can shed light on how the novel is to be read.

Under this framing, the Talmud bears greater resemblance to literature than analytic philosophy. Talmudic thought, like its literary counterpart, resists detached inquiry and is therefore difficult to universalize. The Talmud simply does not make any sense outside of its "plot"—the foundational claims of the world it inhabits. These include that God gave the Torah to the Jewish people and commanded them to perform mitzvot. Beyond these foundational beliefs, the Talmud's arguments are generally inaccessible unless one is already invested in the enterprise of halakhah and its study.

In chapter 4, we saw how the Talmud connects the technical question of how to measure the location of a murdered corpse to the nearest city with the foundational question of how to take the measure of humankind. Even this most basic example assumes a deep familiarity with rabbinic thought and method. One must be aware of: (i) the relevant verses in Deuteronomy; (ii) the textual issues in Deuteronomy that led the Mishnah to focus on the act of measuring; (iii) that minute differences in measurement procedures are a legitimate subject of mishnaic debate;

and (iv) that the Talmud holds these obscure details worthy of deeper investigation.

This is only half the story however, for whereas the Talmud speaks in the legislative tone, literature does not. Above, we offered some account as to why the Talmud expressed its ideas as law, but whatever the reason, the result is a different experience for the reader. Effective literature conveys its ideas by creating an emotional connection with the audience through compelling plots, characters, and descriptions. The Talmud benefits from yet another connection; the reader is assumed bound by its laws.

Hence the exacting rituals of the showbread, the precise time to recite the *Shema*, the particular nature of a worker's eating rights—these serve as effective metaphors because the specifics of each mitzvah matter. In this way, the process of framing an issue in halakhic terms both depends on and generates buy-in to the system as a whole. For if the Talmud's incessant legislation were merely a symptom of a collective obsessive-compulsive disorder, why mine its legal details for any meaning or content?

The rabbis assume that a niggling detail in the laws of Shabbat can engender a conversation about the ideals of manhood and even about humanity's ultimate destiny. The reverse is equally true. Assessing the ideal man, or the value of human wisdom, or the goals of a legal system, is inextricably tethered to the small matters of halakhic observance. In tying these ideas together, the Talmud imparts a claim that is alternately maddening and compelling: that the starting point for human exploration and self-actualization is that man stands commanded to live by God's Torah. The rest, as it were, is commentary.

PART III

Between Torah and Law

HALAKHAH IN THE
POST-TALMUDIC PERIOD

Introduction to Part III

The last generation of rabbis mentioned in the Talmud lived in the fifth century, but the process of redacting, refining, and editing the Talmud continued thereafter. At some point between the sixth and ninth centuries—the specifics remain debated—rabbis ceased to see themselves as creating Talmud and instead began to comment on and summarize the massive work that lay before them. Halakhic writing thus shifts from the Talmudic text, which tends to amalgamate persons, eras, and opinions, to works published by individual rabbinic scholars. This shift offers us a clearer view of the authors involved as well as of the time, place, and circumstances in which halakhah was developed and practiced.

This transitional period of Jewish history corresponds to the era between the fall of the Roman Empire in the fifth century and the reemergence of learning and culture in medieval Europe of the tenth and eleventh centuries. Though much is known about the Roman period, and even more about the later Middle Ages, the intervening centuries are effectively dark (to evoke the term by which they were once known), with comparatively few surviving cultural records or artifacts. Much the same is true of halakhah and its history. The richness of the Talmud illuminates the era between the second and fifth centuries; from the tenth century onward, both rabbinic and external sources provide a sense of how halakhah was implemented and its impact on the structure and governance of Jewish communities. But the roughly 500-year period between these two points is considerably more obscured.

From our perspective, the central shift is from the relatively fluid idea of halakhah reflected in the Talmud to a more "law-ified" and systematic view that served as the backbone for the system of governance in the Jewish communities of North Africa and Spain (*Sepharad*) and northern Europe (*Ashkenaz*). Halakhic analysis thus began to journey away from the give-and-take of the Talmudic sugya toward codification and standardization—a process that continues to this day. Despite this transition from Talmud to law, however, the idea of halakhah-as-Torah continues to present itself at critical junctures. The ensuing chapters discuss how, notwithstanding the push toward codification and standardized application, even in the post-talmudic period, halakhah cannot be understood outside the multiplicity of meanings displayed in the Talmud itself.

9

Transitioning to Law

The Talmud is all halakhah le-ma'aseh [applied law].... It is as if the
talmudic authors told us "this is the law to be applied," for they wrote it
in order that it be performed in practice.

—JOSEPH B. MEIR MI-GOSH (SPAIN; 1077-1141)[1]

The Crystallization of the Talmud

In the centuries following the Talmud's closing, it became both fragmented and crystallized. While the Talmud presents largely undifferentiated discussions that evoke the range of rabbinic thought, in the medieval period what might be classified as Talmud became more narrowly
associated with the regulatory aspects of halakhah. At the same time,
the rest of what might be classified as Torah fragmented into separate
disciplines. This shift is exemplified by the tenth-century rabbinic
leader, R. Sa'adia Gaon of Baghdad. This luminary, who wrote some of
the earliest works of systematic halakhah, was also one of the first rabbis
of the post-talmudic era to discuss biblical exegesis, write religious poetry and liturgy, and engage directly in Greek-style theology, philosophy, grammar, and linguistics. But while the Talmud jumbles these matters together, R. Sa'adia addresses each in a separate work marked by a
distinct purpose and style.

The medieval period thus became a time in which biblical commentary, philosophy, liturgy, religious poetry, mysticism, and ethics—areas

of Torah far less dependent on the technical language of the talmudic sugya—evolved into separate disciplnes. In the course of time, each would come to challenge the primacy of halakhah as the touchstone of Jewish learning and the defining feature of Jewish life. But if these subjects were potential competitors to halakhah, halakhah always sufficed to redress the balance.

Though its subject matter fragmented across many fields, the Talmud remained both the source of practiced halakhah and the foundation of *talmud Torah*, taking precedence over the rabbinic literature that preceded it. Hence the (Babylonian) Talmud generally displaced the Tosefta, the Jerusalem Talmud, the halakhic and aggadic midrashim, and even the Mishnah was effectively folded into the Talmud and read through its lens.[2] These developments, already digested by the time of the later *Geonim*—scholars who headed up the Babylonian academies of the ninth and tenth centuries—became fully entrenched in the work of the *Rishonim*: literally, the "first ones," a term applied to the halakhic authorities of North Africa, northern Europe, and then Spain in the eleventh, twelfth, and thireenth centuries.

The consensus regarding the Talmud's centrality brought two related issues to the fore. The first relates to its *text*. How should it be read and approached? What are the goals of its study and the aims of *talmud Torah* more generally? The second speaks to the Talmud's *law*. How should it be practically applied as a system of governance? What should be made of its non-applied rules? And how should communities respond to idealistic rulings that make governance impossible?

This chapter takes up each issue in turn.

The Talmud's Text: Halakhah and the Goals of Talmud Torah

The period of the Rishonim saw the emergence of two contrasting views of *talmud Torah*. The first, which follows the lead of talmudic sugyot oriented toward determining the correct halakhic view, reads the Talmud as a proto-law code focusing on its legal rules. In this model, *talmud Torah* is a functional project whose goal was to tame the talmudic wild into digestible black-letter rules (principles of law commonly known and rarely disputed) of halakhic practice.[3] Though the appeal of this approach is obvious from the perspective of halakhah-as-governance, it has difficulty accounting for the many talmudic sugyot that are notoriously long on analysis and short on unambiguous conclusions.

The opposing view, anchored in a different set of talmudic features, sees Torah study in devotional terms. But while it may account for a number of the Talmud's more peculiar features explored in part II, this approach makes it difficult to engage the Talmud as an authoritative basis of halakhic practice—the view that came to dominate the rabbinic world following the closing of the Talmud.

Correlating with the different approaches to the Talmud, three distinct styles of halakhic writing emerged. First, and reflecting the functional view, are works that aim to summarize and codify halakhah into rules of practice. Second, and reflecting the devotional view, are works of commentary that expand on talmudic discussions as acts of Torah study. Finally, there are works known as *she'elot u-teshuvot*, literally questions and answers or, in Latin, *responsa*. These record specific questions asked of and answered by rabbinic authorities. As they often demonstrate how halakhah was applied to specific cases, this final category is partially analogous to the role of case law in common-law systems.

Different attitudes toward the centrality of Talmud-centric study in the hierarchy of Jewish values emerged during the period of the Rishonim. For example, should the focus of *talmud Torah* be understood broadly (i) to cover all departments of Torah, including study of Bible, Hebrew grammar, Mishnah, midrash, aggadah, liturgy, mysticism, philosophy, and moral teachings apart from what appears in the Talmud or (ii) focus more narrowly on the Talmud and particularly its legal elements? Similarly, is Torah study (i) one of several elements of a well-rounded religious life or (ii) the near-exclusive locus of religious energy and commitment?

Though the alignment is far from exact, the first clause of each pairing resonates with the functional approach to *talmud Torah* which tends to de-emphasize the Talmud as a method and reads halakhah as a conventional legal system. The second clause resonates more closely with the idea that *talmud Torah* is a form of religious devotion and an outlet of creativity.

On this basis, we can point to a broad if imperfect generalization: Sephardi halakhists tended toward the functional view, while their Ashkenazi counterparts favored the devotional one. By recasting halakhah as legal directives, rabbis of medieval Iraq and Spain separated halakhah's regulatory functions from its expressive content. Notably, these same communities pioneered rabbinic forms of Greek-style philosophical theorizing, and were more open to the intellectual culture of the non-Jewish world. It comes as no surprise that Maimonides, the towering Sephardi figure who worked more than anyone to shift Jewish law and thought away from the talmudic form, was both the Talmud's greatest codifier and, in his *Guide of the Perplexed*, the author of Judaism's most influential work of philosophy. In northern Europe, by contrast, *talmud Torah* adopted a more devotional model. These scholars were fiercely loyal to the Talmud as both a method and as a text, and wrote little in the way of reflective inquiry, systematic theology, or philosophy.

The Functional View of the Geonim and R. Isaac Alfasi

The Geonim who flourished in ninth and tenth-century Babylonia produced some of the earliest works of talmudic synthesis and interpretation. While their influence would be somewhat eclipsed by the Rishonim who followed, the Geonim were responsible for developing three core distinctions that impact halakhic thinking to this day.

First, they proposed a sharp line between halakhah and aggadah. Halakhah was tagged as authoritative, legal, and significant, whereas aggadah was deemed flamboyant, allegorical, and of lesser status.[4] Later rabbinic thinkers generally followed the Geonim; in fact, it would take until the fifteenth and sixteenth centuries—well after the period of the Rishonim—before sustained commentaries on the Talmud's aggadah were written.[5] Moreover, in almost every era, the treatment of aggadah pales in comparison to its halakhic counterpart, as a glance at the layout of the standard printed page of Talmud graphically communicates. A page with a large block of talmudic text that contains relatively few comments by medieval writers, suggests that the material is light and aggadic. By contrast, a page whose surface area is largely consumed by commentators signals a sugya rich in analytical halakhic concepts. The message is clear: the Talmud is about halakhah (see figures 9.1 and 9.2).

Second, the Geonim pointed to a distinction within the category of halakhah itself: between the black-letter ruling accepted as practiced law (called *halakhah le-ma'aseh* or *halakhah pesuka*), and the vast literature of debate, analysis, and contending opinions known as the discussions, or the give-and-take (*shakla ve-tarya*), or the style of the Talmud. Much of the Geonim's work involved winnowing the talmudic dialogue down to a legal conclusion, separating rabbinic speculation from legally binding rules.

Finally, the Geonim distinguished between elements of halakhah that apply in the post-Temple exilic era of *galut* (what came to be known as "in our times" or "in these days") and elements that apply to the ideal halakhic realm described by the Talmud. The latter set came to be known as *dina de-talmuda* (the law of the Talmud), and is often contrasted with the rules and norms that actually governed post-talmudic life.

In separating halakhah from aggadah, winnowing the Talmud to legal conclusions, and focusing on the halakhah that applies in the exilic present, the Geonim presented halakhah in conventional legal terms. One of the most prominent exemplars of this tradition is R. Isaac Alfasi of Fez (1013–1103), known by his acronym and hereafter as Rif. His summarizing commentary, *Sefer ha-Halakhot* (often referred to as "Rif") skips over the aggadic portions of the Talmud, as well as those treating the Sanhedrin's procedures and Temple sacrifices, and deals only with the legal sections deemed then-currently applicable. In other respects, too, the work reads like a stripped-down version of the Talmud, offering a synopsis of the central arguments but generally avoiding its more speculative detours. Rif's work is thus less of a commentary on the Talmud than a summary of rules that can be gleaned from it. In it, halakhah comes close to a system of legal regulation.

עין משפט נר מצוה

נ.

הזהב פרק רביעי בבא מציעא

מסורת הש"ס

רבינו חננאל

הגהות הב"ח

שוה שש בחמש מי נתאנה מוכר יד מוכר על העליונה רצה אומר לו תן לי מקחי או תן לי מה שאוניתני איבעיא להו פחות משתות לרבנן לאלתר הויא מחילה או בכדי שיראה לתגר או לקרובו ואם תמצי לומר בכדי שיראה לתגר או לקרובו מאי איכא בין שתות לפחות משתות איכא דאילו שתות ידו על העליונה רצה חוזר רצה קונה ומחזיר אונאה ואילו פחות משתות קנה ומחזיר אונאה מאי תא שמע חזרו לדברי חכמים סברוה פחות משליש לר' טרפון כפחות משתות לרבנן דמי אי אמרת בשלמא פחות משתות לרבנן בכדי שיראה לתגר או לקרובו ולרבי טרפון כל היום משום הכי חזרו אלא אי אמרת פחות משתות לרבנן לאלתר הויא מחילה ולרבי

FIGURES 9.1 and 9.2. A side-by-side image of Bava Metzia 50a and contrast to Berakhot 58a

רבינו חננאל

[א"ר ירמיה בן אלעזר נתקללו שכינה שומרון נתברכו שאמרו רשומרון למורש משום וכו'. נתקללו השמר. שומרון שנתברכו לערי השדה למטע כרם. נשמתו ובל. נול לרלא. וכו' הקם לבית מלך משמע וכו' ריש גרגיתא. כותים. מש"ע מ"ד חו שדמיונם ע]

תורה אור השלם

1. וְשֹׁמְרוֹן אֶשְׂמֶהָ לְעִי הַשָּׂדֶה לְמַטָּעֵי כָרֶם וְהִגַּרְתִּי לַגַּי אֲבָנֶיהָ וִיסֹדֶיהָ אֲגַלֶּה:
מיכה א'

2. בּוֹשָׁה אִמְּכֶם מְאֹד חָפְרָה יוֹלַדְתְּכֶם הִנֵּה אַחֲרִית גּוֹיִם מִדְבָּר צִיָּה וַעֲרָבָה:

3. בּוֹשׁוּ כִּי תוֹשָׁעָה עֲלֵיכֶם אִישׁ לֹא יֵדַע אִישׁ אֲנָשִׁים וְחָכְמַת בָּרָא:

4. וַיֹּאמֶר צֵא וְעָמַדְתָּ בָהָר לִפְנֵי ה' וְהִנֵּה ה' עֹבֵר וְרוּחַ גְּדוֹלָה וְחָזָק מְפָרֵק הָרִים וּמְשַׁבֵּר סְלָעִים לִפְנֵי ה' לֹא בָרוּחַ ה' וְאַחַר הָרוּחַ רַעַשׁ לֹא בָרַעַשׁ ה':

5. וְדָוִד בֶּן יִשַׁי מֶלֶךְ מִכֹּל יַשָׁי שְׂשׁ יִשַׁי נֶחְשָׁב וַיְנַצְּחוּ לַצֵּחַ בְּבֵית יהוה וְגַם בַּמְּלֵאכֶת עֲבֹדַת בֵּית הָאֱלֹהִים:

6. וְאַחַר הָרַעַשׁ אֵשׁ לֹא בָאֵשׁ ה' וְאַחַר הָאֵשׁ קוֹל דְּמָמָה דַקָּה:

הוא ראה אוכלוסים על גב מעלה בהר הבית אמר ברוך חכם הרזים הוא היה אומר כמה יגיעות יגע אדם הראשון עד שמצא פת לאכול חרש וזרע וקצר ועמר ודש וזרה וברר וטחן והרקיד ולש ואפה ואח"כ אכל ואני משכים ומוצא כל אלו מתוקנין לפני אני משכים ומוצא כל אלו מתוקנין לפני וכמה יגיעות יגע אדם הראשון עד שמצא בגד ללבוש גזז ולבן ונפץ וטווה וארג ואח"כ מצא בגד ללבוש ואני משכים ומוצא כל אלו מתוקנין לפני כל אומות שקדרות ובאות לפתח ביתי ואני משכים ומוצא כל אלו לפני היה הוא אומר אורח טוב מהו אומר כמה טרחות טרח בעל הבית בשבילי כמה בשר הביא לפני כמה יין הביא לפני כמה גלוסקאות הביא לפני כל מה שטרח לא טרח אלא בשבילי אבל אורח רע מהו אומר מה טורח טרח בעל הבית זה פת אחת אכלתי חתיכה אחת אכלתי כוס אחד שתיתי כל טורח שטרח בעל הבית זה לא טרח אלא בשביל אשתו ובניו על אורח טוב מהו אומר זכור כי תשגיא פעלו אשר שוררו אנשים אבל אורח רע כתיב לכן יראוהו אנשים וגו' יחזק רב שקיל צנא ודרי ליה על כתפיה אמר גדולה מלאכה שמכבדת את בעליה ר' יהושע בימי שזן וגו' רבי יוחנן הרואה אוכלוסי ישראל אומר ברוך חכם הרזים דמות פרצופיהן דומים זה לזה ואין פרצופיהן דומים זה לזה

10. עֹשֶׂה גְדֹלוֹת עַד אֵין חֵקֶר וְנִפְלָאוֹת עַד אֵין מִסְפָּר:
איוב ט'

11. וַיִּרָא יִשְׂרָאֵל אֶת הַיָּד הַגְּדֹלָה אֲשֶׁר עָשָׂה ה' בְּמִצְרַיִם וַיִּירְאוּ הָעָם אֶת ה' וַיַּאֲמִינוּ בַּה' וּבְמֹשֶׁה עַבְדּוֹ:
שמות י"ד

12. וְיוֹם הַשְּׁמִינִי וגו'

רב נסים גאון

נביאים האחרונים הם יחזקאל וזכריה ומלאכי [משם דאיתין] מפני ששראל אלא וכו'

The Devotional View of Tosafot

In contrast to the Sephardi view exemplified by Rif, the Ashkenazi halakhists of northern France and Germany saw Torah study as continuing
the process of the Talmud itself. In fact, *Tosafot* (additions or glosses),
the most important commentary authored by various rabbinic figures
in twelfth- and thirteenth-century Ashkenaz, acts as a mirror image to
Rif's *Halakhot*. While Rif reduced the Talmud to legal rules, Tosafot
performed "Talmud" to the Talmud. In the same way that the Talmud
worked to resolve contradictions among its various sources of authority,
Tosafot sought to reconcile contradictions among talmudic passages.

Like the Talmud, Tosafot lacks a conceptual structure, proceeding
instead along the lines of the Talmud's own haphazard system. Similarly,
it regularly mixes flashes of conceptual brilliance with plodding discussions of technical minutiae in a manner reminiscent of the Talmud's
free-association among genres and topics. Finally, Tosafot like the Talmud is not the composition of a single author, but was written and refined over generations, reading like a group blog guided by an anonymous voice that leads the reader through its various questions and
answers.[6]

Early on, Tosafot was recognized as one of the preeminent commentaries on the Talmud, and when the entire Talmud was first printed in
the early sixteenth century, Tosafot appeared in the margin, an influential position it has occupied ever since. Beginning then and continuing
into later times, a group of super-commentaries (commentaries on
commentaries) subjected each line of Tosafot to the same level of detailed analysis commonly afforded to the Talmud itself. As a result, what
is referred to as learning a page of Talmud has long meant studying the
Talmud together with the line-by-line commentary of Rashi on the
inner margin and the dialectical analysis of Tosafot on the outer. In talmudic commentary, as in real estate, location is everything.

Tosafot and Rif present a study in contrasts, with Tosafot drawing its
inspiration from the very aspects of the Talmud that Rif seeks to downplay. Rif tries to reshape the Talmud into a more manageable form; Tosafot counters that much of the Talmud's content is embedded in its

form. Rif focuses on *halakhah le-ma'aseh* (the practiced law in the present), while Tosafot's interest spans the entire Talmud, practiced or otherwise. Rif favors what we can describe as the Talmud's plain meaning; and when two talmudic passages conflict, Rif determines which is correct. Tosafot favors reconciliation, bending passages toward each other until a single principle emerges. While Rif tends to condense lengthy talmudic discussions into fewer and tighter phrases, Tosafot builds expansive interpretive structures from a single talmudic phrase.

The tension between these two approaches is evident in the writings of a thirteenth-century scholar of the Sephardic milieu who urged that young students "not work hard to delve into the various glosses of the Tosafot and their ilk, which were composed by a great multitude of shifting authors, for it is all a waste of time." Instead, this writer recommends focusing on the true purpose of Torah study: "the explication of the mitzvot and the conclusions of the laws, customs, and rulings."[7]

Indeed, the divide between Rif and Tosafot mirrors the competing understandings of what the Talmud is and how it is held to apply. For Rif, the actual text of the Talmud belongs to the past, while the work of the present is to cull and reformat its rules for application. Rif thus follows the Geonic distinctions between accepted and rejected views, and between operative and defunct or suspended halakhot. From Tosafot's perspective, however, the entirety of the halakhic corpus is perpetually alive and open for analysis. The central question is not whether a given view is accepted or in force, but how it interacts and influences other statements in the Talmud.

None of this is to suggest that Tosafot is uninterested in halakhic practice. Tosafot's reading of a sugya is often highly relevant to how the halakhah came to be implemented and remains the basis of Ashkenazi practice to this day. Furthermore, when practiced halakhah is at odds with a talmudic statement, Tosafot will often aim to reconcile or explain the difference. Yet unlike Rif, Tosafot approaches the Talmud as a seamless web of rules and concepts to be explored through the varied dialectics of *talmud Torah*. Like the Talmud, Tosafot weaves intricate textual analysis, conceptual-analytical insights, pragmatic concerns, and normative halakhic pronouncements into an undifferentiated literary unit.

But while Tosafot clearly mimics the Talmud's style, when it comes to aggadah, Tosafot's approach is reminiscent of the line developed by the Geonim and Rif. Tosafot rarely addresses the Talmud's aggadah, nor does the commentary discuss biblical narrative, spin aphorisms to encourage religious devotion, or contemplate theology or religious philosophy—all staples of talmudic aggadah. Works of this sort existed in medieval Ashkenaz, and some even emerging from the Tosafot school, but this material was kept separate from the mainstream works of Talmud study. This narrowing of what counts as Talmud would hold sway over rabbis and thinkers for centuries to come.

Maimonides' Mishneh Torah

Maimonides may be the most influential Jew to have lived since the close of the Talmud, and is certainly the most studied rabbinic personality. Although it is difficult to summarize his influence, three qualities stand out. First, Maimonides is one of the very few accepted as a leading authority both in the field of halakhah and Jewish philosophy; to this day his legal code, the *Mishneh Torah,* and his philosophical treatise, *Guide of the Perplexed,* remain starting points of discussions in their respective fields. Second, nearly every group and denomination, from Sephardi to Ashkenazi, Reform to Ultra-Orthodox, Ḥabad ḥasidim to Lithuanian talmudists, wants to claim Maimonides as its intellectual forebearer. Third, because Maimonides' imprimatur carries so much weight in discussions of Jewish law and philosophy, the rabbinic and scholarly Jewish worlds are treated to never-ending debates as to what Maimonides "really" meant.

Mishneh Torah is one of the most significant halakhic works ever written; another project aimed at codifying the entirety of halakhah would not even be attempted until late in the nineteenth century, and Maimonides' conceptualization of the entirety of halakhah has yet to be surpassed. Maimonides starts from Rif's assumption that the Talmud needs to be pared down to legal rules, but then invents his own method for recording and classifying them. Whereas Rif excerpts Talmudic deliberations, Maimonides eliminates them entirely. Further, though *Mishneh Torah* issues thousands of declarative rules, unlike any work produced before or after, it offers no halakhic defense of its conclusions or even indicates the talmudic source of the ruling in question. *Mishneh Torah* also omits the names of the talmudic rabbis associated with each ruling, and forgoes the Talmud's elliptical Aramaic for the cleaner lines of mishnaic Hebrew. The treatise also departs radically from the Talmud's more haphazard organization, for the first time presenting halakhah in a conceptualized framework marked by principles, corollaries, and exceptions, a feat that would not be matched by later works. Taken together, these features cast *Mishneh Torah* as paradoxically the most influential—and least talmudic—work on the Talmud.

Each of these decisions on Maimonides' part was deliberately intended—and deeply controversial. In the first of a long line of criticisms leveled against *Mishneh Torah*, R. Avraham b. David of Provence, a contemporary of Maimonides known as Ra'avad (1125–1198) wrote:

> He sought to improve but he did not improve, for he has forsaken the method of all authors who preceded him; they adduced proof and cited authority for their statements. . . . Now I do not know why I should retract my tradition and my proof on account of the work of [Maimonides]. . . . Why should I be governed by his choice if it seems wrong to me, and I do not know whether the holder of the opposing view is entitled to deference? This is simply overweening pride in him.[8]

In almost every area of Jewish law or thought, determining Maimonides' view is a complicated and contested process, and understanding his view of halakhah is no exception. On the one hand, he is an even more thoroughgoing functionalist than Rif. More than any halakhist of note, Maimonides has relatively little patience for the Talmud's give-and-take. The introduction to his *Mishneh Torah* states that one of the goals is to present the Talmud's conclusions in a clear and organized manner, thereby obviating the need for the Talmud itself. Whether Maimonides actually sought to replace the Talmud or merely to reduce its centrality is itself the subject of frequent disagreement, but the real point is that no other talmudist would dare entertain such an audacious claim.[9] Maimonides was transparent in saying that the goal of the *Mishneh Torah* was to employ "clear language and concise form so that the entirety of the oral Torah is presented before all without the need for questions, answers, or debates,"[10] in effect the opposite of the Talmud. In his halakhic *Mishneh Torah* (and even more so in his philosophical *Guide of the Perplexed*), Maimonides consciously eschews the Talmud's method in favor of cleaner, and neater forms of reasoning, resembling more of the Greek approach.

Maimonides further promotes the functional account of Talmud study by deeming philosophy to be a critical element of religious activity and study. In fact, a credible argument can be advanced that, at least for the elite, Maimonides holds that philosophical and theological knowledge partakes of a higher form of Torah study than the Talmud itself.[11]

Yet the idea that Maimonides is interested only in the bottom-line legal conclusion forces us to reconsider what legal conclusion really means. For a functionalist in Rif's mold, the meaning of this term is rules of applied halakhah. But this is not quite true of Maimonides, who codified the Talmud in its entirety. What, then, does it mean to devote whole books to the laws of sacrifices or ritual purity: some among the many laws cited by Maimonides that do not apply in the present era? True, these laws may have future significance—that is, in the messianic era—but consider that Maimonides also devotes an entire chapter of the *Mishneh Torah* to the laws of the non-existent rebellious son and another to the non-existent rebellious city, laws that the Talmud itself claims never would apply.[12] How can a law have a bottom line when it is purposefully designed not to be applied? Whereas Rif entirely omits these topics from his work, Maimonides rules on the myriad specific details included within them.

Further, in contrast to Tosafot and other Ashkenazic scholars, *Mishneh Torah* contains relatively few discussions of post-talmudic developments or insights into how halakhah was actually practiced. This is significant not only because legal doctrines inevitably shift when applied, but because Maimonides is known to have issued rulings to specific individuals and contrary to (or at least more nuanced than) the pure halakhah codified in the *Mishneh Torah*.[13] Thus, notwithstanding its declarative code-like structure and its professed desire to move away from the Talmud, when it comes to defining halakhah, *Mishneh Torah* in many ways parallels the Talmud itself. Both combine the idea of laws that are applied every day with an ideal conception of halakhah that stands outside of time and space.

Blends of Ashkenaz and Sepharad

Though the majority of halakhic writing by Rishonim can be placed along the continuum drawn between Rif/Maimonides on the one hand and Tosafot on the other, two intermediate viewpoints merit special mention. The first is the commentary of R. Asher b. Yeḥiel (c. 1260–c. 1328), known as Rosh, who began his life in Ashkenazi Germany and later migrated to Spain. While Rosh's commentary is built on Rif's platform of winnowing the Talmud into accepted legal rulings, it incorporates Tosafot's innovations and transforms them from talmudic commentary into rules of halakhic practice. Rosh's commentary is also more attuned to Tosafot's style, and carries a more analytical, talmudic flavor than its Sephardi predecessor. In fact, Rosh might best be characterized as a Tosafot-inspired commentary on Rif. In putting the devotional practice of *talmud Torah* in service of the functional goal of determining correct operative rule, Rosh comes close to bridging the gap between these two understandings.

Another midpoint emerges from the line of Sephardi Rishonim beginning with Naḥmanides, (known by the acronym Ramban; 1194–1270; Girona), and flowing through to his heirs, Solomon b. Aderet (known by the acronym Rashba; 1235–1310; Barcelona), Yom Tov of Seville (known by the acronym Ritva; c. 1260–1320), and Nissim b. Reuben (known by the acronym Ran; 1320–1376; Barcelona/Girona). Reflecting the functional orientation of Sephardi scholars, these rabbis wrote mainly on tractates of practical relevance and maintained a more organized and focused style than Tosafot. Yet they were also influenced by the devotional and dialectic approach of Tosafot, frequently expanding on Tosafot's discussion in roughly the same style. In captioning their commentaries as *ḥiddushim* (loosely translated as novel interpretations), Ramban and his successors emphasized the intellectual and creative aspects of Talmud study—a position far closer to Tosafot than their Sephardi predecessors.

The combined influence of Tosafot on the Ashkenazi side and Ramban and his progeny on the Sephardi side cemented two ideas into the mainstream of rabbinic consciousness. First, that the Talmud was something to be learned and understood on its own terms; second, that the goal of halakhic interpretation is to offer the most compelling account of the entire body of talmudic evidence taken together.

Living between Tosafot and Maimonides

We can view much of the subsequent tradition as playing out between the lines drawn by Tosafot on the one hand and Rif/ Maimonides on the other. At one end, *talmud Torah* embodies the religious and creative impulse to expand the depth of the halakhic system. Here, halakhah is first an interrelated web of texts and concepts to master and secondarily legislated rules to govern society. Stated in other terms, halakhah speaks first to the student of the sugya and secondarily to the performer of the mitzvah. We thus find limited interest in the distinction between real and ideal halakhah and little concern over how halakhah might succeed in arranging human affairs.

The opposing side, for its part, is drawn to a more conventional portrait of halakhah as law. Here, *talmud Torah* aims to convert the talmudic expanse into manageable rules of conduct. Hence, the issue of how the rules apply and how they might feasibly regulate stand at the forefront of halakhic inquiry.

Though we have described Tosafot and Rif/ Maimonides as exemplifying each pole of the spectrum, these positions are hardly fixed. Over time, Maimonides was transformed from a codifier into a talmudic commentator. Conversely, subsequent halakhists relied on Tosafot's talmudic commentaries to establish the backbone of Ashkenazi halakhic decision-making. As the centrality of Tosafot's additions began to approach that of the Talmud itself a familiar pattern emerged. Just as early waves of commentators sifted out legal rules based on even the slightest inferences from the Talmud, later writers extracted additional rulings based on inferences made from Tosafot's commentary itself.

Surveying the tradition culumatively, we see the following compromise emerge: regarding the sections of the Talmud practiced "in these days," the trend runs strongly in favor of Rif/ Maimonides, as even the competing Ashkenazi views were assimilated into the framework developed by the Geonic and Sephardi codifiers. But when it comes to thinking about what the Talmud is and how it ought to be studied, the balance shifts toward Tosafot. Despite Maimonides' massive influence, few followed his attempts to eliminate talmudic reasoning; all of the later codifiers show their work and justify their rulings via talmudic citations and argument.

Indeed, Tosafot's adoption of the talmudic approach would come to dominate not only how the Talmud is read but how all significant halakhic texts, including Rif's *Halakhot* and even *Mishneh Torah,* were processed. No sooner had *Mishneh Torah* attained authoritative status, than a network of commentaries developed around it, forcibly pulling Maimonides' lean and oracular text back into the dialectical chaos typical of the Talmud. For many latter halakhists, *Mishneh Torah* was less a definitive code of halakhah than evidence of how Maimonides interpreted the talmudic sugya. Perhaps the ultimate irony emerged in the late nineteenth and early twentieth centuries, when some of the most extreme expressions of devotional *talmud Torah* were published as commentaries, no less, to Maimonides' *Mishneh Torah*, a topic we will return to in chapter 12.

As a result, though Maimonides remains one of the most influential halakhists, who worked mightily to replace the Talmud's convoluted dialogue with crisp rules of law, in the long run of Jewish history his project largely failed.

The Talmud's Law: Halakhic Governance in the Post-Talmudic Period

So much for the questions of how, and to what end, the Talmud should be *studied*. The post-talmudic era, however, also raised the more practical dilemma of how talmudic law should be *administered*. As discussed in Part I, the task of enforcing the Talmud's criminal and even civil law runs from difficult to downright impossible. It therefore makes sense to ask: as communities began to adopt the Talmud as the basis of their public and administrative law, how did the system actually work?

Responding to the challenge of governance, medieval halakhists built on the ideas of sub-halakhah already presented in the Talmud and discussed in chapter 3. Courts and communal councils relied on the talmudic authorization that courts may "flog and punish in ways that do not accord with the law." (b.Sanhedrin 46a; b.Yevamot 90b). Thus, medieval courts ordered that offenders have their hands, noses or tongues amputated, be placed in stocks or be branded, or have their heads and beards shaved off as a form of public shaming, even though none of these punishments has any basis in formal halakhah.[14] True, such harsh punishments were relatively rare; but instances of imprisonment, infliction of "lashes of rebelliousness," assessment of civil and criminal fines, and various social sanctions backed by the threat of excommunication were considerably more common.[15] In civil-law cases, courts deployed talmudic statements affirming the community's inherent power to legislate, the idea that secular law or commercial custom could prevail over Torah law, and that a court had the power to create or destroy property rights as needed, to work around many of the Talmud's impractical rules.[16] In adopting these statements as precedents, communities were able to rely on the *authority* of the Talmud, even as they circumvented the specific *rulings* of the Talmud that proved too cumbersome for effective governance.

Although I've described these procedures as sub-halakhic, the degree to which they adhered to the dictates of formal, talmudic halakhah varies considerably. In some cases, rabbis used sub-halakhah to enforce the core substantive principles of talmudic law. For example, if A commits an intentional tort by punching B in the face, the resulting damage is classified as a civil fine. The Talmud rules that such civil fines could not be assessed in Babylonia, because only judges formally ordained in the land of Israel possessed the authority under Torah law to impose them. In response, the tenth-century Babylonian Gaon, Sherira, held that local courts (staffed by rabbinic judges lacking formal ordination) should assess the amount of damage theoretically due under talmudic law but then keep the amount secret, all while nudging the parties towards a settlement that approximated the assessed value of the claim.[17] In examples like this, the two systems seem to operate as one. Sub-halakhah was used to overcome a technicality, thus allowing the substantive aspects of the Talmud's formal rules to be implemented.

In other cases, however, rabbis did everything in their power to *prevent* substantive talmudic halakhah from governing. One example comes from the great threenth-century Barcelonan leader, Rashba, who wrote a responsum to members of a taskforce charged with ensuring adherence to religious practices. The taskforce asked Rashba whether the testimony of close relatives—those most likely to know about the level of religious observance in the home—was valid or whether they had to abide by the Talmud's rules of evidence that prohibited family members from testifying for or against each other. Rashba responded as follows:

> [The formalities of the halakhic rules of evidence] were stated only regarding a court that rules according to Torah law such as the Sanhedrin. . . . But those who act to establish public order do not judge according to what is written in the Torah precisely, but based on the necessities of the time and based on the authority of the government. For if this were not the case, they too could not penalize anyone financially or corporally, as we do not adjudicate fines and penalties outside of Israel. . . . Likewise they could not flog anyone, because a halakhic court does not flog unless there has been *hatra'ah* [lit. warning; the procedure was discussed above in chapter 2]. But all these matters apply only in courts that operate according to Torah law.[18]

In another responsum, Rashba elaborates upon his reasoning as follows:

> If the appointees find the witnesses trustworthy, they are permitted to impose monetary fines or corporal punishment as they see fit. This preserves the world. For if you were to restrict everything to the laws

stipulated in the Torah and punish only in accordance with the To-rah's penal code in cases of assault and the like, the world would be destroyed, because we would require two witnesses and prior warn-ing. The rabbis have already said that "Jerusalem was destroyed only because they restricted their judgment to Torah law." How much more so outside the Land of Israel, where there is no Torah authority to impose penalties, and the unscrupulous will "breach the fence of the world," and the world will become desolate.[19]

Rashba's approach to talmudic law is at once astonishing and obvi-ous: astonishing in that he advocates for a sub-halakhic system that runs wholly contrary to the letter and spirit of the talmudic law. Yet obvious because, as soon as we start thinking about how the Talmud's laws of evidence, criminal prosecution, and punishment will apply to actual criminals, claimants, and defendants, it becomes clear that they cannot serve as the basis of a functioning apparatus of government.

Notably, while Rashba works hard to make sure the laws of the Sanhedrin will not be implemented in practice, he does nothing to detract from their status as normative halakhah. Quite the opposite: he does not for a moment assume that the law of the Talmud is wrong, superseded, invalid, or even impracticable. The law of the Talmud is fully in force—it just does not apply "now." Even though these sound like short-term accomodations, in reality they span the lived history of halakhah. Talmudic law, argues Rashba, applies to the Sanhedrin—the ideal embodiment of Jewish law. The actual work of governance, however, is necessarily different. Hence the sub-halakhah that in real-ity governs is neither bound to nor limited by the formalities of tal-mudic law.

Roughly two generations later, Ran (R. Nissim of Gerona), a student of Rashba's students, offered a theoretical grounding for this approach. In a homiletic essay, Ran directly addresses one of the most basic ques-tions regarding halakhah and governance: how can a society possibly live under the system of non-functional and non-applied law set forth in the Talmud's tractate Sanhedrin?

In response, Ran authored one of the few theoretical accounts of the halakhic system written prior to the nineteenth century. His central insight was to distinguish between two spheres of Jewish law. The first is the pure halakhah, which reflects the ideal mode of social ordering. The second is the realm of civil administration, which Ran calls the king's law (roughly paralleling our term "sub-halakhah") and which operates as a necessary corrective in light of an imperfect reality. The Talmud's rules of criminal procedure, according to Ran, are designed to ascertain the absolute truth of an alleged criminal's culpability. Counterintuitively then, the primary purpose of the ideal halakhah is not to govern society but to serve as the vehicle through which the divine spirit flows to the Jewish people.

When projected on to reality, Ran continues, this regime may produce adverse results. For this reason, halakhah (though maybe *here* the correct term is Jewish law) maintains an alternative system of civil administration, the king's law, which is unconstrained by the formalities of halakhic process and designed to meet the needs of the hour. Originally, this set of laws was administered by the political authority represented by the Davidic monarch. With the demise of the monarchy, however, the king's law was transferred to the rabbis and their courts, who are called upon to ensure the social order.[20]

In Ran's account, present-era rabbinical courts fulfill two distinct roles. First, they are called upon to adjudicate the true halakhah without any regard for consequences or administrative effectiveness. This is the role of the ideal Torah law. Their second function combines legislative and executive roles. Under the banner of the king's law, rabbinic courts are empowered to employ sub-halakhic practices on an as-needed basis to benefit the social order.

Writing in the fourteenth century, Ran was the first to make explicit what has been latent all along. Not only do parts of halakhah not work, *they are not designed to work.* Yet for Ran, this is hardly a defect, since halakhah is foremost a spiritual discourse concerned with establishing a relationship with God, and only secondarily a system of societal administration. To the extent both functions can be accomplished together, the two spheres operate as one. But when actual governance cannot rest on such lofty premises, the roles are divided: halakhah governs in theory, while sub-halakhah rules in practice.

Ran's ingenious scheme addresses some of the major questions about halakhah, but it also generates a host of other concerns. First among them is the matter of scope. Ran's essay speaks only to the matter of capital punishment. Is his theory limited to that case, or can it extend to other areas of impractical halakhah? The latter seems reasonable in other areas of criminal law and possibly in some segments of civil and commercial law. But does there come a point at which even ritual laws become so unworkable as to be designated as merely ideal and require an alternate sub-halakhic regime? Would Ran apply his analysis to alleviate the economic difficulties resulting from the prohibition against charging interest (*ribbit*), the mandate that all farmers leave their land fallow every seventh year (*shemittah*), the requirement that all land sales be reversed during the jubilee year (*yovel*), or the difficulties of divesting from all leavened products (*ḥametz*) on Passover? What about some of the more onerous restrictions of Shabbat? One suspects the answer is no, as there are surely limits as to just how much of Torah law Ran would permit to be displaced by the king's law. His essay, however, provides little guidance on where this line should be drawn. Not surprisingly, contemporary scholars continue to debate the matter.[21]

In many ways, Ran's bright-line distinction between the ideal Torah law and the functioning system of sub-halakhah is too neat to fit the messy facts. In his system, Torah law appears as fully ideal, whereas the king's law is wholly consequential. But even in the case of capital punishment, we have already encountered (in chapter 2) at least *some* talmudic hesitation regarding practical consequences.[22] And as we will see in the next chapter, from the Mishnah forward, halakhic literature contains numerous examples where (apparently) ideal halakhah is interpreted in light of practical concerns. Ran correctly points to the two poles that animate halakhic discourse. It is less clear, however, that the full range of halakhah can be cleanly divided into these mutually exclusive categories.

10

The Idea of Halakhah in the Codes

Those who are drawn to issuing practical guidance according to the *Shulḥan Arukh* rule in matters of Torah in ways that do not accord with the correct halakhah, as they do not know the source from where the ruling is derived, and they make up reasons of their own accord and thus multiply disputes within Israel.

—JOEL SIRKES (1561–1640)[1]

There is no doubt that [the *Shulḥan Arukh* and the work of R. Moses Isserles] were written by God's hand . . . . The spirit of God flowed through the authors so that their words would be directed toward the correct halakhah even without the author's intent, and the will of God was accomplished through their hand.

—JONATHAN EIBESCHITZ (1690–1764)[2]

MORE THAN ANY OTHER WORKS of halakhah, the treatises that have come to be known as "the Codes" (see below) offer the starkest contrast to the idea of halakhah-as-Torah traced in previous chapters. For while the Talmud, Tosafot, and even Maimonides' code engage halakhah on a variety of levels, the Codes' express interest is to frame halakhah as black-letter directives that govern Jewish life of the exilic present.

The gulf between the Talmud and the Codes can be seen by contrasting almost any talmudic sugya with the corresponding provision in the

Codes. In chapter 5, we discussed the mishnaic debate over whether a sword may be carried on Shabbat. In the Talmud, this seemingly minor regulation birthed a discussion over the image of manhood and the nature of the messianic era. The Codes, however, present this as a flat legal rule with nary a trace of the philosophical, theological, or metaphoric ideas developed in the Talmud.

> Anyone who goes out with an object that is not an adornment and is not something usually worn, but carries it in its normal fashion, is liable. . . . Therefore, a man should not go out with a sword, or a bow, or a shield . . . and if he did, he is liable for a sin offering. (*Shulḥan Arukh* OḤ §301:7).

Given the style and function of the Codes, conventional wisdom holds that they state only *halakhah le-ma'aseh*—the binding law that applies in the present era—and no more. Using more formal terms employed by legal scholars, the Codes establish halakhah's "rule of recognition," that is, the test for determing which rules are legally binding. In traditional Jewish practice, the halakhah stated in the Codes is law in the most direct and immediate sense of the term.

But is this description wholly accurate? This chapter will argue that the conception of halakhah developed in the Talmud is so deeply rooted in the structure of rabbinic thought that even works expressly devoted to a functional account of halakhah never fully realize their goal. Using three examples, we'll see that while the Codes succeed in establishing authoritative rules of practice that replace the Talmud's *text,* they are less successful in supplanting the talmudic *method.* Instead, even the most functional works of black-letter halakhah tend to replicate—rather than to resolve—the complexity embedded in the rabbinic understanding of halakhah.

The Halakhic Codes: A Brief Introduction

The medieval halakhic tradition yields three major works typically classified as codes: Maimonides' *Mishneh Torah*, discussed in chapter 9; R. Jacob b. Asher's *Arba'ah Turim* (Four Rows, or divisions), hereinafter known as *Tur*, written in Spain in the early 1300s; and R. Joseph Caro's *Shulḥan Arukh* , written in S'fat, Israel, then published in Venice in the mid-1500s.

Maimonides stands as halakhah's unparalleled conceptual thinker and systematizer. Yet for all its brilliance, the organizational scheme set forth in his *Mishneh Torah* failed to take root. Though his rulings exerted considerable influence over how *Tur* and especially the *Shulḥan Arukh* formulate their rules, his methodology proved too attenuated from its talmudic source to pass the test of time. For most communities, *Mishneh Torah* was transformed into a work of talmudic commentary while *Tur* and especially the *Shulḥan Arukh* became regarded as the definitive codes of Jewish law. In what follows, we'll refer to these latter works collectively as the Codes.

Arba'ah Turim

R. Jacob b. Asher's approach to drafting *Tur* differs from Maimonides in several important ways. First, *Tur* retains more of the Talmud's syntax and conceptual structure, lending it a more talmudic feel than *Mishneh Torah*. Second, whereas Maimonides writes in the declarative tones of a legislator—or as R. Asher, R. Jacob's father, complained, "like Moses, prophesying from on high"[3]—*Tur* reverts to the more traditional practice of placing competing positions alongside each other, often leaving it to the reader to reach the conclusion via implication or inference.

A third difference lies in the image of halakhah displayed in each work. Because Maimonides omits names, citations, analyses, disputes, and most post-talmudic developments, his work evokes an ideal law that stands outside of time and place. *Tur,* by contrast, is considerably more attentive to how medieval halakhists effected the transition of halakhah from the Talmud into a functioning legal system. Thus on the one hand, *Tur* offers a less complete account, as it omits the laws of purity, agriculture, the Sanhedrin, and Temple rituals. Yet, by including the views and practices of different authorities and communities, it paints a far richer picture and provides a living account of how medieval authorities read and applied the Talmud.

Tur divides practiced halakhah into four "rows" or main divisions. *Oraḥ Ḥayyim* covers the halakhah of daily life, Shabbat, and the holidays. *Yoreh De'ah* enumerates such ritual laws as those pertaining to kashrut, idolatry and relationships with non-Jews, the prohibition against lending with interest, charity, conversions, mikveh, and others. *Even ha-Ezer* deals with the laws of marriage, divorce, and family property. *Ḥoshen Mishpat* sets forth civil law and procedure. When R. Joseph Caro later adopted *Tur*'s architecture as the foundation for his *Shulḥan Arukh*, *Tur* became the presumptive gatekeeper for determining which halakhot are of ongoing practical relevance under the diasporic conditions of exile.

Beit Yosef and Shulḥan Arukh

Roughly 200 years following *Tur*'s publication, R. Joseph Caro authored an extensive commentary to it titled *Beit Yosef* (House of Joseph). *Beit Yosef* not only cites the talmudic sources for *Tur*'s halakhot but collects additional rulings and opinions not cited by *Tur* (in particular, those emerging from Sephardic authorities) and engages in a discursive give-and-take with the relevant material.

The encyclopedic nature of *Beit Yosef*, however, makes it too much like the the Talmud to function as a useful code. For this reason, toward the end of his life, R. Caro compiled a brief summary—headnotes, really—to *Beit Yosef* that he titled *Shulḥan Arukh,* evoking the metaphor of a set table where all the laws were comfortably placed before the reader. Much sparser and even more declarative than Maimonides' *Mishneh Torah*, this work focuses exclusively on the black-letter rules relevant to practice. For R. Caro, *Beit Yosef* was the *magnum opus,* whereas the *Shulḥan Arukh* was meant as a primer for beginners or a quick reference guide for scholars who had mastered *Beit Yosef*.[4] There is little indication he envisioned it would become the definitive code of halakhah.

Nevertheless, the work caught the attention of R. Moses Isserles (acronym: Rema) of Cracow, Poland, then in the midst of writing a similar work. From Rema's perspective, the central flaw of the *Shulḥan Arukh* was its adoption of both the methods and the customs of Sephardi scholars at the expense of Tosafot and Ashkenazi religious culture. Abandoning his separate project, Rema looked to remedy these flaws by interjecting his own comments and emendations into the *Shulḥan Arukh* and appending critical glosses to the end of R. Caro's paragraphs, often shifting the meaning in the process.[5] Though these glosses are relatively brief, they continue the Ashkenazi practice of including the rudiments of legal analysis and of encoding multiple opinions into R. Caro's otherwise oracular text.

Rema thus became the first in a long line of commentators to unpack the tidiness of R. Caro's lean text and pull it back toward the dialectical tradition of Tosafot and the Talmud. Since 1580, the two works have been routinely printed together. Since the combined text reflected the scholarship and customs of both Sephardi and Ashkenazi communities, it became the foundational code of halakhah.

Are the Codes Really Codes?

Before engaging the Codes directly, a word is in order about the nature of their authority. The conventional understanding in modern law is that a code is a document issued by a legislative body that draws its authority from a formalized act of a political entity. In the United States, the Uniform Commercial Code is law because it has been adopted by the legislatures of the states, and the Federal Bankruptcy Code and Internal Revenue Code are law because they were created by acts of Congress. In practice, no analogous halakhic body exists (though in theory a reconstituted Sanhedrin might be one). Rather, each halakhic code is the product of its single rabbinic author, which might be more accurately described as a restatement than as a code as modern lawyers use the term.

Still, because these works gained authority over time, later halakhists accepted them as binding, and granted them code-like status. Even so, it has remained a matter of debate whether their rulings are *the* halakhah or simply reflect the halakhah.[6] Thus, later halakhists occasionally register a disagreement or qualification on the basis of an alternative textual reading or competing communal practice—though this is typically directly accomplished by qualifying or working around the Codes without challenging their authority.

Should Codified Law Be Applied in Practice?

Let's now return to the discussion of *p'sharah*, or compromise, first broached in chapter 7. The Talmud seems to conclude that a judge ought to present litigants with the option of either choosing *p'sharah* or abiding by the standard legal ruling of Torah law (*din*, or *din Torah*). This statement of law is recorded in *Tur*, but then followed by an additional ruling:

> The judges are *required to distance themselves in all possible ways* so as not to accept upon themselves to adjudicate according to the law of the Torah . For the hearts have been considerably diminished, and we have learned in the first chapter of the Jerusalem Talmud, tractate Sanhedrin, "In the days of R. Shimon b. Yoḥai, the adjudication of monetary laws was suspended." (emphasis added).[7]

The Shulḥan Arukh dispenses with the talmudic citation, but it too, records that judges are to "distance themselves in all possible ways" from deciding in accord with Torah law.[8]

The statement is significant for what it says about the idea of halakhah in both the Talmud and the Codes. R. Shimon b. Yoḥai was a rabbi of the middle of the second century, who lived at least one generation before R. Yehudah ha-Nasi disseminated the Mishnah. At face value, then, the passage from the Jerusalem Talmud assumes that most of the Mishnah, and the entire body of talmudic civil law, was developed *after* the "real" civil laws of the Torah ceased to be implemented by rabbinic courts. Notably, an alternate textual tradition suggests that application of the Torah's monetary laws were suspended as far back as the days of Shimon b. Shetaḥ, a figure who lived six or seven generations prior to the Mishnah.[9] On this reading, the *entirety* of recorded halakhic civil law emerges after the "real" civil laws of the Torah were no longer practiced.

Of course, it is hard to take either variant of the Jerusalem Talmud at face value. Not only do the Mishnah and Talmud go to great pains to establish the precise details of the civil law, but talmudic literature is replete with stories that, so far as one can tell, decide cases on the basis of Torah law.[10] Even granting the Jerusalem Talmud some literary license, however, it is clear that *Tur*, for its part, appears unshaken by the thought that halakhah emerged from a context where its rules were not recommended as practical guidelines for courts. And that is instructive to how both *Tur* and the *Shulḥan Arukh* understood their own projects.

The laws of *p'sharah* are located toward the beginning of *Ḥoshen Mishpat*, the civil-law section of the Codes, where they are followed by more than 400 technically intricate code sections that work mightily to establish the Torah law on the given topics. All the while, however, the Codes rule that judges are called upon to *avoid* adjudicating a case pursuant to Torah law, and should do so only as a last resort. The rationale for this approach is explained by R. Joel Sirkes (Poland, 1561–1640) in his commentary, *Bayit Hadash*, who explains that since "the hearts" of later generations "have been diminished," it is difficult to determine halakhah. [11] This reduced mental and spiritual capacity generates a risk of judicial error. In order to shield the judges from the grave sin of ruling in legal error, it is better to decide the case in accord with the less formalized standards of *p'sharah,* which by definition cannot reach a result contrary to halakhah.

In sum, this approach maintains that the true halakhah is far too holy to risk mishandling in practice. Again, it is hard to imagine that *Tur* or the *Shulḥhan Arukh* means this literally. The overall goal of *Ḥoshen Mishpat* is to establish the ideal and true law of the Torah, a project seen as a holy vocation. In their respective works, both R. Jacob b. Asher and R. Caro approvingly cite numerous *responsa* that apply Torah law to specific cases, and we have every reason to believe they hoped judges would consult their codes as questions arose. And yet, at some level, each holds that the laws God spoke to Moses at Sinai, that binds the Jewish people to God, that reflects the intellectual and religious output of generations of halakhic scholars, that framed their personal, communal, and religious identities—that this law is best served when *avoided in judicial practice*. Such a view is only possible if at some level, the Codes—that is, *even* the Codes—understand the ideal halakhah as a holy corpus to be studied rather than necessarily applied.

What "Halakhah le-Ma'aseh" Means in *Tur*

Another complexity stems from how the individual sections in *Tur* are organized. In several instances, a section of *Tur* begins by stating a broad rule derived from the Mishnah that sounds as if it will apply in many cases but is then significantly narrowed as the paragraphs proceed. In a number of laws relating to relationships between Jews and non-Jews, this proclivity is taken to the extreme. Not only is the scope of halakhah cut back, but *Tur* concludes that in the present era, the laws in question do not even apply.

For example, Section 148 of *Yoreh De'ah* opens by citing the mishnaic teaching that three days prior to a non-Jewish holiday, Jews must curtail commercial interactions with non-Jews who engage in foreign worship. The accepted rationale for this rule is that if a business deal is success- fully concluded close to a holy day, the non-Jew will offer praise to his god upon visiting the church or shrine for the festival. This is problem- atic, because the Jew will be deemed the proximate cause of an act of foreign worship. After assessing the Talmud's give-and-take, *Tur* cites Tosafot's view that the prohibition applies only to commercial interac- tions involving ritual items used in worship services. From a practical perspective, this introduces a significant area of exception, since accord- ing to Tosafot, most items traded in commerce remain outside the scope of regulation.

Tur then proceeds to a similar discussion about the validity of accept- ing loan repayment from non-Jews in the days prior to their holidays. Here, too, the broad prohibition established by the Mishnah is followed by an analytical discussion of the rules of the Talmud, and finally by the conclusion that "in our time" loan repayment is like "saving the money from being lost to non-Jewish hands." Consequently, most of the restric- tions will not apply.

The pattern of presenting the broad mishnaic rule followed by cur-
tailing exceptions is repeated in several related contexts before the section concludes as follows: (*Tur* YD §148).

> In these days, however, . . . all these [prohibitions mentioned in this
> chapter] are permitted. For [non-Jews] do not really engage in for-
> eign worship, and they do not go to the house of worship and praise
> their god. And even though they donate money to their priests, one
> is permitted to lend them money since the priests do not use this
> money for sacral purposes but consume the money on food and
> drink.
>
> Moreover, since the majority of our livelihood is dependent on
> [non-Jews], and we engage with them in commerce during the rest
> of the year, if we would separate during their holy days they would
> show animosity toward us, and thus it is permitted. . . . Likewise we
> learned . . . : "When are these laws stated? When the Jew has no rela-
> tionship with the non-Jew; but when he has a relationship, it is per-
> mitted since he only seeks to curry favor." Similarly it has been stated:
> "If he enters the city and found them celebrating, he may celebrate
> with them, for he seeks only to curry favor."

Much is packed into these lines, not least the striking claim that non-
Jewish religious practice (Christian, in this case) is essentially insin-
cere—"they do not go to the house of worship and praise their god"—
and the assertion that donations to medieval churches were used solely
to pleasure the priests rather than for sacral purposes. Our center of
interest, however, lies in the structure of this section of *Tur*, which opens
with an elaborate discussion of the halakhic rules, only to conclude the
rules do not apply. Nor is this structure unique. In fact, the discussion
in the very next section, section 149, on the prohibition to participate
in commercial fairs on feast days dedicated to deities and saints, likewise
concludes these laws are not currently applicable. Section 151 also begins
with a broad prohibition against selling certain animals before concluding that it no longer applies. And section 153 opens with the mishnaic
rule prohibiting Jewish travelers from leaving their livestock in the barn-
yards of idolaters' inns for fear the latter will commit bestiality, only to

conclude that, since in our days "we assume they are not suspected of this act," doing so is permitted.

As we've stressed, unlike the Talmud or even contemporary American codes, *Tur* is the product of a single rabbinic author. We can assume that at the outset of each section, R. Jacob knew full well that the broad statement of law will be substantially narrowed and eventually held not to apply. Were *Tur*'s sole purpose to set forth the practiced halakhah, the work could have omitted a given chapter altogether (as in the case of the Temple and capital-punishment laws that are not applicable in our days) or included a brief statement declaring that certain laws are not currently in force, as in the case with many agricultural halakhot applicable to the land of Israel.[12] But in this case, *Tur* does neither. Instead, each section offers a detailed discussion in no way distinguishable from the operative sections. Then, after the talmudic sugya has been rehearsed, we learn in the concluding lines that the pertinent laws are no longer in force.

To a degree, the structure of these sections is driven by the halakhah's historical development. The broad prohibition outlined in *Tur* mirrors the statement found in the Mishnah, which is then scaled back as its application narrowed in practice. Seen this way, *Tur*'s discussion of the talmudic material is similar to the *Background* or *History and Development* sections found in modern codes and restatements. Their purpose is to provide context for the law's current interpretation, allowing drafters to show their work and justify the conclusion.

But an important difference remains. Modern codes use the background material to support conclusions regarding the state of the law *at present*, which is why this information typically appears in footnotes or in a section graphically set apart from the current black-letter rules. In *Tur*, the opposite is true. The bulk of the analysis found in Section 148 is devoted to the non-applied law embedded in the Talmud and the Rishonim. It is only afterward that *Tur* shifts to how the law functions in these days.

Moreover, unlike modern codes, *Tur* does not recognize mishnaic rules as legal history—law that once governed but since superseded.

Rather, the Mishnah reflects law that is universal, that has never ceased and will never cease to apply. The law as practiced is just a temporary accommodation, even if "temporary" refers to much of lived history of halakhah.

In this sense, *Tur* implicitly relies on some variation of Ran's distinction between ideal Torah law—which for *Tur* is the law of the Talmud—and rules through which society is actually governed. Like Ran, *Tur* assumes that Torah law can be relevant even in the absence of its practical application. Just as the laws of the showbread apply even in the absence of the Temple, so, too, prohibitions against aiding foreign worship apply even if not practiced. This is why *Tur* opens that section by codifying the ideal, expressive, and thought-shaping halakhah which teaches that, in principle, a Jew should be so repulsed by foreign worship so as to avoid any association with it, however remote. By the end of the section, however, *Tur* has shifted to addressing halakhah as a more immediate regulatory concern. Here, recognizing that because "in these times" Jews live politically and economically subservient to non-Jews, prudence mandates a different course of action. [13]

But while *Tur*'s presentation recalls Ran's distinction, it also points to the difficulty of drawing a clean line between the two types of law. In Ran's system, Torah law represents the true ideal law untainted by practical considerations, while the king's law reflects concessions to practical realities. For *Tur*, the division is much blurrier. Each section we've cited begins with the ideal halakhah of the Mishnah yet concludes by setting it aside for practical concerns. In the course of discussion, however, it is never quite clear where the former ends and the latter begins.

Finally, it is worth focusing on how the very act of including non-applied halakhah in the Codes enhances its potential impact on actual halakhic practice. In this regard, we might consider Rema's comments to the conclusion of Section 148:12 of the *Shulḥan Arukh*. After rehearsing *Tur*'s account of how the state of non-Jewish religious belief renders these laws no longer applicable, Rema adds: "nevertheless, a pious individual should distance himself from joining non-Jewish celebrations, if it can be done in a way that does not result in animosity."

In Rema's comment, the halakhah has come full circle. The Mishnah begins with a broad prohibition against social and commercial interactions in the run-up to the holidays. As these halakhot became more legalized and concrete, political and economic considerations required them to be narrowed and eventually read out of practice. In Rema's gloss however, the discussion shifts back toward the Mishnah's original rule. Though the plain reading of the Mishnah no longer reflects a universally binding legal decree, the Mishnah has become an aspirational norm taken up by pious individuals on a case-by-case basis. Notably, this aspirational reading of the initial mishnah has become codified and established as black-letter halakhic practice.

The Codes as a Locus of Talmud Torah: The Case of Debt Collection

We've been focusing on cases where the gap between the two functions of halakhah is explicit. But while such examples can be found, they are not the norm. For the more common pattern, let's look at the halakhah of debt collection, where, rather than being deemed inapplicable, the halakhah is simply narrowed until it covers only a small range of relatively insignificant cases.

Section 97 of the *Ḥoshen Mishpat* section of *Tur* records several talmudic rules that, from a modern legal perspective, are unusually protective of impoverished debtors. For example, if a debtor cannot repay a loan, the creditor is forbidden from pressuring him; in fact, the creditor must take care not to cross the debtor's path lest the debtor be embarrassed by his mere presence. A creditor is also forbidden from confronting his debtor directly; instead a court-appointed agent must mediate any interaction between them. Further, neither the creditor nor agent may enter the debtor's home to seize property for outstanding debts, and finally, under no circumstances may any party seize millstones or other items used by the debtor to "maintain sustenance."[14]

Considering these regulations, we might expect the practiced halakhot of debt collection to be equally debtor-friendly. Yet, in just a few lines these idealistic halakhot undergo several critical limitations.

Whereas most halakhists held the category of items used to "maintain sustenance" includes income-generating capital equipment and tools of trade, *Tur* approvingly cites a minority position that limits the protected assets only to household items used in end-stage food preparation.[15] Economically, this offers substantially less protection to the debtor since the more valuable income-producing tools fall outside the scope of halakhah's protection.[16]

A second limitation is even more dramatic. *Tur* maintains that the Torah's regulations apply only when the creditor can easily locate other assets belonging to the debtor. But if no alternate assets are found, or if the debtor is late in making payments, the court agent may enter the debtor's home and seize whatever he finds.[17]

Tur offers two lines of support for this position. The first is sub-halakhic and rests on the impracticality of the Talmud's regime. *Tur* cites the thirteenth century Spanish authority, R. Meir Abulafia, stating: "Though this rule [narrowing the scope of the halakhah] is not expressly stated in the Talmud, and I have not seen my teachers engage in this [issue], I have written what appears logical to me, for this is the work of heaven."[18] The second line of support is based on the view that the talmudic law applies only to cases where the creditor is seeking security while the loan is still due. Once the loan comes due and the debtor is unable to pay, however, a court officer may enter the home to seize any and all assets in satisfaction of the debt. If, moreover, the debtor is presumed to be hiding assets to avoid repayment, *Tur* rules the debtor "may be beaten until his life is extinguished."[19] Similar statements are found in the corresponding sections of the *Shulḥan Arukh*.[20]

In contrast to the case of non-Jewish holy days, neither *Tur* nor the *Shulḥan Arukh* holds the laws of debt collection do not apply "in these days." Surely if a creditor were to enter a solvent debtor's home and seize a fork, knife, or poultry shears, serious Torah prohibitions would be violated. In this sense, the halakhot continue to serve as applied law (*halakhah le-ma'aseh*). But as a practical matter, the Codes interpret the talmudic law to cover only a small range of commercially insignificant cases—for while tools of trade and industry may serve as meaningful collateral, household cutlery and crockery generally do not. When processed through the Codes, the debtor protection laws come to apply mainly to insignificant household objects, while valuable capital assets are exempted from protective regulations.

At one level, this unevenness is a function of the law's history. Though the actual halakhah becomes increasingly favorable to the creditor, *Tur*'s commitment to talmudic precedent means that the debtor-friendly laws remain on the books even as the scope of their application shrink. Because this pattern is repeated throughout, the Codes end up including a fair share of regulations that apply in only the thinnest and most formal sense of the term. Nevertheless, even as these laws do little in the way of regulating conduct, they establish the reader's expectations that the relationship between the halakhah outlined in the Codes and the practicalities of governance is more complex than "rules of applied law."

The impact of *talmud Torah* on the Codes becomes even more pronounced as we shift from *Tur*—meaning the code-like work written by R. Jacob b. Asher—to the composite printed work we might call "*The Tur*," in which R. Jacob's thirteenth-century text is surrounded by a coterie of later commentaries. Since the 1716 printing that established the framework for most subsequent editions, each page of *The Tur* contains a relatively small amount of R. Jacob's primary text surrounded by the longer and more analytical works of *Beit Yosef*, R. Joel Sirkes's *Bayit Ḥadash,* and R. Joshua Falk's (Poland; c.1555–1614) interlocking system of analytical comments and notes known as *Drishah* and *Prishah*. Together, these works transform *Tur* from a code of halakhah into *The Tur,* a text that itself became the object of Torah study, further blurring the line between studied and applied halakhah.

The point is brought home in comparing the issues addressed by the halakhic codifiers with the methods of debt collection prevailing at that time. Because Polish Jews of the seventeenth and eighteenth centuries frequently engaged in commerce and moneylending, the practices of debt collection were of great relevance and urgency to the community. Throughout this period, we find communal enactments and sub-halakhic practices that significantly expand the rights and remedies available to aid creditors in collecting their debts. [21]

For example: under talmudic law, an insolvent debtor is required to submit his assets to the court but is not otherwise imprisoned or subjected to punishment. Over time, this position changed. By the thirteenth century, more forceful tactics came to be employed, particularly against debtors suspected of hiding assets or gaming the system. Eventually, these practices migrated from sub-halakhah into established halakhah, becoming codified in Rema's glosses to the *Shulḥan Arukh*. Yet halakhic authorities continued to insist that harsh tactics were permitted only when the debtor was assumed to be hiding assets. Imprisoning or coercing the debtor as a form of punishment for becoming insolvent remained prohibited.[22]

Then, throughout the sixteenth to eighteenth centuries, we find numerous communal enactments explicitly calling for even harsher approaches. In 1624, to take only one example, the Council of the Four Lands—the coordinating political authority of Jewish life in Poland—promulgated an ordinance establishing imprisonment as a routine punishment for debtors who could not repay their loans.[23]

Given this background, we would expect leading codifiers and their commentators to focus on the halakhic propriety of employing harsh sanctions to extract assets from debtors such as: debtor imprisonment, refusal to bury a debtor or his family until monies were repaid, excommunication, and other social/religious sanctions. And yet, owing to the tradition of the Talmud and Tosafot, many of these writers see their role as both expanding the discourse of the talmudic sugya and stating rules of practiced law. Thus, *Bayit Ḥadash* offers three significant comments to the material under discussion. The first investigates whether the prohibition on seizing the tools of the debtor's trade applies universally or only when the tools are at that moment in use by the debtor.[24] A second discusses whether someone violating the prohibition against seizing assets is liable for the punishment of lashes.[25] Notably, the relevance of these discussions to the commercial practices of the era is indirect at best. Biblical lashes were not even administered in talmudic times, much less in seventeenth-century Poland. And in an economy revolving around trade and moneylending, rules that apply exclusively to end-use kitchenware were of minimal commercial importance.

At the same time, this does not mean the commentators were uninterested in practical matters. As in the Talmud, the halakhah of the Codes crosses the continuum between theoretical expressions of *talmud Torah* and functional regulation. Hence *Bayit Ḥadash*'s third major comment directly engages a number of core issues emerging from sub-halakhic practice.[26] Can a debtor be forced into labor to pay off his debt? (No) Should a court enforce a debtor's contracted promise to accept imprisonment for failure to pay? (No) Can a debtor with funds who refuses to pay be imprisoned? (Yes) Is one justified in relying on the enactment of the Council of Four Lands to imprison an impoverished debtor? (No)

In a code of applied law, one would expect the pressing legal questions of the era to take center stage. Yet here, quite the opposite is true. The issues most relevant to debt collection are recessed deep within the commentary, and enjoy no priority over the lengthy and largely theoretical discussion regarding the seizure of millstones and poultry shears. Finally, though *Bayit Ḥadash*'s disapproval of the Council's act is clear, the critique lacks the verve and acuity that typifies the rest of the work.

I have focused on *Bayit Ḥadash* because, in the author's self-conception, the work is narrowly trained on the halakhah presented in *Tur*. In fact, the introduction to *Bayit Ḥadash* criticizes R. Joshua Falk Katz' rival commentary, *Drishah,* for overemphasizing talmudic analysis and promoting novel interpretations and at the expense of deciding the practical issues at hand.[27] True to form, in the case of Section 97, *Drishah*—authored by the rabbi who was arguably the era's greatest authority on commercial halakhah—wades deep into the laws governing millstones with nary a reference to the question of debtor imprisonment or other forms of communal legislation or common commercial practice.[28]

The Transition to *Shulḥan Arukh*

While the parameters of what counts as applied halakhah are defined by *Tur*, the *Shulḥan Arukh* is what came to be known as the definitive code of Jewish law. Standing alone, the text of the *Shulḥan Arukh* is indeed considerably more code-like than *Tur*. It contains few of *Tur's* moral and aggadic exhortations, less of the law's developmental history, and much less debate and discussion. These differences, however, only accentuate the gap between the base text of the *Shulḥan Arukh* and the astonishingly complex network of learning and commentary that developed around it.

With each ensuing publication, the *Shulḥan Arukh's* spartan language became further crowded out by glosses, commentaries, and eventually commentaries on the commentaries. The 1864 edition, which has become somewhat standard, includes up to fifteen different commentators on a page whose graphical complexity is staggering (editions published in recent decades aim to simplify the layout, but at least one prides itself on maintaining the page formatting of the older printing). For roughly 200 years following its publication, the *Shulḥan Arukh* became the primary locus of both practiced halakhah and *talmud Torah*. Other scholars began to build their own works on its platform, and previously uncategorized responsa were organized to correspond to its sections (*simanim*).[29] These trends solidified the Codes, and in particular, the *Shulḥan Arukh's* standing as the definitive works of practiced halakhah, and transformed their section headings from a simple numerical scheme to a method of conceptualizing the corpus of applied halakhah.

When drafted, R. Caro assumed that scholars could review the entire *Shulḥan Arukh* every thirty days. As the work has been received however, even highly accomplished scholars require thousands of hours to wend through its massive and heavily annotated tomes.

The Shulḥan Arukh as a Secondary Talmud

A survey of Jewish communal legislation from seventeenth- and eighteenth-century Eastern Europe reveals that communities adopted far more creditor-friendly methods of debt collection than permitted by formal halakhah, and these enactments were greeted with varying degrees of rabbinic approval and apprehension. With this background, we can evaluate how the commentaries featured on the pages of the *Shulḥan Arukh* understood their role in explicating halakhah.

At one end of the spectrum we find works whose primary interest is applied halakhah in its most straightforward sense. Exemplifying this approach is R. Abraham Tzvi H. Eisenstat's (1813–1868) *Pithei Teshuvah*, (a play on words that can either mean "gateway to the responsa" or "gateway towards repentence"), a commentary that usually collects responsa and applies halakhic principles to novel situations. With regard to debt collection, the author takes notice of the debtor-imprisonment legislation and the halakhic unease surrounding it.[30] Though less of a defining feature of the work, the commentary known as *Kessef Kedoshim* by R. Avraham David Wahrmann (Galicia, 1771–1840), discusses the legitimacy of communal legislation permitting a creditor to freeze a debtor's assets pending litigation, though notably, in a parenthetical comment.[31] These are examples where the commentators squarely address issues at the forefront of commercial practice.

Most commentators, however, stay within the parameters established by commentaries of *Bayit Ḥadash* and *Drishah* on *Tur*. (The author of *Drishah* also wrote a leading commentary to the *Hoshen Mishpat* section of the *Shulḥan Arukh*). Exemplifying this approach is the commentary colloquially known as *Shakh* (by R. Shabbtai ha-Kohen, Vilna, 1622–1663), which vacillates between citing responsa addressing practical issues and extended elaboration of talmudic concepts, sometimes with scarcely a reference to the Codes themselves. Overall, the works of the first wave of commentators on the *Shulḥan Arukh* play the role of classical interpreters. They trace the laws back to the Talmud and Rishonim, analyze the text to resolve tensions between R. Caro and Rema, and address interstitial questions not explicitly raised in the base-level texts. And on occasion, also rule on issues emerging from practice.

At the non-practiced pole, we find commentators who use the *Shulḥan Arukh* as a springboard for a conceptual analysis of halakhic ideas. The most famous among this group is R. Aryeh Leib Heller (Galicia, 1745–1812), the author of *Ketzot ha-Ḥoshen*, which along with its frequent interlocutor, *Netivot ha-Mishpat* (by R. Jacob Lorberbaum, Poland, 1770–1832), became canonical when published on the bottom of the base text's page in the 1862 edition.[32] *Ketzot* saw the specific rulings of the Codes and their first-wave commentators as guideposts for identifying halakhah's underlying conceptual structure. The work therefore shifts the conversation away from the *Shulḥan Arukh*'s text and back to the Talmud and its medieval commentators and, methodologically, to the practice of using legal rules to discuss foundational questions of halakhic jurisprudence. Building on this older tradition, *Ketzot* propelled it to new levels of sophistication.[33]

While formally a commentary on the *Shulḥan Arukh*, *Ketzot* is generally approached as a central text of *talmud Torah*. Its conception of halakhah is dominated by the ideal law of the Talmud and is therefore comparatively less interested in the sub-halakhic practices and innovations prevailing in practice. In fact, though *Ketzot* has appeared in the standard editions of the *Shulḥan Arukh* since the early 1860's, it was first published as an independent two-volume work (volume 1 in 1788 and volume 2 in 1796).[34] Notably, the second volume of the standalone edition does not even include the text of the *Shulkhan Arukh* itself which *Ketzot* is ostensibly commenting upon. In the introduction to the second volume, this omission is explained in terms of saving on printing costs,[35] but, as scholars have noted, R. Aryeh Leib's assumption that he could print a commentary to the *Shulkhan Arukh* without the base text speaks volumes about the conceptual relationship between the two.[36] In more recent decades, *Ketzot's* proper focus of attention is seen to be not so much the Codes as the Talmud. Jewish bookstores now carry a work titled *The Novellae of Ketzot Ha-Ḥoshen on Tractate Bava Batra*, which, inspired by how the work is often studied, rearranges the comments on the *Shulḥan Arukh* as a sequential commentary to the Talmud itself! [37]

So much for *Ketzot's* form. In substance, its discussion of the laws of debt collection display little interest in communal legislation, debtor imprisonment, or the contractual devices employed by seventeenth- and eighteenth-century commercial parties. Instead, *Ketzot* uses the technical language of halakhah to explore the foundational assumptions of the Torah's regulatory scheme, prefiguring the work of the Briskers we'll discuss in chapter 12. On the topic of debt collection, *Ketzot* draws on the Talmud's quasi-philosophical inquiry (b.Temurah 4–6), asking whether an act performed in violation of a Torah prohibition is legally valid (albeit prohibited), or whether the Torah's prohibition renders the act entirely meaningless.

In the narrow sense, this question concerns whether a creditor who seizes the debtor's assets in violation of halakhah nevertheless acquires valid title to them in satisfaction of the debt, or whether the Torah's prohibition renders the creditor a simple thief. *Ketzot*, however, is less interested in the rule itself than in what it teaches about the structure of halakhic thought. In other words, what sort of legal system is halakhah? One that gives primacy to physical acts, or to legal status? And how is a conflict between the two resolved?

While the question is anchored in a technical matter, it also peers into a broader jurisprudential realm: does halakhah construct social and economic reality or does it reflect already existing conventions? Within a system of religious law, this question touches on the relationship between the divine will (which prohibits the seizure of assets) and human freedom (which seizes them anyway). These questions emerge in the Talmud and have been broadly debated in the literature of jurisprudence and theology. For *Ketzot*, there is nothing unusual about drawing this discussion into the legal code's technical treatment of debt collection.

How Unique Are the Halakhic Codes?

At this point, we may pause to ask whether this situation is unique? Surely halakhah is not the only system to display a gap between "laws on the books" and "law in action." In fact, it is very common for practices on the ground to outpace official legal pronouncements, and for codes and treatises to quickly become outdated. For example, modern American law students spend a semester learning the law of criminal procedure that detail the rights afforded to defendants. From the textbooks, one may get the impression that the accused have a vast array of such rights to deploy against the government in court. In reality however, these rules exist only in the law books, as since upward of ninety percent of criminal cases are resolved via plea bargains, with the defendant waiving all rights to challenge the government's actions.

The difference, however, is that in the American context, the impulse of a treatise writer is to identify the gap and narrow it. A good criminal-procedure treatise is written against the background knowledge that the formal rules apply to a vanishing set of cases. The text therefore focuses on those doctrines that remain relevant, and on how legal practice shifts in light of the diminished importance of the formal rules. Indeed, if current trends persist, criminal-procedure law will eventually be replaced by the law of plea-bargaining. Similarly, while a century ago the doctrine of "consideration" in contracts and the "rule against perpetuities" in real property were prominently featured in every American casebook and treatise, today they are viewed as possessing little content and command correspondingly less space in each succeeding edition.

In the case of the *Shulḥan Arukh* however, while the law recorded in the Codes may decrease in practical relevance, its status as an object of Torah study remains constant. As Torah, the Codes are significant beyond whether they accurately present current law. A compelling example can be found in the laws of acquisitions. Under talmudic law, a sale or contract is binding only if the parties indicate their agreement through a prescribed transactional formality known as a *kinyan* (acquisition). Over time, however, the ritualized *kinyan* fell into disuse as parties began to demonstrate their agreement by signing contracts, shaking hands, or issuing other verbal declarations. Though such transactions lack a formal *kinyan* status, they were validated under the talmudic principle that a contract engaged per the "customs of the merchants" (i.e., the way commerce functions) generates binding obligations. Though this notion is only briefly mentioned in the Talmud, it has become the basis of the majority of commercially significant contracts.[38]

Yet this trend is hard to detect in the pages of the Codes, which all devote numerous sections to the manifold details of the formal *kinyan*. Perhaps owing to their desuetude, especially in yeshivas, these Code sections became something of a secondary Talmud. Scholars like *Ketzot* would probe how the Rishonim, Codes, and their leading commentators resolved difficult passages in the Talmud, focusing on how their rulings inform the core conceptual questions of property, ownership, and contractual justice in halakhic thought. By contrast, the single section dealing with the imminently practical custom of the merchants is visibly devoid of the analytic commentary common to other code sections. In the eyes of many halakhists, the custom of the merchants is a form of sub-halakhah that describes what people actually do, yet offers few insights into the true and ideal halakhah that is studied.[39]

Conclusion

This chapter hardly claims that the Codes do not contain applied halakhah; nothing could be further from the truth. In fact, Code sections relating to the cycles of daily, weekly, and yearly rituals, as well as the laws of kashrut in its various forms, have defined the practiced law for observant Jews for nearly half a millenium. Entire communities have undertaken considerable expense to conform to even a minute inference based on the language of the Codes, their commentaries, or even their super-commentaries. In these cases, whether past or present, the Codes stand as governing law in virtually every sense the term can be understood.

Nevertheless, precisely because *Tur* and the *Shulḥan Arukh* are the most code-like documents in the tradition, one should be sensitive to the many ways in which they complicate the conventional understanding of a code. In moving from the laws of Shabbat, prayer, kashrut, and the personal status of marriage and divorce, to matters of civil law, civil procedure, and marital property law, halakhah in the Codes begins to drift from governing regulations toward a body of knowledge to be studied. In these sections, we find scholarly interest gravitating toward commentators like *Ketzot* who draw conceptual halakhic insights from the text rather than focus on end-user application. With the passage of time, parts of the *Shulḥan Arukh* itself morphed into a secondary Talmud—a space where devotional *talmud Torah* and practiced law live side-by-side.

Notwithstanding attempts to the contrary, the Codes inevitably embody the complex and fluid definitions of halakhah. This can be seen both within the text of the Codes themselves and, even more so, in the surrounding commentaries that have come to dominate their pages. No sooner did the Codes attain authoritative status then they became focal points for the uncode-like methods of devotional *talmud Torah*. And just as the Talmud combines both applied and learned laws under the heading of halakhah, the Codes do the same, now even under the heading of applied halakhah or *halakhah le-ma'aseh*.

11

The Idea of Halakhah in Responsa

Th[e] phrase [it is halakhah but not to be applied] has been common currency in [the responsa] literature for well over seven hundred years, ever since the days of Rashba, (d. 1315). How ubiquitous it is may be seen from the Bar-Ilan Responsa Project. The project's data bank yields no less that eighty-seven instances of its use in the sixteenth century alone.

—HAYM SOLOVEITCHIK [1]

AS NOTED ABOVE, a third style of halakhic writing emerged in addition to talmudic commentaries and codes. These are known as *responsa* (singular: *responsum*), questions posed to and answers given by renowned halakhic figures. In the era of the Geonim—early in the post-talmudic period—responsa covered nearly all forms of rabbinic thought: ritual and monetary cases, issues of theological belief, translations and interpretations of Talmudic words and phrases, and more. Later, as the center of the Jewish world shifted from Babylonia (Iraq) to Western Europe and North Africa in the period of the Rishonim (roughly in the late 1100s), talmudic commentaries and codes became more dominant. By the fifteenth century, however, responsa once again gained in significance, tending now to focus on civil disputes and the application of halakhic principles to novel situations.

Scholars have treated responsa as the halakhic equivalent of case law in a common-law legal system. In that sense, they may offer the clearest expression of halakhah as a governing system developed in the *beit din* (court) as opposed to a system of learned law anchored in the *beit midrash* (rabbinic academy). This view is attractive for a several of reasons. While commentaries and Codes take the Talmudic text as their starting point, responsa are usually stimulated by real-world events. In addition, the Talmud and Codes have become objects of *talmud Torah* and are often studied sequentially with the aim of mastering the corpus. Responsa, by contrast, have rarely attained an equivalent canonical status and tend to be consulted on an as-needed basis. The difference is apparent in how the genres are customarily printed. In editions of the Bible, Talmud, and Codes intended for study and discussion, the base text is normally surrounded by layers of commentary, drawing the reader into the inter-generational discussion taking place on the margins of the page; collections of responsa are generally published as stand-alone works with nothing other than the responsa's text printed on the page. In this way, too, and perhaps even more so than the Codes, responsa present a version of halakhah uncomplicated by the educational and expressive aspects of *talmud Torah.*

The view of responsa as equivalent to case law is generally accurate—at least as it relates to specific responsa or specific rabbinic respondents. Many do employ a conventional definition of law, and their goal is to rule on matters of halakhah with the expectation that the ruling will be applied. And yet, as with the Codes, the ethos of the Talmud and the ideal of *talmud Torah* are so powerfully enmeshed in rabbinic consciousness that it can be hard, *even in the responsa literature,* to pinpoint the frequently shifting lines among legal rulings, talmudic analysis, and rabbinic study and speculation.

One source of complication is the institutional context, or lack thereof, in which responsa are typically written. Following the Geonic period, responsa are not generally court documents—that is, judgments written by a court to the parties (known as a *p'sak din*)—but the learned opinions of scholars often prepared as consultative documents for use by the judges or others involved in the case.[2] What is more, the entire issue of courts and judges is relevant only in the context of civil litigation, as matters of ritual halakhah stand outside the court structure entirely. In the latter, validity of responsa depend more on the prestige and authority of the authoring rabbi than the institutional authority of the court and its infrastructure.

We can put this in perspective by looking at a few examples.

Terumat ha-Deshen is a well-known fifteenth-century collection of responsa penned by R. Israel Isserlein (Central Europe, 1390–1460) which exerts a profound influence on the formulation of halakhah in R. Joseph Caro's *Shulḥan Arukh*. According to a longstanding tradition, the questions presented in this work did not emerge from actual cases but were posed by R. Isserlein himself to address halakhic matters deemed worthy of discussion.[3] This in no way diminishes the importance of the work, but it does challenge the bright-line distinction between analytic-talmudic commentary—in which theoretical questions of Torah study are *de rigueur*—and responsa that allegedly address real-world issues.

As noted in the epigraph to this chapter, scholars have also noted that the responsa literature is replete with such terms as *le-halakhah ve-lo le-maʿaseh* (that is, halakhah but not for implementation): a clear statement that a particular responsum shares more with academic Torah study than with practiced law.[4] A good example here is found in the collection *Shvut Yaakov* by R. Jacob Reischer, a leading Central European respondent of the eighteenth century. R. Reischer discusses the case of two young men, dubbed Reuben and Simon, who are traveling together and begin to fight. Reuben pulls out a knife but is overpowered by Simon, who kills him in an apparent act of self-defense. Before embarking on his halakhic analysis, R. Reischer explains that "even as in these times we do not have authority to judge capital cases, I will not refrain from examining the issue as a matter of Torah law—by way of study and debate rather than as an actual ruling."[5] Although the case cannot be resolved pursuant to the formal laws of the ancient Sanhedrin, the incident, whether real or made up, offers an occasion for expounding on the theoretical approach taken by relevant halakhic sources.

Past events are likewise seized upon as starting points for detailed analysis. R. Yair Ḥayyim Bacharach (Worms, 1638–1702) recounts a famous case that took place in Worms during the great disaster of 1636—two years before his birth—in which a brilliant and beautiful daughter of a wealthy man fell ill. Because of the upheaval, no one could tend to her until a tall, handsome butcher's apprentice appeared. Offering to nurse the maiden to health, the young man contracted with the father for her hand in marriage if she survived. The father agreed, but later reneged as it was beneath his daughter's dignity to marry the impoverished simpleton. After presenting this story—which some have noted draws freely on a familiar trope in many a traditional fable[6]—the responsum analyzes the halakhic validity of agreements made under duress, in this case, the maiden's ill-health.

In roughly the same period, we find examples of halakhic interest in *golems*, Frankenstein-like creatures produced via esoteric means. One issue is whether a golem can be counted in a *minyan*—that is, for purposes of constituting a prayer quorum. It was addressed in a pair of responsa by R. Tzvi Hirsch Ashkenazi (Central Europe, 1656–1718) and his son, R. Jacob Emden (1697–1776).[7] The discussion was carried forward into the late nineteenth century, and touched upon in *Mishnah Berurah*, a commentary to the *Shulḥan Arukh* that remains a primary source of practiced halakhah to this day.[8]

Reflecting the considered opinion of esteemed halakhists, these responsa blur the line between talmudic commentary and decisions of legal practice. Just as the Talmud could retell the story of the quarrel between David and Saul to analyze the laws of betrothal and marriage, R. Bacharach could adopt the themes of a popular folktale to address the laws of contract. Similarly, just as the Talmud could open a discussion of the essence of personhood by way of the technicalities of *eglah arufah*—the ritual (Deuteronomy 21) of slaughtering a calf in atonement for an unsolved murder—so too, seventeenth- and eighteenth-century rabbis recast the issue of what constitutes human life by raising the question of whether a golem counts in making up a minyan. Indeed, the debate over this issue in the responsa literature could later come to figure in practical decision-making. In recent decades, the "golem" responsa have been cited in halakhic discussions of cloning, in-vitro fertilization, and genetic engineering.[9]

To press the matter further, in the eighteenth century, some of the most analytically significant works of Torah scholarship were published in the form of responsa. To some extent, this is a function of the available genres. Commentators, after all, are limited by the base text upon which they are commenting, and codifiers must draft a concise and comprehensive account of all the talmudic rules. Only responsa presented the classical halakhic writer with a clean slate, and leading halakhists used this freedom to develop a more conceptual account of the talmudic sugya.

Exemplars of this approach include collections of *responsa* such as *Sha'agat Aryeh* by R. Aryeh Leib Ginzberg (1695–1785), *Noda be-Yehudah* by R. Yeḥezkel Landau (1713–1793), *Ḥatam Sofer* by R. Moses Schrieber (1762–1839), and the responsa of R. Schreiber's father-in-law R. Akiva Eiger (1761–1837). Within these works it is not uncommon to find a responsum that could easily have been published as a theoretical-analytic essay emerging from the *beit midrash*.

To a large degree, these works foreshadowed developments in the nineteenth century, when halakhists began to publish essays on the Talmud's sugyot directly—sometimes in books captioned as responsa. In the introduction to one such work of responsa, *Beit ha-Levi*, R. Yosef Dov Soloveitchik (1820–1892) explains that he has written in the spirit of dialectical analysis among friends (*pilpul ḥaverim*); for that reason, he has confined his conclusions to the book's index/summary, and even there they serve as halakhah-but-not-for-implementation (*le-halakhah ve-lo le-ma'aseh*).[10] Likewise, in introducing his work *Aḥiezer*, R. Ḥayyim Ozer Grodzinski (1863–1940) notes that the responsa therein are not intended to "rule on matters of halakhah for the general public" but to offer insights on the weighty matters of talmudic analysis for "interested persons who study regularly."[11] A more extreme exemplar of this trend is found in *Hitorerut Teshuva* by R. Shimon Schrieber (Hungary, 1850–1944), the grandson of the aforementioned R. Moses Schrieber. Not only does the book's introduction state that one should not rely on his rulings in practice, but literally *every page* of the book contains a header issuing the following disclaimer: "One should not rely on this ruling in any manner, as explained in the Introduction."[12]

Finally, even responsa that strive to reach definitive conclusions can be opaque when it comes to exactly which meaning of halakhah is in play. Take a responsum by R. Jacob Ettlinger (Germany, 1798–1871), dealing with a talmudic statement we first encountered in chapter 8: "Better to be thrown into a blazing furnace than embarrass another in public" (b.Sotah 10b). After reviewing different readings of this state-ment, R. Ettlinger concludes that as a matter of halakhah, one must indeed give oneself over to death rather than shame another person publicly.

But how, then, would R. Ettlinger rule should an actual case arise? Would he really consign a person to death rather than avoid embarrass-ing another, or would he find a mitigating factor to hold the halakhah in abeyance? We can only speculate—although, to the best of my knowl-edge, in the past thousand years there is no instance of this rule being invoked in its literal form. Indeed, had R. Ettlinger published his discus-sion not as a responsum, but instead in his well-known commentary to the Talmud, *Arukh la-Ner,* we might easily assume his goal was to rein-force the Talmud's view that shaming can be so severe that *at some level* it may be worthy of the ultimate sacrifice; but not to advocate for a lit-eral death sentence. And so we must ask: to what degree does publica-tion in, specifically, a work of responsa change these assumptions?

Finally, inasmuch as some *responsa* are best understood as articles of Torah study cloaked in the garb of decisional law, other rulings con-spicuously labeled "not for practice" can exert considerable impact on practiced halakhah. One of the best examples of this trend is another responsum by R. Ettlinger, this one dealing with the seemingly innocu-ous question of the ritual status of wine.[13]

The Talmud rules that Jews are forbidden to drink wine handled by a non-Jew. Medieval authorities extended the ban to wine handled by Jews who flagrantly violated Shabbat, which in prior periods meant in-dividuals or small groups who acted out of rebelliousness. In 1860,

R. Ettlinger was asked whether wine handled by rapidly secularizing German Jews was similarly prohibited. Standing behind this narrow question was one the era's most important halakhic issues: the status of the many Jews who left traditional practice and violated halakhah with neither compunction nor a sense of guilt.

Under talmudic law, Jews who purposefully throw off "the yoke of heaven" are subject to civil, social, and criminal sanctions. Historically, these rules applied to heretics and traitors who formally broke away from the community. In the nineteenth century, the question was whether these sanctions applied to the masses of rapidly secularizing German Jews and, particularly, the generations born into an increasingly non-observant society. Were such persons analogous to the wicked blasphemers, or was another designation more apt?

The stakes were high, as a stringent ruling would write, from a halakhic perspective, most Jews out of the Jewish story. Moreover, in many instances, the break with tradition was far from complete. R. Ettlinger noted that some Shabbat-violating Jews would attend synagogue in the morning, recite the traditional Shabbat prayers, and then head off to the secular world.

The issue was approached through a bifurcated analysis. From a formal legal perspective (*me-ikar ha-din*), wine handled by a flagrant Shabbat violator was prohibited, just as if it had been touched by a non-Jew. But R. Ettlinger then switched tracks, noting his uncertainty as to whether the "sinners of our day" were indeed the "flagrant violators" depicted in the classical sources.

The responsum then tentatively suggests that perhaps the better analogy for secularizing Jews is the one referred to as the captured infant. The Talmud (b.Shabbat 67–70), refers to a child who, through no fault of his own, has been raised in non-Jewish society and is therefore not responsible for failing to adhere to halakhic practice. Notwithstanding his Shabbat violation, that person is treated with compassion rather than contempt, and faces none of the punitive measures that generally apply to those who violate Shabbat as a means of conscious rebellion. R. Ettlinger contemplates extending this analysis to those "captured" by the *zeitgeist*, reasoning that adherence to the mores of secular society is a sign of spiritual infancy, not rebellion.

While the captured infant is hardly held up as a halakhic ideal, R. Ettlinger's move reclassifies non-observant Jews from vile sinners who must be excommunicated (or worse) to lost souls who deserve pity and ought be encouraged back into the fold. Though analogies can be found in some medieval rulings,[14] R. Ettlinger appears to be the first (albeit hesitantly) to suggest a halakhic approach for keeping the Jewish people together in an era when secularizing Jews began to vastly outnumber those committed to halakhah.[15]

Interestingly, the responsum opens with a prefatory headnote printed just before the main text instructing the reader that its ruling is not *halakhah le-ma'aseh*,—it is *not to be implemented* in practice. Though it remains uncertain whether this cautionary note was placed by R. Ettlinger himself or by his son who published the volume,[16] the headnote, together with the responsum's tentative tone, underscores both the novelty and the centrality of this new halakhic attitude toward secularizing Jews. [17] R. Ettlinger's ideas proved prescient. In time, the responsum gained support from leading rabbis and was widely cited.[18] To this day, the captured infant remains one of the dominant halakhic paradigms through which observant Jews engage their secular brethren.

The fluidity of the genre enables this responsum to accomplish some-what contradictory goals. On the one hand, in labeling the responsum as not for practical application, R. Ettlinger (or his son) tentatively stakes out a far-reaching position without fully committing himself to the social, religious, and political consequences that may follow. In this way, the responsum functions like a law-review article, allowing the au-thor to test out an idea without enshrining it into law. On the other hand, because responsa are closely associated with decisional law, R. Ettlinger's position became influential among later halakhic authorities. This may have been exactly the intention of R. Ettlinger's son, who in the volume's introduction declares that his father's responsa should not be relied upon in practice, yet in the same sentence expresses the hope that subsequent authorities will use these responsa in support of their own halakhic conclusions.[19]

Conclusion

Viewed as a whole, there is little doubt that responsa indeed tilt in the direction of applied halakhic case law. The examples surveyed here, sitting as they do near the opposite, non-applied end of the spectrum, are among the exceptions. And yet, like the Codes and the Talmud that came before them, responsa embody a more complex definition of halakhah than a term like case law can convey. Even Menachem Elon, the leading proponent of the responsa-as-case-law theory, conceded that the "fine-spun dialectics (*pilpul*) and extremely subtle distinctions (*ḥillukim*) fashionable in the *yeshivot* in Poland in the sixteenth century . . . had a strong influence on the respondent's approach and analysis," resulting in the inclusion of "theoretical discussions of the Talmud and Rishonim that were not directly relevant to the question posed."[20]

The upshot is that while responsa are surely a form of rabbinic case law, this is by no means their exclusive function. As with the Codes, even in texts explicitly styled as applied halakhah, the halakhah may apply in a more removed sense. Because the rabbinic tradition makes it difficult to disentangle the practical job of answering legal questions from the spiritual drive to immerse in the Sea of the Talmud, each form of halakhah inevitably contains elements of both.

Thus, whether our point of reference is the Talmud, the Codes, the commentaries, or the responsa, the result is substantially the same. Halakhah is concurrently a system of governing rules and practices, a forum for legal analysis, a platform of religious expression, and an object of devotional study.

12

Halakhah's Empire

THE YESHIVA AND THE
HOUSE OF BRISK

[Torah study] is a total, all-encompassing and all-embracing
involvement—mind and heart, will and feeling, the center of the
human personality—emotional man, logical man, voluntaristic man—
all are involved in the study of Torah. Talmud Torah is basically for me
an ecstatic experience, in which one meets God.

—JOSEPH B. SOLOVEITCHIK [1]

Return to the Talmud

For nearly 200 years following the publication of the *Shulḥan Arukh*, the
study of halakhah focused on the ever-expanding network of commentaries printed on the margins of its pages. But by the late eighteenth
century, in a movement typified by the commentary known as *Ketzot*
explored in chapter 10, Torah study in Eastern Europe had begun to turn
back to the Talmud itself. The shift assumed an institutionalized form
in 1802 with the founding of *Yeshivat Etz Ḥayyim* (the Yeshiva) by the
students of the famed Vilna Gaon (1720–1797). Located in the small
town of Volozhin between Vilnius and Minsk in modern-day Belarus,
the Yeshiva quickly became the nerve center of the influential Lithuanian school of Talmud study.

The turn from the *Shulḥan Arukh* back to the Talmud was accompanied by a parallel change in the conception of Torah study. Rather than the summarizing and codifying works surrounding the law Codes, the central aim of study was now to expand and explain the system of interlocking legal ideas. This created the environment (as we saw in chapter 9) in which Maimonides' code, the *Mishneh Torah*—one of the most black-letter texts in the entire canon—became a work of devotional *Torah lishmah*, Torah study for its own sake.

Though the idea stretched back to talmudic times, the Yeshiva's theology pushed it to extreme forms. Torah study was primary to all spiritual endeavors, and understood to sustain the physical existence of the cosmos itself. In a work termed the "theoretical blueprint for the great nineteenth-century Torah academies,"[2] R. Ḥayyim of Volozhin, the Yeshiva's founder, wrote: "If all the world, from one end to the other, were . . . void even for one moment of our study and meditation on Torah, then immediately [everything] would be destroyed and revert to chaos and nothingness."[3]

In line with these theological claims, the Volozhin Yeshiva innovated around-the-clock study rotations of to ensure that no moment would ever be bereft of Torah. It likewise emphasized mastering the entire body of the Talmud, making few distinctions between its applied and its non-applied sections. And even in locations where only a subset of the Talmud came to be studied, as at several of the Yeshiva's offshoot institutions, the curriculum gravitated to the analytically rigorous parts of family and commercial law, typically at the expense of the more practically relvant topics such as the laws of prayer and blessings, Shabbat and holidays, kashrut, and other facets of daily life.

A similar ethos was reflected in the student body. Those who flocked to the Yeshiva came not to train as practitioner-rabbis who would then go on to serve in the field. Rather, they entered with the aspiration of becoming accomplished Talmud scholars.

Alongside its emphasis on devotional *Torah lishmah*, the Yeshiva raised the parallel concept of *bittul Torah*—the shameful abnegation of Torah—to new levels. In this understanding, any moment *not* devoted to Torah study required specific justification. Eating, sleeping, family affairs, and all other activities were to be kept to a bare minimum, as even the slightest excess might constitute *bittul torah*.[4] A walk in the park, or any form of recreation or amusement, was looked down upon when not banned outright. In this milieu, rabbis and their students would boast of how little they slept, how they never read a non-Torah book, and how uninformed they were about anything other than Torah. The goal was a near-fanatical emphasis on processing all of life through the filter of halakhah—a worldview both celebrated and criticized in the justly famous poem, *ha-Matmid*, by the modernist master Ḥayyim Naḥman Bialik, himself an alumnus of Volozhin's Etz Hayyim Yeshiva.[5]

But the most enduring legacy of Volozhin lies in what has come to be known as the Brisker method of talmudic analysis. Brisk refers to the town (Brest-Litovsk in present-day Belarus) where the method was refined after the demise of Yeshivat Etz Hayyim of Volozhin in the 1890s. Its leading practitioner was R. Ḥayyim Soloveitchik (1853–1918) who, while teaching at the Yeshiva, developed the approach which was later disseminated across a network of institutions in Eastern Europe. Although the communities of Brisk, Volozhin, Ponovizhe, Telshe, Mir, and others were all destroyed in the Holocaust, the names of the towns live on in the contemporary yeshivot that bear their name. More significantly, the understanding of halakhah initially developed in these towns continues to influence Torah study to this day.

Of course, not all of Torah scholarship followed the Volozhin-Brisk method. Though any halakhist worth his salt deplored *bittul Torah* and prized Torah study, the extremes of the Volozhin system were far from the norm. Since at least the early-modern period, Sephardic halakhists were considerably less invested in the refined distinctions and talmudic dialectics that typify traditional Ashkenazic study, but instead, focused on drawing practical conclusions from prior source material, a trend continued well into the twentieth century. In fact, R. Ovadya Yosef, arguably the greatest Sephardic halakhist of the last two centuries, devoted a section of the introduction to his massive work of (highly practical) responsa to criticizing the the method of study prevailing yeshivot emerging from the Volozhin tradition. But R. Yosef reserved particular ire for the Brisker practice of centering study on the laws of the Temple's offerings and and purity regimens that have limited practical relevance in the present era. [6]

Much closer to Volozhin's native sphere of influence, such leading authorities as R. Israel Meir Kagan, the author of *Mishnah Berurah*, and R. Yeḥiel Michael Epstein, the author of *Arukh ha-Shulḥan,* composed influential codifications that remain the basis of Ashkenazi practiced halakhah today. Even the movement's fellow travelers, rabbis who generally shared the Briskers' Talmud-centric worldview—including such figures as *Ḥatam Sofer* (R. Moses Schreiber, Hungary 1762–1839) and *Ḥazon Ish* (R. Abraham Isaiah Karelitz, Belarus/Israel, 1878–1953)—remained outside and perhaps even hostile to the analytical method of Volozhin-Brisk.[7]

Since the idea of halakhah as a system of thought reaches its fullest articulation in the orbit of Volozhin, to investigate this corner of the rabbinic universe is to appreciate both its strengths and its limitations. The Briskers' nothing-but-Talmud approach did not allow them to articulate their methodological underpinnings or philosophical assumptions. That task was undertaken by R. Joseph B. Soloveitchik (Belarus/ New York, 1903–1993), the scion of the Brisker dynasty and grandson of the movement's founder. Though loyal to his family's methodology, the younger Soloveitchik parted ways with his forefathers by also highly valuing philosophical and secular education, to the point of earning a doctorate in philosophy from the University of Berlin. In time, R. Soloveitchik became one of twentieth-century America's most influential halakhists and theologians.

R. Soloveitchik's dual training in both Talmud and philosophy enabled him to describe the Brisker method and its underlying theology in terms unavailable to his ancestors. His insights frame our discussion below.

The Brisker Method: Examples

Before we assess the Brisker method, a few examples will help introduce its style and substance.

According to the Talmud, legal title to a movable object is acquired by way of a physical act known as *kinyan*, a term encountered in chapter 10. Typically, this involves demonstrating ownership by lifting the object in question into the air. But since the Talmud does not state how much lifting is required, a debate on the question ensued among medieval commentators. Some require a height of three handbreadths (about nine inches), while others only a single handbreadth (three inches).

The Brisker interprets this debate by probing the nature of the act of lifting itself: What is the legal impact of lifting the object into the air? Does it: (i) *effectuate* the transfer of legal rights; or (ii), does it merely offer *evidence* that a transfer of ownership has taken place. To the Brisker mind, each of the contrasting opinions assumes one of these positions. The view that insists on nine inches holds the act of lifting is meant to evidence the transfer of ownership, hence a more pronounced motion is required. By contrast, a minimal motion of only one handbreadth is sufficient if the lifting is simply a mechanism for transferring ownership. In other words, just as the Talmud understood in another context that a debate over a few inches could represent different views on the nature of humanity (see the discussion in chapter 4), the Brisker converts a difference of six inches into an inquiry about the nature of a legal formality.[8]

To better understand the Brisker approach, consider for a moment the explanations that are *not* on offer: for instance, that the two positions reflect the commercial customs of their respective time and place, or the different legal regimes of their host cultures, or simply different intuitions about which approach makes more practical sense. To the Brisker mind, these circumstantial explanations do not warrant the name "halakhah." Only fundamental or conceptual accounts addressing the essence of each rule are acceptable. Historical, contextual, sociological, or realist thinking has no place in the Brisker worldview, an issue we will return to below.

The second example highlights the way in which Briskers saw the world through a halakhic filter. The Torah prohibits wearing an article of clothing that contains wool and linen fibers woven together. An exception, however, exists in the case of *kohanim* (priests) serving in the Temple in Jerusalem and whose uniforms, according to Torah law, *must* combine wool and linen. For them, the mixing prohibition is suspended.

The scope of this exception, however, is debated by two twelfth-century authorities. One view finds the exception applicable whenever the uniform is being worn in the Temple compound. The other rules more stringently, holding that mixed-fiber garments are permitted only when the *kohen* is actively performing his official duties.[9]

From the Brisker point of view, this dispute touches on what it means for a *kohen* to wear his vestments. The first approach tends toward a colloquial definition; hence so long as the uniform is being worn, the mixing prohibition is suspended. The second maintains that simply wearing the vestments is not enough; rather, the *kohen* must have, in Brisker parlance, the "legal status of wearing" them. And that "status of wearing" is determined not by whether the garment is physically covering the *kohen's* body, but by whether the *kohen* is engaged in a halakhically significant "act of wearing."[10]

The distinction between ordinary wearing and "the halakhic act of wearing" may be more easily visualized if considered first in a less exotic setting. Imagine a law under which a police officer can make a valid traffic stop only while in uniform. Should an ordinary civilian put on a uniform, a stop made by him would be invalid, as no one thinks the mere act of wearing a uniform transforms a civilian into an officer of the law. But now suppose a uniformed officer who is off-shift and returning home from work and sees a motorist running a red light. Can the off-duty officer initiate a valid traffic stop, or not?

In the Brisker perspective, the answer would depend on the nature of the requirement to be in uniform. On the one hand, since the officer is commissioned and his clothes identify him as an agent of the state, he may be considered in uniform and thus authorized to make the stop. This is roughly the position that emphasizes the physical presence of the uniform. The opposing view, however, maintains that an off-duty officer in uniform is no different from an actor who dons a police costume. Yes, the actor is *physically* wearing a uniform, but he is not in uniform as the law understands the term. Adopting the Brisker's language, the off-duty police officer is similarly not engaged in an "act of wearing" that generates the "halakhic status of being uniformed." Hence, the ensuing traffic stop is invalid.

In each of our examples, the Brisker approach points to a central tension embedded in almost every legal act. Take the example of a party entering into a contract. On the one hand, there is the physical and observable act of signing the document. On the other hand, the physical act initiates a more abstract, conceptual, and, for the Brisker, metaphysical act or moment that generates legal obligation. This becomes clear once we realize that not every contract needs to be signed, or that even if the pages stamped "Contract" atop are lost, the legal obligation remains in force.

In both halakhah and American law, the *idea* of a contract is a more abstract concept than either the physical act of signing, or the sheet of paper labeled "Contract." In the Brisker view, to understand the essence of halakhah requires penetrating behind the observable and physical trappings of its rules and reaching the essential elements at work. Brisker Torah study, therefore, invests considerable effort in distinguishing the temporal and circumstantial aspects of a given halakhah from the principles that animate its internal structure.

The Brisker Conception of Halakhah and Its Study

The Methodology of Talmud Torah

Brisker analysis draws its inspiration from talmudic sugyot that probe the legal architecture of a given rule or the conceptual source of existing disputes; these sugyot often begin with the phrase *ibaei lehu* (they queried) and/or *mai beinaihu* (what is the source of the disagreement). But whereas the Talmud will occasionally hint at questions like, "What is the nature of a transactional formality?" or "How does a uniform confer authority?" the Briskers confronted these matters directly. Therein lay their primary innovation.

Related, is the Briskers' target audience. Take for example R. Israel Meir Kagan's *Mishnah Berurah,* the authoritative nineteenth-century codification of practiced halakhah. That work is plainly addressed to a person on the verge of performing a mitzvah, the pious but average Jew who confronts halakhic questions in the context of its practice. In this setting, *Mishnah Berurah* is designed to serve as a reliable guide, ensuring and encouraging the meticulous observance of halakhah under every imaginable scenario.[11]

By contrast, the Briskers addressed themselves to the scholar encountering halakhah through in-depth study of the talmudic sugya. In doing so, they adopted the Talmud's practice of writing on non-practiced halakhah, melding various halakhic disciplines into a single framework and investigating long-rejected positions right alongside the views codified in the *Shulḥan Arukh.* Thus, for all its analytical acuity, the classic Brisker exposition says little about which view is correct. And while Briskers surely assumed their readers were fully committed to halakhic practice, the paradigmatic encounter with halakhah was as a medium of Torah study.

Halakhah as Reflecting Fundamental Ideas

The Briskers also promoted the view that there was no such thing as a merely technical halakhah; every legal rule—even a rejected position—can teach something about the nature of halakhah itself. A few inches of space in the transference of legal rights can be shorthand for how changes in legal status are triggered; whether an off-duty *kohen* may wear his vestments—hardly an issue that kept nineteenth-century Jews up at night—probes the relationship between inherent authority and its external manifestation.

In his admiring reconstruction, R. Joseph Soloveitchik described his grandfather's method as follows:

Torah scholars used to denigrate those who studied the laws of kashrut: only those who were about to enter the rabbinate would study this area of the law. Who could guess the day would come when these laws would be freed from the bonds of facticity, external and common-sense explanations, and become transformed into abstract concepts . . . ? Suddenly the pots and the pans, the egg and the onion, disappeared from the law of meat and milk. . . . The laws of kashrut were taken out of the kitchen and removed to an ideal halakhic world . . . constructed out of complexes and abstract concepts.[12]

This theme plays out in numerous Brisker writings that show how obscure halakhic data address questions occupying lawyers and theologians to this day. These include whether tort damages are meant to vindicate a plaintiff's property right or to compensate for injury,[13] whether an agent steps into the shoes of the principal or merely acts on his behalf,[14] whether required mitzvah-activities, such as lighting Shabbat candles or hearing the *shofar*, focus on the process of performance or the result of the mitzvah having been performed,[15] or as discussed in the Preface, whether the initiation or conclusion of the sexual act is legally significant. These analytical inquiries not only clarify talmudic conundrums but speak to foundational concepts like ownership,[16] property rights,[17] tort liability,[18] marriage and divorce,[19] the obligation of giving charity,[20] the prohibition on charging interest,[21] liability for intentional bodily harm,[22] fasting,[23] and prayer.[24] In the Brisker's hand, myriads of halakhic details that are neither intuitive nor relevant are recast as meaningful indicators of halakhah's conceptual structure.

The Omnipresence of Halakhah

A related feature touches on the question of where or when halakhah exists. The discussion of the *kohen's* uniform is undertaken by a nineteenth-century Brisker analyzing a debate between twelfth-century authorities over a fourth-century text describing the workings of an even more ancient institution. As we note in the Introduction, from a historical perspective, this method is hard to justify. Surely, the best evidence of how the Temple historically operated is to be found in sources close to it in time and place, not in halakhic reconstructions written nearly two millennia later. But the Briskers saw halakhah as an omnipresent reality that stands outside of time: thus, there is nothing unusual or untoward about folding the nineteenth, twelfth, fourth and first centuries into a single halakhic framework. To the Brisker, the question of how the Temple functioned is halakhic, not historical. Authoritative statements of halakhah from any period are therefore more relevant than historical materials from the era of the Temple's existence.

Though the ahistorical approach to halakhah does not originate with the Briskers, in their hands it became a foundational belief. This is made evident in R. Joseph Soloveitchik's analogizing the halakhist to the mathematician or physicist who

> engages in complex and difficult calculations involving the manipulating of ideal mathematical quantities that, at first glance, are wholly lacking in the music of the living world and the beauty of the resplendent cosmos. It would seem as if there exists no relationship between these quantities and reality. Yet these ideal numbers that cannot be grasped by one's senses, these numbers that are meaningful only from within the system itself, meaningful only as part of abstract mathematical functions, symbolize the image of existence.[25]

Take the equation of 2+2=4. This statement does not "exist" in any specific time and place; nor does its truth depend on having two objects that can be added to two other objects. In R. Soloveitchik's understanding, it is an ontologically true statement that simply *is*. Likewise, equations accounting for how planets revolve around the sun are mathematical truisms that exist whether planets actually revolve around the sun or not. In R. Soloveitchik's view, what mathematicians and physicists might say about the ruling concepts in their own fields is equally true of such halakhic concepts as, for instance, the Sanhedrin's rules concerning capital punishment. It makes no difference whether the Sanhedrin stands or not, or whether its cumbersome procedures ever succeeded in deterring crime. Such circumstantial factors cannot impinge on the inherent truth of these halakhic propositions.

Halakhah in the Physical and Social World

The halakhah-as-physics argument is based on a midrashic statement encountered in chapter 4: "the Torah is the blueprint for the world." In the theology of Brisk, this means that specific halakhic rulings are conceptually and temporally prior to reality itself. The depths of this commitment are drawn out in the following statement attributed to the originator of the Brisker method, R. Ḥayyim Soloveitchik:

> One may think that the reason the Torah instituted [commandments such as charity and performing acts of kindness] is in order for society to function. But in truth, it is the opposite. *Because* there is a commandment not to murder, *therefore* murder leads to destruction. Similarly, because the Torah commanded to give charity, such an act sustains the world. . . . Thus the universe is created in accordance with the Torah, and Torah is the blueprint of creation. For in truth, a universe could be created in which murder would sustain society and charitable acts would destroy it—is the hand of God limited? . . . . All is in accord with what is written in the Torah; and not that the Torah was given on the basis of reality.[26]

This passage starkly outlines the Brisker understanding of the relationship between halakhah and society. It asks us to envision the halakhah of marriage and divorce in the absence of men and women, and the laws of debtor and creditor in the absence of commerce or money. To the degree that this is a correct apprehension, then halakhah is truly more akin to mathematics than a legal system designed to regulate society. R. Joseph Soloveitchik (the grandson) wrote, "[t]here exists an ideal world and a concrete one, and between the two only an approximate parallelism prevails. . . . [T]he mathematical world has no desire to apprehend the concrete world *per se* but seeks only to establish a relationship of parallelism and analogy."[27] Thus, "[t]he theoretical halakhah, not the practical decision, the ideal creation, not the empirical one, represents the longing of halakhic man."[28]

In sum, the *real* halakhah is the ideal in God's mind. That which happens on earth is a rough approximation at best.

The Briskers' preference for the halakhic over the human provides the context for several of their unique formulations. Take the ungainly phrase, "legal status of wearing the uniform" discussed above. Here, the term "legal status" is meant to distinguish the observable act of wearing the uniform from the halakhic "status of wearing a uniform." Elsewhere, Briskers argued that water halakhically unfit for a mikveh is *not water*, and that an unowned ox is simply *not an ox*. (In the Talmud, an "ox" is an animal that generates liability for its owner when it gores; since an un-owned ox does not create liability for anyone, the Briskers entertained that it might "not be an ox.").[29] When the Briskers studied the laws of the Temple or Sanhedrin, they did not focus on the buildings or institutions of ancient Jerusalem, but on the *legal construct* of the Temple or Sanhedrin that stand eternal in the divine realm. The Briskers' "deepest ideal is not the realization of halakhah," wrote R. Joseph Soloveitchik, but rather the "ideal construction which was given to [man] from Sinai, and this ideal construction lasts forever."[30]

Contrast the Brisker idea of halakhah-as-reality with how modern courts in the West deal with the analogous tension between "legal" and colloquial understandings of common terms. Courts have been asked to rule on whether a chicken is a "chicken" within the meaning of a contract;[31] whether a tomato is a fruit or a vegetable for purposes of customs regulation;[32] whether Pringles are "potato crisps" under British tax law[33]; and whether a gun bartered for drugs is "used" during the commission of a crime.[34] Though the reasoning in these cases may surprise ordinary speakers of English, the courts do not typically adopt Brisker postulates. Modern courts assume the colloquial definition establishes the baseline, and they seek to explain why the specialized legal meaning should nevertheless take precedence over what the word *really* means.

The Briskers, however, start from the other end. The real meaning of water is the substance deemed valid for a *mikveh*. The compound H_2O is, at best, an approximate parallelism of the ideal halakhic standard.

The Beit Midrash and the Beit Din

For all their talmudic prowess, the Briskers were notoriously reticent about deciding questions of practical halakhah. As R. Joseph Soloveitchik reflects, "many of the greatest halakhic men avoided . . . serving in rabbinical posts" and were "reluctant to render practical decisions." Even when necessity "compel[led] them . . . to render practical decisions," this was only a "small, insignificant responsibility which does not stand at the center of their concerns."[35]

Their quietism was not born out of an indifference to halakhic practice. To the contrary: the Briskers were fierce—even radical—traditionalists who frequently advocated for halakhic stringencies far beyond the accepted norm. Likewise, in the political sphere, Briskers were at the forefront of the fight against reformist and social movements that looked to define Judaism in terms other than submission to halakhah. Instead, the anti-practice bias stems from their understanding of the nature of halakhah itself: it is not something of the here and now, but something that like God, stands beyond material reality. *Real* halakhah deals not with the avaricious businessman or the insolvent debtor, but with refined halakhic concepts such as the "legal status of a debt" and the "ideal construction of a loan." If the Sanhedrin's cumbersome procedures failed to deter criminals—what of it? And if the Talmud's debtor/creditor laws made commerce difficult, of what concern is this to halakhah? True halakhah is not found in a *beit din* where criminals are tried and litigants square off, but in the *beit midrash* where the divine presence resides when holy texts are studied.

While this lofty view may be suited for the academic confines of a yeshiva, the reality was and is more complex. For as we have seen, the pure law of the Sanhedrin was buttressed by sub-halakhic methods of enforcement, and the rigid standards of commercial law were often modified by local practice, communal legislation, and the responsa literature. The Briskers did not necessarily deny these innovations, and were generally content to live within the accepted norms, but these sources and and practices were generally precluded from the yeshiva curriculum. Halakhah exists in God's supernal realm, thus neither Jewish moneylenders, the commercial practices of Gentiles, nor the exigencies of the time can affect a legal system that predates the creation of the universe itself.

The Domain of Halakhah

As R. Joseph Soloveitchik saw it, halakhah "wishes to objectify religiosity."[36] Pushed to its limits, this means that every Jewish—even every human—experience must be mediated through halakhic categories. This idea, too, has more ancient roots. In chapter 1 we saw that while the Bible relates the story of David and Saul as an epic focusing on themes of leadership, politics, family, and jealousy, the Talmud transforms it into a halakhic debate over the technicalities of betrothal law. In the Talmud, this is but one of several methods of reading, for the Briskers, it became the central interpretive tool.

Social Policy

The idea that halakhah predates creation means that its rules are hardwired into the fabric of the universe. Thus, if some rules proved too burdensome on commerce, or enabled wealthy creditors to oppress impoverished debtors, there is simply nothing to be done about it. In the Bible, the prophet Elisha miraculously spares the son of a destitute woman from being sold into debt-slavery. (2 Kings Ch. 4). But this role is reserved for a miracle-working prophet empowered to change reality, not for the halakhist who must operate within it. To be sure, the founder of the movement, R. Ḥayyim Soloveitchik, was renowned for his acts of piety and charity. [37] But these stemmed from his personal sense of obligation to assist the poor and destitute, not his understanding of the nature of halakhah and its ability to adapt to social conditions. The halakhah that God studies with the angels in heaven consists of objective principles beyond the reach of humans. As the younger Soloveitchik saw it, his grandfather "fought a war of independence" on behalf of halakhah, granting it "full autonomy" from the contextual factors of human society. Thus

> Any psycholization or sociologization of halakhah strangles its soul . . . If halakhic thinking depends on personal variables, it loses its objectivity and devolves into a subjectivity lacking all substance . . . Rather, Reb Chaim . . . created a complex set of halakhic categories and an order of *a priori* premises through a process of pure postulation. Halakhah is not conceived of in historical-political or sociological terms . . . Reb Chaim re-coronated halakhah with the crown of complete independence.[38]

The Religious Experience

Another impact of Brisk touches on the nature of halakhic spirituality. In the austere religious economy of Brisk, experiences of divine love and grace, or expressions of unity with the transcendent commonly described as religious or spiritual, are demeaned as ephemeral and lacking in theological rigor and content.

The tension becomes evident in the Brisker analysis of the Passover seder. Traditionally, the seder represents the foundational moment of Jewish education as families gather around a festive table to re-enact the birth of the nation. The Talmud speaks of several practices and concepts designed to construct the mood and experience of the seder. One such is *herut*, translated as liberty or freedom, typically understood as the reason behind the requirement to recline (as in the custom of the ancient aristocracy) and the obligation to drink four cups of wine (which only the well-off could afford). With regard to the wine in particular, the Talmud notes the rabbis instituted this practice *derekh heyrut* (in the way of freedom) (b.Pesahim 109b and 117b).

But how can one be commanded to feel free? Is freedom the *interior state of mind* one strives to obtain through the seder rituals? Or is freedom the *halakhic status* that results from fulfilling the designated requirements?

The Brisker is preternaturally suspicious of amorphous concepts such as "the human experience of freedom," and tends toward the latter approach. Hence the Talmud's term, "way of freedom" (*derekh ḥerut*) is subtly transformed into the Briskerized "legal status of freedom" (*din ḥerut*).[39] Changing only two Hebrew letters, the Brisker shifts the locus from a human experience into an objectified halakhic status. Freedom becomes an independent legal object (*ḥeftzah*, in Brisker terminology) governed by its own postulates that depends neither on the psychology of the individual or sociology of the group. Whether the rituals of the seder in fact move participants toward a meaningful religious experience is not a question Briskers tend to ask.

Taken to the extreme, Brisker theology leads to a view where a child does not cry over the death of a parent but responds through the halakhic requirements of mourning. Couples do not love, but fulfill the halakhic duties of copulation and procreation. Children, spouses, friends, and relatives are not ends in themselves but vehicles for the fulfillment of halakhic obligations. Most of course, did not take it to such extremes, but in yeshiva circles, stories circulate of pious rabbis who went to great length to disengage human emotion from halakhic practice.[40] R. Joseph Soloveitchik contrasts a Brisker's (surely hypothetical!) walk through the forest with that of an ordinary spiritual seeker. Both encounter glowing sunrises and soothing sunsets as well as rivers and streams, mountains, and valleys. But while the spiritualist stands in awe of the majesty of God's creation, the Brisker dismisses this subjective religiosity and turns instead to the halakhic questions at hand. The streams: do they qualify for use as a mikveh? The mountains: do they demarcate a separate domain for Shabbat? Sunrise, sunset, and twilight: what halakhic obligations does each entail?[41] The recurring message is clear: the Torah is the blueprint of reality, and halakhah is the prism through which it is viewed.

A common criticism of Brisk, therefore, is that its adherents serve halakhah rather than God. Opponents argue that Brisker theology denudes the religious person from the religious quest, transforming the spiritual aspirant into a halakhic robot who feels neither pain nor passion, zeal nor faith, grace nor doubt.[42] The Brisker however, is not so easily moved, and retorts that only the rigor and precision of halakhah provides the objective certainty required to actualize God's will.

The Success of Brisk

Our reconstruction of the Brisker method answers some of the most basic questions regarding halakhah: why are rabbis so concerned with every minor detail, yet rarely comment on its overall structure? Why is there so little analysis of halakhah's theory of politics or its approach to governance? Why is halakhah frequently oblivious to elisions of time and space? What accounts for the centrality of Torah study? Finally, why does halakhah crowd out competing forms of human expression?

To the Brisker, these questions all miss the point. Halakhah is not primarily about regulating the social sphere but a system of divinely ordained concepts that undergirds the spiritual—even physical—universe. Torah study is not about crafting law to govern society but the founding act of Jewishness that strives to master God's wisdom. As R. Joseph Soloveitchik passionately describes:

> When I sit down to learn Torah, I find myself immediately in the company of the sages of the *masorah* [halakhic tradition]. . . . The Rambam [Maimonides] is at my right, Rabbenu Tam at my left. Rashi sits up front and interprets, Rabbenu Tam disputes him; the Rambam issues a ruling and the Rabad objects. They are all in my little room, sitting around my table. . . . Those who transmitted the Torah and those who received it come together in one historical way-station."[43]

The version of Torah study reflected in this soaring passage refers to a specific group of halakhists who flourished near the end of nineteenth century. To be sure, the Briskers engendered their fare share of critics. From Sephardic (and some Ashkenazic) halakhists for focusing too much on Talmudic analytics while neglecting practical questions of law, and by Hasidic and religious existentialists who faulted them for worshipping the law rather than God. From the more liberal side, for creating vision of halakhah that is walled-off from basic social, moral, and historical considerations, and from the more conservative side, for placing creativity and ingenuity, rather than simply mastery and submission, at the center of Torah study.

Yet because the Brisker method takes the assumptions of the talmudic sugya to their farthest conclusion, Brisk's core ideas resonate with a broad cross-section of rabbinic thinkers. Even while the range of that thought is more diverse than the Brisker conception allows, the method exerts a strong pull on the entire field of halakhic theology. In every era in which significant works of halakhah have been produced, whether prior to or after Brisk, one finds the sensibilities that reach their fullest expression in the Brisker method.

13

The State of Halakhah and the Halakhah of the State

Having lain dormant for centuries, upon the advent of the State of Israel [questions of religion and state] suddenly burst upon the scene with a vengeance, confronting us existentially with what had previously been purely theoretical issues. . . . A hiatus of fifteen or twenty centuries in the application of any Halachic area would pose severe difficulties, even if the practical situation in the area had remained relatively stable. How much greater the difficulty when that area has radically altered.

—AHARON LICHTENSTEIN[1]

The Social and Religious Background

The traditional halakhic "constitution" is based on the belief that God revealed both the written and oral Torah to Moses at Mount Sinai. The oral Torah was passed down through the generations until it became crystallized in the Mishnah and Talmud. Following the completion of the Talmud, halakhic authority was vested in the scholars of each generation, later to be embodied in the *Shulḥan Arukh* along with its commentaries, responsa, and associated communal practices. In brief, this constitution requires each Jew to live in accordance with the halakhah outlined in the Talmud, as understood by its subsequent rabbinic interpreters.

For centuries, the broad outlines of this constitution prevailed. Rabbinic authority was a normative force within the community, and those who openly rejected its foundational norms were considered outside the fold. Though it is unlikely that the average Jew was either aware or interested in the details of Shabbat observance set forth in the commentaries and super-commentaries on the *Shulḥan Arukh,* flagrant disregard of the central Shabbat laws entailed social (and often political) consequences.

This religious dynamic was buttressed by several factors, the most salient of which was that Jews lived in *galut* (exile) as a subjugated minority within a Christian or Muslim orbit.[2] Though circumstances inevitably varied, non-Jewish authorities tended to govern the Jews under their domain through the internal institutions of the Jewish community (a political arrangement often known as corporatism). In these small homogeneous communities, governance was effectuated through a relatively un-theorized mix of formal halakhah, sub-halakhah, and other lay and rabbinic methods and institutions. Since Jews could not typically live freely within the general society, the community's ultimate power lay in its ability to banish or excommunicate those violating its core commitments.

To the extent one could name a dominant political theory for this arrangement, it may have been best captured by the rabbi in the musical *Fiddler on the Roof* who, when asked about the proper blessing for the Tsar, replied: "May God bless and keep the Tsar . . . far away from us!"[3] Operating in the context of exile, halakhists had little need to deal with questions of theory, legal or political, or address the structural issues of statecraft and legal enforcement. Indeed, prior to the onset of modernity, there is scant rabbinic reflection on such topics.

Over the past 250 years or so, this landscape changed in several critical ways. Politically, the rise of the nation-state centralized power in the hands of state institutions at the expense of indigenous rabbinic and communal organs. Socially, emancipation and increased freedom of movement and trade made it easier for Jews to reside within Gentile society, reducing the cost of abandoning communal norms. Together, these two developments shrank the rabbinic sphere of influence. At least from an external perspective, halakhic observance increasingly became a matter of voluntary commitment rather than a framework enforced by communal bodies empowered by non-Jewish officialdom.

The consequences also played out at the level of religious consciousness. Starting in Western Europe and moving eastward, large numbers of Jews came to reject the theological tenets of the halakhic constitution. In the nineteenth century, new forms of Jewish identity were adopted, ranging from a full-throated secularism that dismissed the authority of Torah and halakhah *in toto*, to the rise of competing denominations that rethought various doctrines of Jewish theology in light of modernity, to efforts to recast Jewish identity on social, national, ethnic, or ethical grounds. After more than two centuries, the result is that less than twenty percent of world Jewry now adheres to the classical halakhic constitution.[4] (For a number of reasons, mainly demographic, that figure is projected to rise in coming decades.)

And all this does not take account of what, for the purposes of our subject, is the most fateful development of all: namely, the emergence of Zionism and the establishment of the State of Israel. After two millennia of *galut*, Jews founded a state and re-entered the mainstream of national and political history, marking the first time since before the mishnaic era that Jews attained sovereignty and independence.

The effect on Jewish reality could not be more dramatic. If, in the traditional arrangement, world Jewry was a largely believing community generally bereft of political power, today it is a largely secular community that, in the State of Israel, expresses full political autonomy. To complicate matters further, although Israel's founding fathers conceived of the state in mainly secular terms, recent demographic and political shifts have brought the question of its religious and halakhic character to the fore. Indeed, among those who adhere to the halakhic constitution, there is a growing sense that halakhah should play a decisive role in the governance of the Jewish state.

In its most basic form, this sentiment is easy to understand. Over the long course of *galut*, Jews studied and celebrated their law in prayerful anticipation of its eventual restoration. Surely, then, halakhah should serve as the foundation for any Jewish state. But this raises two related questions. First, to what extent can halakhah become, or merge with, modern state law? Second, how is the answer to that question affected by the fact that the majority of the Jewish population in the Jewish state itself do not subscribe to the halakhic constitution, and that a recognizable minority of the state's citizenry is not even Jewish?

In both popular and scholarly media, the discussion over the relationship between halakhah and the state tends to center on the second issue, often presented in the form of the presumed fit or misfit between halakhah and democracy. On this view, the silent presumption is that the difficulty is not converting halakhah to the law of a modern Jewish state, but simply whether that is something to be promoted (as its adherents wish) or thwarted (the wish of its many detractors). But this way of framing things obscures a number of fundamental questions regarding the nature of halakhah itself.

Throughout this book, we have argued that halakhah straddles the conceptual gap between law and theology, the *beit din* and the *beit midrash, galut* and sovereignty. In line with this understanding, I propose to bracket the issue of "halakhah and the non-halakhic society," and focus instead on questions that center on the concept of halakhah itself. Specifically, what are some of the differences, typically in degree, between halakhah and state law that make it challenging to simply graft halakhah onto the law of the state? This will lead us to investigate the extent to which halakhah is optimally designed to perform the functions of modern state law. After assessing these issues, we'll conclude by considering the most appropriate role for halakhah in contemporary Israel.

Halakhah and State Law: Design and Structure

State and Halakhic Categories

Though state law fulfills many roles, its primary function is to order society by determining whether the state (or individuals petitioning it) is permitted to take action against a person violating its laws. This posture is embodied in the law's familiar dichotomies: whether conduct is legal or illegal; whether a criminal defendant is guilty or not guilty; whether a civil litigant is liable or not liable. For much the same reason, state law tends to avoid commenting on the moral or spiritual status of its citizens. The modern state does not generally investigate whether a given conduct is good, moral, nice, or advisable, but only whether the machinery of state should be employed to do something about it. This is true even when a state's legal categories try to split the difference between not-guilty and innocent, as when the Securities and Exchange Commission sends a "no action" letter or when criminal prosecutions are dismissed with *nolo prosequi*, the Latin formula for "unwilling to prosecute."

In contrast to state law, halakhah maintains an active set of in-between categories that do not break neatly along a simple yes/no dichotomy.[5] For example, it is quite common for halakhah to differentiate between actions approved *ex-ante* (*le-khathila*, i.e., actions ideally recommended) and those merely tolerated *ex-post* (*be-di'eved*, i.e., minimally acceptable, though far from ideal). This core halakhic distinction has no clear parallel in Western state law, which, notwithstanding some recent attention to "best practices," is concerned with whether a legal duty is fulfilled, not whether it is fulfilled in optimal fashion.

Nor is halakhah shy about using moralistic language. One whose observance extends beyond baseline standards is described favorably as a Torah scholar (*talmid hakham*), one who admires the rabbis (*mokir rabbanan*), a member of the community in good standing (*haver*), one who acts beyond what the law requires (*lifnim mi-shurat ha-din*), one who walks in the path of the pious (*be-derekh tovim*), and among those who elevate mitzvah observance (*mehadrin*). Alternatively, a person who skirts halakhic boundaries is deemed to act inappropriately (*shelo kehogen*), in ways displeasing to the rabbis (*ein ruah hakhamim noha heimenu*), as a boorish simpleton (*am ha'aretz*), immoral as the residents of Sodom (*middat sedom*), and a scoundrel within the boundary of law (*naval be-reshut ha-torah*)—even as formal punishments are rarely issued for these lapses.

The rabbis also castigate civil litigants who insist too strictly on their legal rights (*shurat ha-din*), are deemed untrustworthy (*mehusar amanah*), give cause for legitimate grievance (*taromet*), engage in actions prohibited though not legally punishable (*patur aval asur*), or are liable under the laws of heaven though exempt under the laws of man (*patur be-dinei adam ve-ḥayav be-dinei shamayim*). The Talmud even crafts a special formula to curse persons who renege on their deals but haven't technically breached their contracts (*mi she-para*). Finally, in light of the large number of unresolved halakhic disputes, pious Jews are lauded either for their stringency (*ḥumra*) or for performing an obligation in a way that satisfies multiple halakhic views (*la-tzeit le-khol ha-deot*). By contrast, those who choose to rely on an especially lenient view (*kulla*), or on a position rejected by the clear majority of authorities (*da'at yaḥid*), are evaluated in less favorable terms.

In sum, while the categories of state law are designed to differentiate between law-abiders and law-breakers, halakhic regulation is intimately bound up with the rabbis' roles as teachers, scholars, spiritual guides, and theologians. Its categories thus assume a more variegated and complex forms that are designed to channel the community's religious and moral outlook.

Talmud Torah and the Rule of Law

The idea known as "the rule of law" is at the foundation of the modern legal order. In its most minimalist form, it requires the state to enforce its laws in an equal and predictable manner. Hence legal and administrative decisions are to be grounded in rules set forth in advance, rather than reflecting the preferences of the officials tasked with administering them. More bluntly, the rule of law means that the law, not the police officer, decides who gets arrested; the law, not the bureaucrat, decides which drugs will obtain FDA approval; the law, not the judge, decides who wins a lawsuit.

In support of these goals, an influential legal theorist like the late Supreme Court Justice Antonin Scalia could state that law is ideally flat, bureaucratic, formulaic, and unambiguous—indeed, that a boring and repetitive formalism is one of the law's primary virtues.[6] For the less law leaves to the judicial imagination, the more it can be predicted in advance; and the more it can be predicted in advance, the greater protection it affords from arbitrary and unequal application.

This conception of the rule of law, however, presents a difficult fit for a legal system in which the Talmud is the foundational text and Torah study is one of the highest religious callings. In Part II we demonstrated how the Talmud favors legal argument, literary nuance, and cultural exploration over black-letter rules. This structure can effectively foster moral development and impart religious meaning, but as thousands of post-talmudic debates attest, extracting a simple rule from a talmudic sugya is a daunting task. Moreover, as we saw in chapters 9–11, even with the advent of halakhic codes in the post-talmudic era, halakhists remain torn between stating operative rules of law and wide-ranging *talmud Torah*.

Thus, even as halakhah can be quite formal (some would argue, excessively so), its attraction to rule-based formalism is based on different assumptions than those that operate in state law. Halakhah's formalism is born from a desire to fulfill God's command with a degree of precision that only strictly applied rules can provide. Proponents of state-law formalism by contrast, rarely bring up any such concerns, framing its value as its ability to curb judicial discretion and enhance legal predictability. The typical formalist argument thus holds that the law should consists of hard-and-fast rules and minimize any fact-specific balancing tests that make the outcome hard to predict.[7]

These considerations, however, are decidedly less prominent in halakhic writing. On the contrary, a long line of rabbinic thought celebrates the difficulty, intricacy, and complexity of arriving at a halakhic conclusion. An oft-cited midrash notes that for every 1,000 students to embark on education in Torah, only one will emerge as qualified to issue halakhic rulings.[8] Recent authorities similarly emphasize how a student must invest years in immersive study before acquiring the standing to serve as a halakhic adjudicator, and that only the most skilled rabbis are qualified to rule in halakhic matters.[9] American law, for its part, though requiring that judges be qualified and competent, gives little sense that a judge must display once-in-a-generation talent.

Encoding Halakhah into State Law

These differences between halakhah and state law raise difficulties for any attempts to combine them. For example, in chapter 6 we cited the Mishnah's discussion concerning the amount of food a landlord must supply his farm-laborers. As a matter of "hard" halakhah—that is, a law that can be administered by the state—the Mishnah rules that a master owes his workers no more than a basic meal. As a sacred and learned text, however, the Mishnah's stylistic choices imply a "soft norm," teaching that, at some level, field workers deserve more than law can mandate. Since the study of Mishnah is a holy endeavor, this soft norm, though not enforceable in court, can also serve as a form of halakhah.

Imagine, however, a well-intentioned legislator attempting to encode this mishnah into state law. The decision to include the aspirational norm would lead to uncertainty over what the law is and how a court should apply it. Lawyers would end up replicating the Talmud's lengthy attempt to decipher the rule proposed by this mishnah. As it happens, the French philosopher Emmanuel Levinas understands the Talmud's discussion of this mishnah as a discourse on the nature of human labor and the need for divine aid in providing sustenance.[10] Levinas' insight is fascinating in itself and offers a compelling account of the talmudic discussion. But it would likely do more harm than good if placed into a state's civil code.

Now imagine that our hypothetical legislator simply sticks with the Mishnah's hard law, and ignores the soft norm entirely. That would certainly clarify things, but it would also decouple the halakhically inspired statute from the moral and spiritual teachings of the Mishnah. Much the same is true of several examples discussed in Part II: the worker's eating rights (90–93); the recitation of the *Shema* (104–110); the policies regarding *din* versus *p'sharah* (111–120); and the laws of carrying on Shabbat (84–87). In each case, we saw how the Talmud employs literary allusions, structure, and particular phrasing to deliver its message: the very aspects that would generate confusion if pressed into state law.

To be sure, there are plenty of examples of reductive halakhic thinking that pre-date attempts to combine halakhah with state law. As we saw in chapter 10, codification inevitably divorces halakhah from its native sugya, and in a different way, the Briskers took pride in reformatting the Talmud's oftentime fuzzy categories into hardened legal constructs. But this is only half the story. The Codes themselves became the basis of wide-ranging learning, and scholars continue to debate whether the Codes are the halakhah itself or summaries of the authoritative view of the Talmud (making that *the* halakhah).[11]

At times, we also find halakhists who end-run around the Codes, and push the discussion back to the sugya and its commentaries. The success of Brisk and the yeshiva movement shifted the locus of study back to the Talmud, and these days (as we will see further in the Conclusion) Talmud study is surprisingly popular across a wide array of Jewish communities. Not least, even the Brisker's rigid categories can be shown to address a range of spiritual and social considerations both precluded and preluded by the method's founders; of late, there has been a move to steer a renewed form of Brisker analysis farther in this direction.[12]

This push-and-pull flows from the twin emphases discussed throughout this book: halakhah governs as law imposed from above, and as divine wisdom explored from within. The ideal of *talmud Torah* is for law to be encountered in the sanctified space where regulation, education, and religious reflection meet under the canopy of God's grace. This is undoubtedly one of halakhah's greatest virtues—and simply too tall an order for state law to achieve. Nor is state law designed to achieve it. The state's regulatory apparatus aspires to be flat, univocal, and predicable; the very qualities that, to paraphrase R. Joseph Soloveitchik, strangles halakhah's soul.

Halakhah and State Law: How Law Is Meant to Govern

Another tension between halakhah and state law emerges from their different understandings of what it means for a rule or norm to govern *as law*. In chapter 8 we introduced the concept of a rule of recognition— the line that separates norms that are within the state's jurisdiction to enforce (law) from those that are beyond the state (i.e. ethics, morality, religion, and so on). To say that something is law *within* the state's rule of recognition is to say that it is neither poetry nor literature, neither an aspirational nor religious ideal. Obversely, to say that something stands *outside* the rule of recognition means that no matter how compelling the norm may be, it is beyond the state's power to enforce it.

State law is by its nature premised on establishing clear rules of recognition; halakhah, much less so.

The Aggadic Death Penalty

By way of example, let's return to the debate between the schools of Hillel and Shammai regarding the proper posture for reciting the evening *Shema* (109). Following the school of Shammai, R. Tarfon had lain down on the ground and been attacked by armed robbers. The Mishnah editorializes that he deserved this fate for going against the views of the school of Hillel. For its part, the Talmud raises the stakes even higher, commenting that "one who follows the ruling of the school of Shammai is liable for the death penalty." (*ḥayav mitah*; b.Berakhot 11a).

Harsh medicine, indeed. But the question is: does this ruling lie within halakhah's rule of recognition? It certainly *sounds* legal, and is recorded in the most authoritative of halakhic texts. Should we therefore conclude that police officers of a hypothetical halakhic state should cart off anyone dissenting from Hillel's views to the gallows?

Nor is R. Tarfon's case unique. Across the talmudic corpus, a surprising number of people are held liable for death for fairly minor offenses. They include a Torah scholar who has a stain on his clothing (b.Shabbat 114a), a student with the effrontery to issue a halakhic ruling in the presence of his teacher (b.Berakhot 31b), a mourner who fails to grow his hair wild (b.Moed Kattan 24a), one who learns from a Zoroastrian magician (b.Shabbat 75a), one who eats a consecrated (*terumah*) fig that fell into water containing the ashes of the red heifer (m.Parah 11:3), a non-Jew who observes Shabbat or studies Torah (b.Sanhedrin 58b and 59b), a Jew who fails to study Torah (m.Avot 1:4), one who fails to engage in procreation (b.Yevamot 64a), and one who engages in sexual self-gratification (b.Nidda 13a). In each example, the offender is deemed *ḥayav mitah*—liable for death.

Are these statements law? Some are traditionally viewed as rhetorical flourishes to emphasize rabbinic disapproval. Others signal that God (but not a court) will kill or cut off the individual from the spiritual community of Israel. Still others are understood as mandating court-imposed corporal punishments. Individual cases, not surprisingly, engender disagreement.[13]

In a bureaucratic system of state law, such linguistic imprecision is dangerous. The rabbis, however, were not only legislators but also teachers and preachers—and generally operated outside a system that had authority to execute convicts. Given the multiple roles assumed by halakhah, this form of aggadic death penalty may be quite useful. The Talmud's claim that a (deliberately) childless individual is liable for death stresses an element of responsibility for the metaphorical murder of lives not born. This is probably not law as the state defines the term, but evocative phrasing reinforces communal expectations and is likely to influence the personal behavior of the devout. It can apply as halakhah, even though not as law.

This dual strategy is less suited to state law. States and citizens rely on the predictable and, to a degree, literal meaning of legal language to hold each other accountable. But when faced with a halakhic rule declaring someone liable for death, state law has two choices. It can domesticate halahkah's evocative phrasing, thereby weakening its moral impact. Or, it can use its power to enforce the rule literally, thereby mandating a punishment likely never intended. The second possibility is immeasurably worse, yet both positions are flawed, as neither captures how halakhah aims to regulate.

The Halakhah of War

In the liable-for-death example of R. Tarfon presented above, the accepted view is that the rule is not literally enforced. In other cases, however, the issue is less clear-cut, and the structure of halakhic regulation creates the danger that an aspirational halakhah might be enforced through the state. This concern is especially pertinent in halakhot dealing with governance, social policy, and legal administration. Because these laws were not active during centuries of *galut*, neither the Codes, nor accepted practice, reliably guide their implementation.

A telling example emerges from halakhah's idealistic yet impractical rules of warfare.[14] A statement recorded in *Sifre*, a collection of Mishnah-era halakhic midrash teaches that when a Jewish army lays siege to a city, it must "leave the fourth side open, allowing the enemy to flee." (Sifre, Numbers §157)

One need not be a military expert to see the serious pitfall in activating this halakhah. The point of a siege is to exhaust the food, supplies, and psychological will of the surrounded population and force its surrender. A three-sided siege is no siege at all. The political theorist Michael Walzer noted how this rule offers a prime example of halakhah's *galut*-based mentality in which idealized rules are legislated without regard for how the law operates in practice.[15] To the extent this halakhah is applied, it would have to be either substantially curtailed, limited to idealized conditions, or both.

But how did the tradition deal with this halakhah? Though not recorded in the Talmud, it entered the canon of applied halakhah when Maimonides included it in the section of his code titled, "Laws of Kings and their Wars" (6:7). Echoing the midrash, Maimonides writes that "when a city is besieged to capture it, they do not surround the city from all four sides but rather from three sides, leaving room for anyone who wants to flee to save his life." A similar view was taken by Ramban (Naḥmanides, 1194–1270), who not only considered the rule as applied halakhah, but even criticized Maimonides for omitting it in his formal counting of the 613 foundational mitzvot.

Ramban offers two rationales for this counterintuitive halakhah. First, a humanitarian concern: the law is designed to instill mercy and sensitivity even toward an enemy in wartime. Second, a tactical concern: if enemy soldiers are allowed to retreat they will be less impelled to fight to the death and more likely to accept a bloodless surrender. Notably, Ramban includes a significant limitation not found in Maimonides' code: this halakhah applies only to "wars of choice." But in wars of self-defense, an army is free to impose a four-sided siege.[16]

Nearly six centuries later, R. Meir Simḥah of Dvinsk (today Daugavpils, Latvia; 1843–1926) analyzed the debate between Maimonides and Ramban in terms of the degree to which this halakhah is understood as law. As suggested by his critique of Maimonides' failure to include the ruling in his listing of the 613 mitzvot, Ramban (in R. Meir Simḥah's interpretation) sees it as binding halakhah—law in the conventional sense of the term. For Maimonides, by contrast, it was merely strategic advice, but not an ironclad halakhah binding on Jewish armies for all times. This interpretation is significant because, for many halakhists, Maimonides' code functions as halakhah's rule of recognition. That is, rabbinic statements included within the *Mishneh Torah* are understood to have binding force as law, while those left out are of lesser status, sometimes deemed merely aggadic. In this case, however, R. Meir Simḥah holds that although the rule appears in Maimonides' code, the contours of what it means for applied halakhah remains up for grabs—is it a binding obligation, or merely suggested practice? In fact, in his view, Maimonides and Ramban—two of Judaism's most authoritative halakhists—seem to disagree on precisely that point.[17]

For nearly 2,000 years, this issue lay in the exclusive province of *talmud Torah*. In the course of the 1982 siege of Beirut by the Israel Defense Force, however, it moved from the yeshiva's bookshelf to the popular press. Speaking first on a radio broadcast, and in follow-up article in a leading religious-Zionist newspaper, Chief Rabbi Shlomo Goren (1917–1994) ruled that a complete siege on Beirut violated halakhah. To blunt the impracticality of a three-sided siege, he maintained that while the army was obviously allowed to prevent food and military reinforcements from reaching the surrounded city (though nothing in prior sources spoke to that point), anyone—including enemy combatants—trying to leave the city must be allowed to retreat unimpeded.

Though it may be tempting to write off R. Goren as a naif who could not see past the talmudic page, he was neither a military nor a political neophyte. Having created the position of the IDF's chief rabbi, he served in that capacity for twenty years before becoming the chief rabbi of Israel. An ardent religious Zionist, he was also the primary advocate of constructing a halakhah relevant to the day-to-day administration of the Jewish state. Even a generation after his death, his writings on halakhah and military conduct remain preeminent in the field.

Nevertheless, R. Goren's idealistic view was challenged by R. Shaul Yisraeli (1909–1995), one of the few religious-Zionist rabbis who could stand toe-to-toe with him on matters of halakhah and state. Like his counterpart, R. Yisraeli was committed to incorporating halakhic laws into the working of the modern state, and not prone to dismissing halakhah as impractical or irrelevant. Still, he pointed to the tactical futility of allowing Palestine Liberation Organization militants to escape Beirut and regroup unharmed, especially since the goal of the Israeli militiary's operation was to dismantle the PLO's infrastructure in Lebanon. In halakhic terms, R. Yisraeli explained that whereas both Ramban and Maimonides held this law to apply only to "wars of choice"—a category relevant only to wars fought under effectively messianic conditions—as applied to modern Israeli wars, it was, at best, advisory. To the extent the army's generals thought a lockdown siege was tactically superior, both prudence *and* halakhah required following their lead.[18]

Responding to this line of argument, R. Goren drew on the core ambiguity latent in the term "halakhah." His critics, he wrote, had it backward: the halakhah presented in Maimonides' code is the "real and applied" halakhah; while arguments over which commandments are included in the formal list of 613 mitzvot are of theoretical and academic interest only. In any case, R. Goren was "certain" that R. Meir Simḥah never intended anyone "implement his speculations on Jewish thought (*maḥshavah*) in practice."[19] In fact, Goren held, R. Meir Simḥah signaled as much by publishing his analysis in a work called *Meshekh Ḥokhmah*—a collection of insights into the weekly Torah portions, a book Goren described as a "work of Jewish thought from which we do not derive practiced halakhah." By contrast, had R. Meir Simḥah intended to speak in the normative tone of halakhah, he would have published these thoughts in his commentary on Maimonides' code known as *Ohr Sameaḥ*, a classic work of devotional *talmud Torah* anchored in halakhic materials.[20] Finally, without disputing the military futility of a three-sided siege, R. Goren challenged R. Meir Simḥah's distinction between halakhah as governing law and halakhah as strategic advice, citing numerous cases where halakhah addresses law, ethics, and tactics within a single framework.[21] In the end, he wrote, a Jewish army must place its faith in God's hands, and "we do not involve ourselves in God's mysteries."[22]

This episode underscores the difficulty of mixing spiritual ideals with the realities of governance. Nearly 2,000 years ago, rabbis of the mishnaic era recorded a terse statement promoting an idealistic view of military conduct, with not a word devoted to whether or how this rule should be implemented or applied. From that time onward, it has been read variously as a religious call to recognize the enemy's humanity, a tactical recommendation designed to benefit a Jewish army, or a law that restricts the tactical options available to the IDF.

In the context of the contemporary interaction between halakhah and state, the debate over this heretofore-unapplied halakhah has its own lessons to teach. According to R. Yisraeli, halakhah's rule of recognition must remain fuzzy, its different meanings must be juggled and balanced case by case. In the here and now—that is, until such time when Israel's wars become "wars of choice" fought under ideal halakhic conditions—R. Yisraeli held that the siege rule cannot be applied as "hard halakhah." Nevertheless, the rule still applies as "soft halakhah"— tactical advice and aspirational ideals that may influence policymaking, but do not legally tie the military's hands. This is consistent with the view that so long as the natural order prevails, a subset of halakhot will have greater resonance in the *beit midrash* than in the realm of actualized policy. Ideal halakhic governance must await the messiah: we cannot hasten the end.

For R. Goren, by contrast, the existence of the Jewish state creates a mandate for halakhah to become fully embodied in public law—though even then, this pragmatic military man relied on his theological certitude that God will not allow harm to befall the people of Israel for obeying halakhah. Although in many ways R. Goren agrees with R. Yisraeli that this halakhah of warfare does not belong to the natural order, in his zeal to establish halakhah as the law of the state, he would commit the Jewish army to fight under unnatural conditions.

Halakhah and the Administrative State

Still another and most surprising difficulty in adopting halakhah as state law is that there are *not enough halakhic rules* to administer a state. At first blush, the claim—too little halakhah—may sound absurd. But if we focus not on the volume of law but on its function, it becomes clear why many aspects of state law are not addressed by halakhic standards.

Active vs. Reactive Law

Consider the following example: Joseph is walking on Shabbat and finds Benjamin lying unconscious on the ground. At this moment, two halakhic rules come into play. First, Joseph has an affirmative duty to save Benjamin's life—a halakhah that applies every day of the week. Second, because "saving a life pre-empts Shabbat," Joseph is absolved from responsibility for any Shabbat violations he may incur in the process. (m.Yoma 8:8 and t.Shabbat 9:22).

This structure is typical of halakhic regulation. The rules are directed at an *individual* (Joseph) and instruct how to react to a specific situation. The Talmud and Codes contain a wealth of precedents regarding when and how Shabbat may be violated, the resources Joseph must expend to save Benjamin, and whether Joseph can seek restitution for the time and expenses incurred along the way.

Viewed from the perspective of public administration, however, a different set of features stands out: halakhah rarely speaks about how to *plan* for the situation. In lawyer's terms, halakhah engages in reactive rather than proactive lawmaking. [23] In addition, the laws are generally directed toward individuals rather than public organizations or collective entities. Again using lawyer's terms, there is not much in the way of public law.

What happens if we switch our perspective from the individual to the communal, and from reactive to proactive ways of thinking about law? Imagine that, rather than finding an unconscious Benjamin lying in the street, Joseph is a hospital administrator who must decide how the institution should be staffed for Shabbat. Joseph cannot know how many emergencies will arise, so how should he determine how many doctors should be on call? How many nurses? What about operators to staff the call center or maintenance personnel to stand by in case the medical equipment needs repair? Can the entire infrastructure of a modern hospital be subsumed under the exemption of "saving a life," a term that historically applied only when a discrete emergency was at hand?

The traditional response was to delegate such matters to a non-Jew (known as a *shabbes goy*) expressly engaged to deal with whatever Shabbat violations became necessary. The institution of the *shabbes goy* has been aptly described as a prime example of *galut*-based halakhah.[24] This is because it assumes Jews live among Gentiles who can be hired to do the work that Jews cannot, and more fundamentally, because it provides a solution for individuals or even small communities but offers no vision for what it means to observe Shabbat as a society. Wide-scale implementation of the *shabbes-goy* solution is viable only to the extent it relies on persons not bound by halakhah. In principle, however, a halakhic state is more than just a place where many halakhah-compliant individuals reside; it is where the public, *as a political community*, lives out the vision of halakhah.

Nor is the larger issue limited either to Shabbat or to the *shabbes goy*. On any day of the week, halakhah requires a passerby (Joseph) to drop everything and expend time and money to save Benjamin's life. How does this individual mandate translate to state policy? What emergencies must a halakhic state plan for? What should its health policy look like? How many hospitals are to be built? Should funds be allocated to preventative care and medical research or only to end-stage treatments that expressly stave off death? Since the mitzvah of saving lives is paramount, must the entire Gross Domestic Product of a halakhic state be devoted to healthcare? Who pays, and by what mechanism are scarce health resources to be allocated? And who makes these decisions?

The legacy of *galut* means that one can scour the Talmud and its Codes cover to cover yet find relatively little guidance on such matters of public policy and administration.

Sub-halakhah and the Subsumption of Law

Another reason for halakhah's administrative shortfall owes to the way that sub-halakhah was historically used to respond to the impracticalities of formal halakhah. In chapter 2 we described the many procedural impediments that make it impossible for the Sanhedrin to model a viable system of legal enforcement. Chapters 3 and 9 describe how, in response, sub-halakhic practices emerged to enable communities to regulate conduct notwithstanding the strictures imposed by formal halakhah. Returning to R. Nissim of Gerona's (Ran's) terminology, these sub-halakhic, gap-filling measures constitute the king's law.

In the sixteenth century, the *Shulḥan Arukh's* code of civil law established the sub-halakhic authority as follows:

> Any court, even one comprised of judges not formally ordained in the Land of Israel [that is, judges who cannot administer civil fines or corporal punishments as a matter of formal halakhah], if they observe that the community is flagrantly sinning, they may adjudicate; whether in cases of capital punishment, monetary fines, or any other [corporal] modes of punishment, even if there is no [halakhically] valid testimony as to the facts. . . . And all of the court's actions should be undertaken for the sake of heaven. And this should be done specifically by the great [scholar] of the generation or the aldermen of the town that the community has appointed as a court over itself.[25]

To this, Rema concurs in his gloss:

> And such is the practice that in every town. The aldermen of the city are like the Great Sanhedrin who possess the authority to administer

corporal punishment and to seize assets, as per the custom; even though there are authorities who dispute this.

In these paragraphs, the Codes present a 180-degree shift from the law of the Talmud. For if talmudic law proved too cumbersome to effectively govern, the discretionary authority afforded to government by the Codes is so broad that there seems to be no substantive limit on the polity's sub-halakhic powers at all. It is possible, of course, that within the relatively small and homogenous communities, a strong social consensus regarding the halakhic constitution obviated the need for formal limitations on governmental power. But surely, this is no longer the case. In the current environment, even adherents of the halakhic constitution are unable to coalesce around a single religious scholar or religio-political institution whose authority will be recognized by all.

The historical reliance on sub-halakhah thus presents a double-edged sword. Though it makes rabbinic courts and institutions relevant to legal administration, it re-creates the original problem—in reverse. Talmudic halakhah hamstrings courts with too many regulations while sub-halakhah offers too few constraints on legislative, executive, and judicial power. At least in the modern period, effective governance requires both the freedom to operate (the drawback of formal halakhah), as well as limits on the scope of the government's power (what modern lawyers call constitutionalism). In the end, sub-halakhah's unregulated model is no more viable than the over-regulated halakhic regime it seeks to remedy. Neither succeeds in establishing a framework through which halakhah can realistically govern a modern state.

Halakhah: Unique or Extreme?

In drawing the contrast between halakhah and state law, I have at times presented state law as a wholly formalist statutory system where the sole aim of legal interpretation is to determine the outcome of a case.

Statutes, however, are hardly the only source of American law, and though influential, the claim that legal texts should be understood as flat, two-dimensional tools of regulation is far from its only theory. To take the most obvious example, American judges commonly issue opinions with pluralities, concurrences, and dissents that make discerning the legal rule more like analyzing a talmudic sugya than like consulting a tightly drafted code. Judicial opinions, moreover, are not terse statements of legal rules but dialogical arguments that debate how the law should be written, interpreted, and construed.[26] Some scholars have gone so far as to argue that courts serve an educative and even preaching function that sounds far more like rabbinic discourse than state agents who merely articulate the rules of law.[27] And many citizens obey the law out of a sense of duty and obligation, rather than out of the fear of prosecution and punishment.

More generally, prominent observers note that, like halakhah, state systems contain laws whose most significant function is expressive rather than regulatory. One common example are laws prohibiting flag-burning. The regulatory impulse is probably less about reducing the actual number of flags burned, than the community's desire to disapprove of those who deface its symbols. In a different vein, though anti-discrimination laws are rarely enforced with rigor, the authority and cachet of their status as *law* can have considerable influence on behavior and voluntary compliance in the social sphere.[28] Finally, Robert Cover, whose ideas we have relied upon throughout, explains that law consists not only of a regulatory (imperial) dimension but simultaneously relies on "world-creating" and thought-shaping (paideic) functions that make the state's regulatory apparatus possible. Though Cover famously drew inspiration from rabbinic sources, he theorized about American law generally.[29]

Taken together, these and related accounts suggest that many features associated with halakhah are found within state law as well.

Both here, and throughout this book, my response is that in contrasting halakhah to state law, we should see halakhah as *extreme* rather than *unique*. In other words, while several characteristics ascribed to halakhah are found in other legal systems, the centrality of *talmud Torah* combined with the attenuated relationship between halakhah and governance results in halakhah presenting these tendencies in more demonstrative and concentrated forms.

First, American judges indeed write dialogic opinions whose goals are as much to shape the public and political narrative as to articulate the legal rule in a case. But this is only half the equation. No system of state law demands or even idealizes that citizens will become learned enough to appreciate the nuances of judicial writing. State law is typically mediated through lawyers, bureaucracies, the media, businesses, and social institutions, all of which flatten the law to make it more digestible for the public. Halakhah, and especially the strands of the tradition that tout Talmud study as an ideal, traditionally rely on direct contact with the legal source material, personal relationships with authoritative teachers, and the lived experience of residing within a closed normative community. These, rather than the tools of an administrative bureaucracy, are the agents binding the halakhic constitution together.

Second, like halakhah, state legal systems contain laws that exist mainly on the books rather than in actual practice, and whose impact is more expressive than regulatory. But here, too, the question of degree matters, as even expressive laws are situated within a system of state institutions that makes enforcement possible, even if not probable. Thus, even as instances of flag-burning or social discrimination may go unpunished, the laws prohibiting these activities capture the public's attention because it is possible for the state to prosecute violators. This stands in contrast to the laws of the Sanhedrin, or even the talmudic tort laws, which do not exist within an institutional apparatus that can administer them. These halakhot are relevant not as law that can be applied, but as part of God's Torah—the unending wellspring of teaching. The line between a blistering op-ed decrying flag-burning and legislation that prohibits it, is still clearer than the line between a rabbinic sermon and a formal halakhic prohibition.

Finally, though debates over legal interpretation and application are common to most legal cultures, state systems enjoy far greater capacity to end interpretive disputes through the official acts of their constituted bodies. ("The Supreme Court decided," or "Congress legislated.") And while pockets of fuzziness and theoretical instability are inevitable, the lines of authority between higher and lower courts, between state and federal law, and among the coordinating branches of government have been repeatedly tested and refined over time. By contrast, outside the idealized construct of the Sanhedrin, halakhah maintains few rules of "constitutional" law that structure authority among various rabbis, courts, lay organizations, and communities. Consensus, where it exists, is predicated on shared commitments to communal structure and its underlying theology rather than on formalized rules establishing the jurisdiction of different actors. And finally, in the absence of the coordinating structures of the state, dissenters can simply split off and form their own communities; in many ways, this has been the experience of Judaism in both medieval and modern times.

Nevertheless, seeing halakhah as extreme rather than unique also counsels us to regard any conclusions as appropriately modest. Foremost, the argument of this chapter applies to halakhah *as it presently stands*. While at least since the time of the Mishnah, halakhah has never applied as state law, from a conceptual perspective nothing prevents a Jewish state from convening a Sanhedrin or a constitutional convention to reconstruct halakhah along statist lines. Still, the argument here is that the "state of halakhah"—that is, the deep structure of halakhah described throughout this book—makes it difficult simply to plug-and-play existing halakhah into the law of the state. Any transition of this kind would require both a "constitutional moment" (a conscious break from existing patterns of halakhic development), matched with a spirit of cohesion, institutional authority, and unity of purpose that has eluded the Jewish polity for nearly two millennia.

Second, the extreme-not-unique framework means that, following the line of scholars who study the expressive dimensions of law, renewed study of halakhah may lead us to develop more complex understandings of the nature of law and legal normativity more generally. Halakhah offers—in the extreme—an example of legal normativity that emerges from communal structures and cultural resources beyond the state and where state-based enforcement plays a minimal role. It is thus no wonder that modern legal theorists interested in the phenomenon of non-state law, whether in the form of international law, transnational arbitration, or even bottom-up systems of norms existing within the state, have looked to halakhah as a source of relevant analogy and insight.[30]

Halakhah and State in Modern Israel

Having explored the conceptual difficulties involved in establishing halakhah as state law, we now turn to consider how these factors have played out in the actual State of Israel. Here the historical background can help us understand both why Israel's earlier generations had little to say about the systematic questions of halakhah and the state, and why, in the contemporary milieu, framing Israel's heritage as *Jewish* rather than *halakhic* presents a more workable model for a productive relationship between religion and state.

History and Demographic Background

The founders of modern Israel were largely secular Zionists who had abandoned the halakhic constitution. To this group of Jews, the tensions between halahkah and state were just one further indication that halakhah was unfit for modern Jewish society. These Zionists thus sought to create a Hebrew culture and even a Hebrew law premised on the Bible and other heroic documents of Jewish history, but rather deliberately downplayed the significance of the Talmud and halakhah—texts many blamed for the dead-end of exilic Judaism. In its ideology, art, music, dress, and language, early Zionism sought to liberate the diasporic Jew from the shackles of halakhah on the one hand and from anti-Semitic society on the other. These early Zionists thus had little interest in thinking creatively about adapting halakhah to the modern state. To the contrary, the fundamental incompatibility between these systems offered ongoing evidence of halakhah's irrelevance to the modern condition.

Presented with the same basic facts, the halakhic traditionalists of the Agudat Israel movement (forerunners of today's ultra-Orthodoxy) reached exactly the opposite conclusion. If the state, and the modernity it represented, was fundamentally at odds with halakhah, then the state—not halakhah—was an illegitimate form for organizing Jewish life. Agudists had nothing but disdain for any form of Hebrew culture that was not rigorously halakhic, and, to them, the Zionist state was nothing more than a republic of Jewish sinners. A true Jewish state would be heralded by the prophet Elijah and the arrival of the messianic king who would miraculously transform the state of halakhah to bring forth the State of halakhah.

While the reasons of the two groups could not have been more different, the result was similar. Neither pre-state Zionists nor Agudists were disposed to think deeply about the proper interaction between halakhah and the modern state.

As the era of statehood approached, a relatively small group of religious Zionists emerged who stood between these two poles and saw the emerging political independence as God's down-payment on the messianic prophesies of the Bible. While many recognized the difficulties of creating a state-based halakhah, they held that the rebirth of Jewish sovereignty on sanctified soil would foster a renewed halakhic culture that could rise to the needs of modern statehood. Some optimistic writers envisioned the national legislature as a fount of halakhic legislation, or speculated that the state would reconstitute the Great Sanhedrin, endowing it with the authority to craft halakhah for the modern condition.[31]

In general, religious Zionists saw the tension between halakhah and state as offering a dual challenge: a challenge to move society toward halakhah and to move halakhah toward society. Nevertheless, the movement's small size and relative lack of political clout in the pre- and early state era ensured these discussions remained more academic and aspirational than practical. Despite their belief in the cause, religious Zionists were not much closer than the Agudists or secular Zionists to articulating how a contemporary halakhic state could operate. Subject to one significant exception, explored below, Israel was founded as an essentially secular state whose laws were enacted by a democratically elected parliament (the Knesset).

A Jewish and Democratic State

Much has changed in Israel since those early days. With the State of Israel as an established fact, and the memory of exilic persecution fading into the background, secular Zionism shifted from its emphasis on a nationalistic Jewish, if secular, collective identity toward a liberal cosmopolitanism, premised on the individualistic and universalist ideals. This ethos stresses the right and freedom of individuals to author their own narrative and rejects attempts by the state to slot its citizens into mandated forms of Jewish identity or practice. It likewise hesitates to give Judaism preference over other religions or nonreligion.

At the same time, the expressly antireligious strain of Zionism has lost much of its political and cultural cache, and halakhic observance has become a far more prevalent feature of Israeli culture. Even the Talmud, long the *bête noire* of the Zionist intelligentsia, is making a slow yet steady comeback. Today, the twenty volumes of the classic edition of the Babylonian Talmud serve as the backdrop for televised broadcasts of the Israeli prime minister's public addresses: an image that would have been unthinkable in the era of David Ben-Gurion (1886-1973), Israel's first prime minister.

Moreover, the halakhically observant segments of the population have grown dramatically in both size and influence. Religious Zionism—once a junior partner to the dominant Labor Zionism—has developed its own cultural and political identity. Members of this community now lead mainstream institutions, and have assumed key positions in the military, government, media, academia, and business communities that were once the exclusive province of secular Zionists. What's more, and contrary to the dire prediction of the pre-State Agudists, the Israeli state has proved extraordinarily hospitable to their conception of religious life. Indeed, as the threat of anti-religious Zionism recedes, ultra-Orthodoxy has pragmatically, if haltingly, begun to integrate into and influence Israeli society at large. Indeed, though the main institutions of Israeli society are hardly halakhic, on the whole, they are probably closer to traditional halakhic Judaism today than during the years after Israel's founding.[32]

These cultural shifts are reflected on the legal plane as well. Two quasi-constitutional Basic Laws were passed in the early 1990s that expressly define Israel as a "Jewish and democratic state,"[33] a phrase that has since become shorthand for conceptualizing questions of religion and state.

In the political arena, those two marks of Israel's identity are often cast in opposition. Advocates of a universalistic and individualistic ethos are heard to champion the cause of democracy, while the nationalistic and religious sectors seek to advance the state's Jewish charter. This makes for an adversarial relationship. While, in the 1950s and 1960s, the dominant secularist party was apt to make practical accommodations to the religious minority in the name of national unity, today the two sides stand more equally matched, such that deal-making is perceived as capitulation to the other side.[34]

From our perspective, however, it is worth focusing on the choice of the term "Jewish" rather than "halakhic." For whereas halakhah connotes conforming with the detailed rules of the *Shulḥan Arukh*, Jewish is a more amorphous term that enables a wider array of identities to coalesce under its banner. This is a particularly important feature in a culture where the majority sees itself as decidedly Jewish though not necessarily bound to halakhah. The net result has been a hazy convergence by a majority of Israeli Jews around a public culture that is expressly Jewish, sometimes reinforced via state law, coupled with widespread opposition to using state law to enforce halakhic standards on an unwilling population. To the extent one can talk about consensus over the meaning of a "Jewish and democratic state," this is where it stands.

In this light, it is worth examining a few of the laws that most clearly express Israel's Jewish identity. They include the adoption of the Jewish calendar and the Hebrew language, the Star of David on the national flag, and the menorah as the state's emblem. Though obviously Jewish, none of these symbols are understood as halakhic requirements in the narrow sense of the term. Furthermore, though Israeli laws that establish Shabbat as the legal day of rest, regulate the sale of bread on Passover, and restrict the breeding of pigs and the supply of pork among Jews, clearly derive from halakhic norms, they are not instances of state halakhah but of democratic legislation inspired by the halakhic tradition.

Not surprisingly, the state's regulation is substantially less demanding than the standards set forth in the *Shulḥan Arukh*, and more attuned to the latent difficulties in combining halakhah with the machinery of state law. In fact, it's quite possible that such laws have proved relatively workable due to the extent the state has recast halakhah in a way that leaves breathing room for those outside its frame of reference. As at least one commentator, now a Justice on Israel's Supreme Court, has put it, these laws succeed when seen as a nationalistic expression of public Judaism, yet fail when regarded as a state-sponsored attempt to enforce halakhic identity on the country as a whole.[35]

The utility of the distinction between a Jewish state and a halakhic state can also be seen by recalling how many halakhic rules are decidedly *not* on the agenda of Israel's lawmakers. Blasphemy, adultery, and homosexuality are all cardinal halakhic sins and theoretically punishable by death, yet there is no move to criminalize them in Israel. Likewise, in a halakhic court, women and Gentiles are generally prohibited from serving as judges or witnesses, yet few wish to import these standards into the state's judicial system. The *Shulḥan Arukh* permits the authorities to beat flagrant Shabbat violators, unmarried cohabiting partners, and anyone refusing to perform mandated halakhic obligations. Yet even the most religiously conservative Israeli governments have not sought to adopt these positions as law. Israel's operative definition of "Jewish" thus is both broader and narrower than "halakhah."

Between these poles of relative agreement—"yes" to an unobtrusive Jewish public culture, "no" to impositions of illiberal halakhic rules, "maybe" to mild forms of halakhically inspired legislation—Israelis debate the relative weights of their Jewish and democratic identities. While the state will not invoke halakhah to punish or even prevent premarital or same-sex cohabitation, far more contested is whether it should positively sanction relationships contrary to halakhic norms. Other matters of disagreement center on the degree to which Jewish religious interests should be given priority over other religions and nonreligion, whether public transportation should operate on Shabbat, which commercial establishments should be subject to elements of Shabbat and kosher regulation, and the extent to which the state should tolerate public behavior by private actors that runs deeply counter to religious or egalitarian norms (gay-pride parades on the one hand, gender-segregated busing on the other). Although advocates on the "Jewish" side are often motivated by halakhic considerations, as a legal and practical matter, these questions are decided through the mechanisms of state legislation, the judiciary, and ordinary democratic politics.

Now for the promised significant exception to this preference for a Jewish but not a halakhic state. It lies in issues of "personal status," that is, marriage, divorce, and the definition of who is a Jew. Under Israeli law (with the exception of the Law of Return), these matters are governed by halakhah as determined and implemented by the rabbinical courts and the Chief Rabbinate. In contrast to the Knesset's enacted laws that mediate halakhic principles through a democratic filter, here state law empowers the rabbinic bodies to apply halakhah directly. This arrangement is thus commonly criticized for imposing halakhah upon a population that does not accept its definition of Jewish identity, and for being insufficiently attuned to the gap between halakhah and the needs of modern statehood.

Not surprisingly, the merger of state power and halakhah has become the hottest flashpoint in the divisive clashes between religion and state in Israel—and a source of ongoing friction between Israel and Jewish communities worldwide. Hence, even ultra-Orthodox websites report that when polled in 2013, about two-thirds of Israeli Jews favored dismantling the Chief Rabbinate,[36] and a poll released a year later by a secular organization dedicated to greater separation between religion and state in Israel found that fully seventy-one percent of the Jewish population expressed dissatisfaction with the state's rabbinic institutions.[37]

The gap between distaste for direct application of halakhah and overall acceptance of a Jewish public culture in contemporary Israel has much to teach us about halakhah and state more generally. If, as we argued above, halakhic regulation is ideally encountered in a holy space where regulation, education, and religious reflection converge, then imposing halakhah through state law falls short on every account. Hence, even within populations that accept the halakhic constitution, the Rabbinate is often seen as a government bureaucracy tasked with enforcing state law rather than attuned to the community's spiritual needs and development. These feelings are only exacerbated in populations that maintain a less rigid perspective on halakhah than found in the state's rabbinical bodies, as well as in those that do not subscribe to halakhah's foundational framework altogether.

The Rabbinate and its courts thus personify, as it were, the fact that when halakhic authority is an artifact of state law rather than an autonomous cultural norm, the result is inevitably frustration and disenchantment on all sides. Divorced from the covenantal theology that places the Torah and its study as the primary cultural value, the state's halakhah becomes nothing more than *law* in the most reductive sense of the term—a brute mechanism of state power.

And yet the Israeli experience also demonstrates the possibility of a Jewish state that is not halakhic. True, as a matter of both halakhah and political theory, the distinction between the two terms is not fully coherent. In practice, however, it has produced a society that is meaningfully Jewish, in which large segments of civil society are infused with Torah study, and where certain halakhic values find expression in state law. Though universal agreement on any matter of significance is almost impossible in so factional a polity as Israel, support for these measures can be found even among those not committed to a classical understanding of the halakhic constitution.

Conclusion

WE OPENED THIS BOOK by noting the two features that set halakhah apart from state-based legal regimes. First, halakhah came of age in the form of the Mishnah after the demise of Jewish sovereignty in the first century; as a result, Jews until recently have rarely inhabited a political arena where halakhah could embody the full scope of its regulatory ambitions. Second, the ideal of *talmud Torah,* which understands the study of halakhah as a central aspect of its practice, is a foundational religious requirement that competes with other religious, social, economic, and intellectual pursuits.

From these premises, we went on to see why and how halakhah fulfills so many roles in rabbinic thought and culture: from tasks classically associated with legal regulation all the way to the diverse devotional, spiritual, cultural, and expressive functions performed by its study and practice. Identifying these different roles helps account for some of halakhah's least understandable features: non-applied law, the mixture of halakhah and aggadah, curious turns of talmudic dialogue, the emphasis on Torah study, and the relationship between the *beit din,* the court, and the *beit midrash,* the study house.

Each of halakhah's paradigmatic forms represents a pole that exerts a magnetic force on the field as a whole. At one pole, there is a tendency to see halakhah as a regulatory regime and present it in terms of its discrete behavioral norms. Pushing outward, however, is the other pole, at which halakhah's regulatory structure is mobilized to address wholly theoretical questions of law as well as matters of Jewish thought, philosophy, theology, and ethics. The history of halakhah unfolds along these same lines, as different scholars, schools, and communities play out the tensions embedded in the Talmud itself. Is halahkah primarily law to be applied, or discourse to be studied? God's regulations for life, or the language spoken to the covenantal community? A system concerned with social life, or a conduit enabling the divine spirit to rest upon the Jewish people? These questions reverberate throughout halakhic literature.

In the final chapter we turned back to the question of halakhah and governance, but now in the context of a modern state. Though the combination of halakhah and sub-halakhah may have worked in the small, homogeneous, and partially autonomous communities of exile, several of halakhah's core features make it ill-suited to serve as the legal system of a modern state. This would be true even if the majority of the population adhered to the halakhic constitution; how much more so in the actual State of Israel, where large numbers of citizens do not. But whereas the shortcomings of halakhic regulation are evident in the modern Jewish *state*, these same features may enable halakhah to serve as a regulatory force in Jewish *society*.

We have emphasized how Torah study creates a religious, cultural, and emotional connection to halakhah, the rabbis, and their ideas. By inviting the student into the law's internal forum, halakhah ideally becomes less about commands imposed from the outside than about an internal desire to follow in God's path. Thus, in contrast to the "hard" regulation associated with the bureaucracies of state law, Torah study may operate as a "soft" form of halakhic regulation and enforcement.

Some version of this idea has long been present. The Jerusalem Talmud castigates one who studies Torah with no intention of adhering to what is learned. (y.Shabbat 1:2). And when the Babylonian Talmud debates whether Torah study or halakhic practice is greater, at least one source concludes that "study is greater, for it leads to practice." (b.Kiddushin 40b). This seemingly contradictory statement is understood by the medieval commentator Rashi to mean that a focus on study offers the adherent "two for the price of one." A more mystical account developed in the sixteenth century notes how Torah study molds the human character so that godliness becomes integrated into the individual's intellect and soul. Whereas halakhic practice affects a person's physical actions alone, Torah study penetrates a higher level of mental and spiritual existence.[1]

More recently R. Aharon Lichtenstein stated it this way: "*talmud Torah* is not just informative or illuminating; it is ennobling and purgative." He cites in this connection the Mishnah's accolade (Avot 6:1) of the Torah student as "a friend, beloved, lover of God, and lover of men" whose study enables him to "be virtuous, pious, upright, and faithful." In R. Lichtenstein's account, the "emphasis upon process and its purgative character renders abstruse study both possible and meaningful."[2]

This aspect of halakhic regulation-through-study has taken on increasing significance in the modern era. A number of scholars have tied the success of Brisk, and the yeshiva movement more generally, to the ability of today's traditionalist Jewish society to co-opt the ethos of analytical inquiry and personal improvement that emerged in late-nineteenth-century Eastern Europe.[3] That ethos, would seem even more relevant in the context of a pluralist democracy infused with the values of self-fulfillment and authenticity, even as the community's ability to impose its norms via coercive means has lessened. In this environment, Torah study can be a generator of religious fervor that in turn enables halakhic practice to survive. While the centrality of study may make halakhah a poor basis for the regulatory apparatus of a Jewish state, it can be surprisingly effective in creating a culture of halakhic compliance outside the arena of state power.

This insight was clearly embraced by the leaders of ultra-Orthodoxy in the decades following World War II. With the physical and social structures of traditional communities decimated first by emancipation and assimilation and then by persecution and mass murder, ultra-Orthodox rabbis consciously established Torah study, to the exclusion of almost every other secular—and even religious—activity, as the axis around which communal life revolved. For these communities, full-time study became a boundary marker, both a way of demonstrating membership in the group and a method of segregating it from the larger society. The results in sheer numbers have been phenomenally high: more people may be engaged in intensive Torah study today than at any time in the past.

To be sure, the decision to pursue full-time study as a social goal has entailed economic and political consequences for ultra-Orthodox communities that are the source of considerable agitation, particularly in Israel, where the rest of society is expected to bear the cost. Those consequences must be squarely faced. Still, the ability of ultra-Orthodoxy, out of the ashes of Auschwitz, to create a deeply devout and countercultural society is tribute to the thesis that dedication to Torah study can indeed produce a society centered on meticulous halakhic observance. Torah study is thus not only the product of ultra-Orthodox life, but to some degree also its cause.[4]

Another example is the "gap year" program common in the more culturally assimilated circles of North American Modern Orthodoxy. Each year, thousands of high-school graduates mark the transition from adolescence to adulthood by spending a year in yeshivot in Israel before beginning college. The stated goal of these programs is to strengthen students' Jewish identity and commitment to halakhah before returning home to begin college education. Notably, the most prestigious of these programs are modeled after the Etz Hayyim Yeshiva in Volozhin and emphasize analytical Talmud study on topics not directly relevant to everyday practice—on the theory that time devoted to Torah study will instill respect for and confidence in the rabbinic system overall.

This initiative has a clear parallel in the Israeli setting, as religious-Zionist high-school graduates routinely spend time in yeshiva prior to enlisting in the army. Here again, the goal is to strengthen the resolve for a life of halakhah and classical Jewish values before becoming immersed in the generally secular culture of the Israeli military.[5] Though styles and methods differ, Torah, and Talmud study in particular, are seen as a tools for generating commitment to halakhic observance.

Still another iteration of this same impulse can be found in outreach (kiruv) programs that emerge from the ultra-Orthodox world, but are directed at encouraging non-observant Jews towards a life of classical observance. Rather than introducing that life through a menu of demanding halakhic practices, the journey can begin with an invitation to study Torah and, in the case of young men, Talmud. Like the gap year programs favored by the Modern Orthodox, these initiatives are founded on the belief that greater exposure to the talmudic system can provide a foundation upon which to build an edifice of observance.

In sum, whereas personal commitment to halakhah was once a prerequisite for advanced Talmud study, today the reverse is true: Talmud study is increasingly a tool to strengthen observance.[6]

And that is not all. Though we can detect shifts in emphasis, each of these examples emerges from a world where Torah study and halakhic practice are understood as mutually reinforcing. Throughout the nineteenth century, the intellectual leaders of non-halakhic Judaism—classical Zionists, German Reformers, and East European *maskilim*—generally railed against the Talmud as a collection of rabbinic accretions that distorted true Judaism and was responsible for the stifling morbidity of Jewish thought and life.[7] In recent decades, however, a startling reversal has taken place: for many of the ideological descendants of that pre-state *intelligentsia*, Talmud study is increasingly seen as an exciting, even a chic, pathway toward positive Jewish identity.

Israeli society has thus produced a number of institutions, ranging from not-necessarily Orthodox to expressly secular, that draw on methods of the traditional yeshiva *beit midrash* to teach Talmud to nonobservant populations. In these settings, study is not seen as leading to full acceptance of halakhah but as a promising avenue for creating and transmitting Jewish identity and values. In one striking instance, Ruth Calderon, a former Israeli Knesset member who is a self-professed secular Jew and the founder of such an institution, used her inaugural address to the Knesset to offer a creative reading of a talmudic aggadah—perhaps the first such address by a Knesset member ever. Though Calderon is removed from classical observance, she successfully related the Talmud to issues in contemporary Israeli life in a way that politicians entrenched in the traditional halakhic worldview had not previously appreciated.[8]

Other examples, now from the American scene, include a weekly column in *Tablet*, a nondenominational online magazine, that has tracked the sections of Talmud studied in the *daf yomi* (a page-a-day) system and is the work of Adam Kirsch, a well-known literary critic.

Mechon Hadar, a post-denominational institution committed to a new brand of egalitarian halakhism, offers a curriculum consciously inspired by the classical yeshiva. The non-denominational Limmud conferences that began in the United Kingdom, which have since spread internationally, similarly sponsor sessions devoted to Talmud, as do Federation and other Jewish communal auspices across the United States. And in 2017, Ilana Kurshan's memoir, *If All the Seas Were Ink,* which charts her march through the *daf yomi* cycle, attained widespread readership and acclaim across the Jewish demoninational spectrum.

In the not-so-distant past, text-based Talmud study was almost unheard of outside of Orthodox enclaves and select academic circles. Today, it is increasingly part of the Jewish intellectual landscape. A text once held responsible for alienating modern Jews from Judaism may now carry enough cachet to reel them back in.

From its earliest formulation in the Mishnah, halakhah's regulatory strategy has relied not only on law backed by social and political authority but on the religious and cultural identity forged through Torah study. While the strategy is ancient, the idea translates surprisingly well into the present. Contrary to all expectations, the modern era has ushered in a renaissance of Torah study and religious culture that the founding generations of either American or Israeli Judaism could never have envisioned.

These developments have not only reinforced the imprint of halakhah in its traditional strongholds, but have pressed the Talmud into conversation with Western philosophy and literature, academic scholarship, and the arts—sources previously excluded from the *beit midrash.* Even as the political infrastructure of halakhic enforcement has weakened as compared with centuries past, the culture of Torah remains entrenched within its traditional sphere and now radiates to a broad cross-section of Jewish society and beyond.

According to traditional theology, halakhah, like the Jewish people, will only reach its ultimate fulfillment in the messianic age. Rabbinic commentators have long debated whether this will take the form of a divine reorientation of human consciousness, the miraculous establishment of a utopian halakhah, a renewal of prophecy, or simply the progression of ordinary politics toward its redemptive climax. In the meantime, the decision to entwine a demanding system of regulation within a sanctified framework of religious study and creativity has allowed halakhah to survive and thrive under a vast array of disparate legal and cultural settings.

This is the enduring legacy of the rabbinic idea of law.

GLOSSARY

Aḥronim—Literally "latter ones." Leading rabbis of the seventeenth-nineteenth centuries. Early Aḥronim tended to focus their writing on and around the *Shulḥan Arukh* and its commentaries. Later Aḥronim specialized in developing conceptual accounts of talmudic sugyot (passages). (pages 163–212)

Aggadah—Nonlegal or narrative material found in rabbinic literature that includes creative readings and interpretations of the Bible, theological investigations, mysticism, stories about the rabbis themselves, rabbinic and popular aphorisms, cultural commentary, moral lessons, inspirational tales, and sermonic admonishments. (pages 58–59 and 103–123)

Amora (pl. Amoraim)—Rabbinic scholar from the talmudic period (third–sixth centuries).

Ashkenaz—In the Middle Ages, this referred to an area comprising the northern parts of modern-day France and Germany. As populations shifted eastward in the fifteenth through seventeenth centuries, the term came to include European Jewry more broadly and, in particular, the communities of Eastern Europe. Jews who follow the traditions and customs of Ashkenaz are referred to as Ashkenazim. (pages 146–162)

Bittul Torah—Literally, the abnegation of Torah, typically referring to the derogation of the duty to study Torah. (pages 67–68, 196–197)

Beit din—Rabbinic court.

Beit midrash—Rabbinic study hall. The location where *talmud Torah* classically takes place.

Beit Yosef—Joseph Caro's encyclopedic sixteenth century commentary of *Tur*. The work serves as the basis for Caro's later work, the *Shulḥan Arukh*. (pages 166–167)

Bread of the Presence—(Hebrew: *leḥem ha-panim*, also: showbread). The cakes or loaves of bread presented on a dedicated table in the Mishkan and Temple, as mentioned in Ex. 25 and Lev. 24. (pages 63–64 and 78–79)

Brisker method—A method of Talmud study named after the town of Brisk (Brest-Litovsk in present-day Belarus). Brisk is where the founder of the movement, Ḥayyim Soloveitchik (1853–1918), resided with a circle of students following the close of the Volozhin Yeshivah. Leaders of this movement exemplify the later Aḥronim, and devotees of the method are known as Briskers. (pages 195–212)

Din—Strict or formal justice, as contrasted with a compromise solution or arbitration/mediation. Also, a ruling of a rabbinical court. (pages 111–117, 168)

Ervah—Sexual taboo. Also, the legal term for genitalia. (pages 131–135)

Galut; also, *golus*—Literally "exile." Galut refers to the understanding that, because of sin

Jews inhabit a diminished and compromised political, legal, and spiritual reality (pages 31–32)

Geonim (sing. Gaon)—Rabbis who served as the heads of the Babylonian academies of the ninth and tenth centuries. Geonim also served as communal leaders and halakhic decisors. (pages 146–147)

Greek wisdom—Corpus of "external" wisdom, the study of which is frowned upon (or forbidden) by the Talmud. Later scholars debated which works and disciplines fall into this category. (pages 67–72)

Ḥasidism—Pietistic movement that began in eighteenth-century Eastern Europe, centered on the rabbinic court of a hereditary *rebbe*. Song, prayer, devotional practices, and mysticism, as well as fierce devotion to the teaching and authority of the *rebbe* in all aspects of life, are core values of ḥasidic life.

Hava amina—Stage 1 starting assumption of a talmudic discussion, usually rejected by the *maskana* in stage 2. (pages 94–95)

Ḥiddush (pl. ḥiddushim)—Literally, a novel idea. The term refers either to published works of talmudic commentary and interpretation or to a novel insight regarding the Talmud or point of halakhah. (pages 155–156)

Issur—Prohibition.

Kiddushin—Legal ceremony that affects a woman's betrothal to a man but does not finalize a marriage. (pages 22–23)

Kohen (pl. kohanim)—A priest who performed sacrificial duties of in the ancient Temple in Jerusalem, or a patrilineal descendant of such a person.

Maariv—Daily evening prayer.

Maskana—Stage 2 concluding section of a talmudic discussion that rejects the *hava amina*. (pages 94–95)

Midrash—Rabbinic exegesis of the Bible which can be pursued for either halakhic or aggadic ends. The term can also refer to a particular midrashic text or collection of such texts. "Midrashic" often connotes a non-literal aggadic interpretation.

Mikveh—Pool of water used for ritual immersions. (page 25)

Minḥah—Daily afternoon prayer.

Mishnah—Base text of halakhah embodying the oral traditions of Jewish law compiled in final form in the third century. The Mishnah forms the first layer of the Talmud. (pages 18–21)

Mishneh Torah (abbreviated as MT)—Maimonides' conceptually ordered magnum opus that codifies the legal rules of the entire Talmud and oral Torah. (pages 152–155)

Mitzvah (pl. mitzvot)—Literally, commandment. Any of the 613 commandments that Jews are obligated to observe. The term can also refer to any Jewish religious obligation, or more generally to any good deed. (pages 18–20)

Oral Torah—A broad category that incorporates all the teachings of the talmudic rabbis found in Mishnah, Tosefta, Talmud, and related midrashic collections. It is expressly contrasted with the Bible, which is known as "written Torah." (pages 57–59)

Pharisees—Intellectual (if not historical) predecessors of the mishnaic rabbis. This group was active in the late Second Temple period and often portrayed as in conflict over legal matters with both the Sadducees and the early Christians. (pages 23–26)

P'sharah (also, *bitzua*)—Compromise, but also includes arbitration and mediation. Contrasted with *din*. (pages 120–125)

Rashi—Acronym for R. Solomon b. Isaac, the eleventh century French commentator who authored what are arguably the most influential commentaries to both the Bible and Talmud.

Responsa—In Hebrew, *she'elot u-teshuvot*, or "questions and answers." The term refers to the corpus of questions asked of and answered by rabbinic authorities. These often provide evidence of how halakhah was applied to novel issues and specific cases. They are often compared to case law in common law systems. (pages 186–194)

Rishonim—Literally, "the early ones." Leading rabbis who lived approximately in the eleventh to fifteenth centuries. Though Rishonim were preceded by the Geonim, the general assumption is that the former eclipsed the prestige and authoritativeness of the latter. (pages 143–162)

Sanhedrin—the Jewish high court that according to the Mishnah sat in Jerusalem, consisted of seventy-one members, and adjudicated ritual and capital cases. (pages 32–36, 38, 42)

Sepharad—In the Middle Ages, this referred to the Jewish communities of Spain and Portugal, but eventually came to include those of North Africa, Greece, Italy, Turkey, and Egypt as well as Israel and Iraq. Jews who follow the traditions and customs of Sepharad are referred to as Sephardim. (pages 146–162)

Shema—The prayer consisting of three biblical passages required to be recited twice daily. The three texts serve as an affirmation of Judaism's central tenets.

Shulḥan Arukh—A code of Jewish law written by Joseph Caro in the sixteenth century, built on the platform established by the earlier work *Tur*. Originally intended as a summary of the lengthy *Beit Yosef*, over time, the *Shulḥan Arukh* became the authoritative code of Jewish law. (pages 166–167)

Sub-halakhah—Matters of practice and methods of enforcement not found in formal sources but developed by rabbinic legislation or by communal practice "from the ground up." Over time, many sub-halakhic practices became recognized as formal halakhah and dropped their "sub" status. (pages 46–48)

Sugya (*pl. sugyot*)—Basic unit of organization in talmudic literature. The term can refer to both a textual unit in the Talmud itself or to a conceptual unit of halakhic study.

Talmud—The massive collection of both halakhic and aggadic rabbinic statements that are framed as an exposition of the Mishnah. There are two versions of the Talmud: the Jerusalem (Palestinian) Talmud, completed around the sixth century in Palestine, (abbreviated as y. in the text) and the Babylonian Talmud (abbreviated as b. in the text), completed somewhat later in present-day Iraq. The Babylonian Talmud is deemed the more authoritative and is often simply (and in this book) known as the Talmud.

Talmud Torah—The devotional act of studying the Torah. Though the term applies to both written and oral Torah, the emphasis has traditionally been on the Talmud and other forms of oral Torah. (pages 57–73)

Tanna (*pl. Tannaim*)—Rabbinic scholar from the period of the Mishnah.

Terumah—A form of tithe given to Jewish priests (*kohanim*).

Torah lishmah—The study of Torah as a devotional act, for its own sake. Often contrasted with *she'lo lishma,* which means studying Torah insincerely, for ulterior motives, or for professional advancement.

Tosafot—Literally "additions." The glosses on the Talmud composed by a group of Ashkenazi scholars in the twelfth and thirteenth centuries who became known as Tosafists. Tosafot have appeared on the margins of the talmudic page since the Talmud's first printing.

Tosefta—Cousin-text to the Mishnah which deals with roughly the same topics, albeit in a more loosely edited format. Scholars debate whether Tosefta is more of a "rough draft" or precursor to the Mishnah, or whether it was compiled after the Mishnah to preserve materials edited out of the Mishnah's tighter text.

Tur—A code of Jewish law written by Jacob b. Asher in the fourteenth century. It later became the basis for Joseph Caro's *Beit Yosef* and the *Shulḥan Arukh.*

Tzedakah—Charitable giving, typically seen as a moral obligation. Can also refer to charity or mercy more generally. (pages 118–119)

Volozhin Yeshiva—The most influential yeshiva in Eastern Europe during the nineteenth century and progenitor of most modern yeshivot. The Yeshiva emphasized *Torah lishmah* and provided the fertile ground where the Brisker method was initially developed. (pages 195–196)

NOTES

Introduction

1. Grant Gilmore, *The Ages of American Law* (New Haven: Yale University Press 1977), 110.

2. Frederic W. Maitland, *Why the history of English law is not written: an inaugural lecture delivered in the arts school at Cambridge on 13th October, 1888* (London: C.J. Clay & Sons, Cambridge University Press, 1888).

3. H.L.A. Hart, *The Concept of Law* (Oxford; New York: Oxford University Press, 3rd. ed. 2012), 56–57; 88–90; 102–04; Ronald Dworkin, *Law's Empire* (Cambridge, Mass.: Belknap Press, 1986), 46–86.

4. A similar theme is developed in Sergey Dolgopolski, *The Open Past: Subjectivity and Remembering in the Talmud* (New York: Fordham University Press, 2013).

5. Alasdaire MacIntyre, *Whose Justice? Whose Rationality?* (Notre Dame: Notre Dame Press, 1984).

Chapter 1. The Idea of Halakhah

1. See Y. Y. Neuwirth, *Shemirat Shabbat ke-Hilkhatah* (New York: Feldheim, 1978), §16:23.

2. Scholars who specialize in the historical facts surrounded Jesus's life often raise doubts about whether Jesus and/or Paul in fact had such conversations with the Pharisees, and also how the Pharisaic sect described in the New Testament relates to the group of religious leaders who would later become the mishnaic rabbis. My goal here is not to engage the historical question, but to take a typological view that focuses on the contrasting evaluations of law and the nature of legal argument in the cultures of the Gospels and the Talmud. For this reason, the description of Jesus is not of the historical person, but rather of the persona and core ideas presented within the canonical texts. Similarly, though my analysis of the contestation between Jesus's and the talmudic approaches to law are anchored in Gospel's textual narrative, I place little emphasis on the actual conversations that may or may not have occurred. Instead, my goal is to offer a jurisprudential account of the debate between the emerging Christian and rabbinic traditions.

3. See for example, Justin Martyr, "Dialogue with Trypho," Chs. 14–22; John Chrysostom, "Discourses Against Judaizing Christians," Homily 6 §7.

4. Critiques of talmudic (Pharisaic) legalism reach as far back as the New Testament (Luke

11:37–54; Matthew 23:1–39), and both Jerome and Augustine criticized the Jews for forsaking the Bible's divine law in favor of man-made rabbinic law. In the Middle Ages, the Talmud came under attack in many disputations, though the opposition was generally directed at the Talmud's theology rather than at its legalism *per se*. See Ḥen Merḥavia, *The Talmud in Christian Eyes: Talmudic and Midrashic Literature in Medieval Christendom 500–1248* (Jerusalem: Bialik Institute, 1970) [Hebrew]; David Berger, *The Jewish-Christian Debate in the High Middle Ages* (Philadelphia: Jewish Publication Society, 1979). A summary of this history is usefully presented in Barry Scott Wimpfheimer, *The Talmud: A Biography* (Princeton: Princeton University Press, 2018), 174-187.

Critiques of talmudic legalism began to re-emerge in the early modern period. Following Spinoza, Kant referred to Judaism disparagingly as a "statutory" religion and "not a religion at all." Immanuel Kant, *Religion Within the Limits of Reason Alone* (New York: Harper Torchbooks, 1960), 116. In the nineteenth century, criticism turned again to the rabbis' legalism. Examples include Crawford Toy, *Judaism and Christianity: A Sketch of Progress from the Old Testament to the New* (Boston: Little, Brown, 1890); Goldwin Smith, "The Jewish Question" in Goldwin Smith, *Essays on Questions of the Day* (New York: Macmillan, 1894) and "New Light on the Jewish Question," *The North American Review* 153 (Aug 1891): 129–143. Perhaps most famously, Max Weber accused Jews of using talmudic legalism to rationalize unethical business practices. *Economy and Society: An Outline of Interpretive Sociology* (Berkeley: University of California Press, 1978, 2: 615).

5. See, Chaim Saiman, "Jesus' Legal Theory—A Rabbinic Reading," *Journal of Law and Religion* 23:1 (2007–08): 97–103.

6. An exemplar of this view for the mishnaic and early talmudic periods is Seth Schwartz, *Imperialism and Jewish Society: 200 BCE–640 CE* (Princeton: Princeton University Press, 2001), 101–176. A more general discussion focusing on late antiquity can be found in Catherine Hezser, *The Social Structure of the Rabbinic Movement in Roman Palestine* (Tubingen, Germany: Mohr Siebeck, 1997), 353–404. For the medieval period, see Elisheva Baumgarten, *Jewish Culture and Context: Practicing Piety in Medieval Ashkenaz* especially (Philadelphia: University of Pennsylvania Press, 2014), 138–171. Other well-known studies examining the variety of Jewish practice across history include Lawrence Fine, ed., *Judaism in Practice: From the Middle Ages through the Early Modern Period* (Princeton: Princeton University of Press, 2001); *Jewish Religious Leadership: Image and Reality*, Jack Wertheimer, ed., (New York: Jewish Theological Seminary, 2004); and *Rabbinic Culture and Its Critics: Jewish Authority, Dissent, and Heresy in Medieval and Early Modern Times*, Daniel Frank and Matt Goldish, eds., (Detroit: Wayne State University Press, 2008).

7. Regarding the medieval period, see Talya Fishman, *Becoming the People of the Talmud: Oral Torah as Written Tradition in Medieval Jewish Cultures* (Philadelphia: University of Pennsylvania Press, 2011). For an examination in the modern era, see Ḥaym Soloveitchik, "Rupture and Reconstruction," *Tradition* 28:4 (Summer 1994): 64–130.

8. See for example, J. David Bleich, "Is There an Ethic Beyond Halacha?" *Proceedings of the 9th World Congress of Jewish Studies* (Jerusalem: World Union of Jewish Studies, 1986), 55–62.

Chapter 2. Non-Applied Law

1. Yosef Ḥayim Yerushalmi, *Zakhor: Jewish History and Jewish Memory* (Seattle: University of Washington Press, 1982), 22–24.

2. For example, David Weiss Halivni, *Midrash, Mishnah, and Gemara* (Cambridge, Mass.: Harvard University Press, 1986), 2–3.

3. Aharon Shemesh, *Punishment and Sins: From Scripture to the Rabbis* (Jerusalem: Hebrew University Press, 2003), 206–7 [Hebrew]; Chaim Saiman, "The Halakhah of Jesus' Trial," *First Things* (August/September 2013).

4. See *Responsa Rashba* Vol. 4 §109; Ḥayyim Ḥezkiah Medini, *Sedei Ḥemed*, "Mem" §31 (New York: Friedman 1962); Reuven Margaliot, *Margaliot ha-Yam* to Sanhedrin 81a (Jerusalem: Mossad Ha-Rav Kook, 1957).

5. Maimonides, *MT*, The Laws of Sanhedrin 14:8.

6. Most contemporary scholars assume the Sanhedrin did not function in the exact manner depicted by the Mishnah. First, because contemporanous sources such as Josephus and the New Testament do not portray the Sanhedrin in the same light as rabbinic texts. Further, while extra-rabbinic sources attest to different types of councils, these are not invested with the overarching political and religious responsibilities the Mishnah accords to the Sanhedrin. The two leading studies on the topic are David Goodblatt, *The Monarchic Principle: Studies in Jewish Self-Government in Antiquity* (Tubingen, Germany: J.C.B Mohr, 1994), 77–130, and Joshua Efron, *Studies in the Hasmonean Period* (Leiden; New York: Brill, 1987). Also notable in this regard are Hugo Mantel, *Studies in the History of the Sanhedrin* (Cambridge, Mass.: Harvard University Press, 1961); Howard Clark Kee "Central Authority in Second-Temple Judaism and Subsequently: From Synedrion to Sanhedrin," *The Annual of Rabbinic Judaism* 2 (1999): 51–63; Beth Berkowitz, *Execution and Invention: Death Penalty Discourse in Early Rabbinic and Christian Sources* (Oxford; New York: Oxford Univeristy Press, 2006), 12–19; Lester Grabbe, "Sanhedrin, Sanhedriyyot, or Mere Invention?," *Journal for the Study of Judaism in the Persian, Hellenistic, and Roman Period* 39 (2008): 1–19.

Much the same can be said regarding rabbinic descriptions of Temple ritual. As compared with the material discussing the Sanhedrin, there are fewer contemporaneous extra-rabbinic sources that refer to the details of Temple procedure. Nevertheless, most historically oriented scholars understand that mishnaic accounts of Temple ritual do not necessarily describe the procedures as they historically occurred. See for example, Joshua Schwartz, "The Temple Cult Without the Sages: Prolegomena on the Description of the Second Temple Period Cult according to the Sources of the Second Temple Period," *New Studies on Jerusalem*, 14 (2008): 7–19 (English section); and Joshua Schwartz, "Sacrifice Without the Rabbis: Ritual and Sacrifice in the Second Temple Period according to the Sources of the Second Temple Period," in Alberdina Houtman, et al. eds., *The Actuality of Sacrifice: Past and Present* (Leiden, The Netherlands: Brill, 2014), 123–149.

Recent scholarship on mishnaic descriptions of Temple ritual and the Sanhedrin's procedure have shifted away from attempting to reconstruct the historical reality. Instead, they assume the Mishnah's conceptual and literary units communicate theological, political, and religious meaning through the articulation of ritual, law, and procedure. With respect to the Sanhedrin, two exemplars of this approach are Beth Berkowitz, *Execution and Invention: Death Penalty Discourse in Early Rabbinic and Christian Sources* (Oxford; New York: Oxford University Press, 2006), and Devora Steinmetz, *Punishment and Freedom: The Rabbinic Construction of Criminal Law* (Philadelphia: University of Pennsylvania Press, 2008). Regarding the Temple and purity laws, see for example, Jonathan Klawans, *Purity, Sacrifice and the Temple: Symbolism and Supersessionism in the Study of Ancient Judaism* (Oxford; New York: Oxford University Press, 2006), 175–211; Naftali Cohn, *The Memory of the Temple and the Making of the Rabbis* (Philadelphia: University of Pennsylvania Press, 2013); Ishay Rosen-Zvi, *The Mishnaic Sotah Ritual* (Leiden, The Netherlands: Brill, 2012); Daniel Stökl Ben Ezra, *The Impact of Yom Kippur on Early Christianity: The Day of Atonement from the Second Temple to the Fifth Century* (Tubingen, Germany: Mohr Seibeck, 2003), 19–28; Avraham Walfish. "Ideological Trends in the Description of Temple and Cult in Tractates Tamid and Midot," in *Judaea and Samaria Studies: Proceedings of the Seventh Conference* (1997): 79–92 [Hebrew]; Jeffrey Rubenstein, "The Sadducees and the Water Libation," *Jewish Quarterly Review* 84:4 (1994): 417–444; Ishay Rosen-Zvi, "Orality, Narrative, Rhetoric: New Directions in Mishnah Research," *AJS Review* 32:2 (2008): 242–249.

7. See for example, b.Sanhedrin 19a-b; See also David C. Flatto, "The King and I: The Separation of Powers in Early Hebraic Political Theory," *Yale Journal of Law and Humanities* 20:1 (2008): 97–99.

8. For example, b.Sanhedrin 52b, which explains a seemingly illegal decision issued by the Sanhedrin because at that time the body was controlled by Sadducees who rejected rabbinic halakhah.

9. See the sources cited in note 6 to this chapter.

10. See Ishay Rosen-Zvi, *The Mishnaic Sotah Ritual*, (Leiden, The Netherlands: Brill, 2012), 239–254.

11. For preservation of the past, see David Zvi Hoffman, *The First Mishna and the Controversies of the Tannaim,* Paul Forchheimer trans. (New York, Maurosho Publishing, 1977), 31–37; and J. N. Epstein, *Introduction to Tanaaitic Literature* (Jerusalem, Magnes; Tel Aviv, Dvir, 1957), 36–37 [Hebrew]. As to messianic aspirations, see Klawans, *Purity, Sacrifice and the Temple: Symbolism and Supercessionism in the Study of Ancient Judaism* (Oxford; New York: Oxford University Press, 2006), 175–211. As a response to the loss of self-governance, see Jacob Neusner, "Map Without Territory: Mishnah's System of Sacrifice and Sanctuary," *History of Religions* 19:2 (1979): 103–127, and Shaye Cohen, "The Destruction: From Scripture to Midrash," *Prooftexts* 2:1 (1982): 18–19. As an educational manual see Yaakov Elman, "Order, Sequence, and Selection: The Mishnah's Anthological Choices," *The Anthology in Jewish Literature*, David Stern ed. (Oxford; New York: Oxford University PPress, 2004), 53–80. For establishing rabbinic authority see Naftali Cohn, *The Memory of the Temple and the Making of the Rabbis* (Philadelphia: University of Pennsylvania Press, 2013).

12. The first was Nissim ben Reuven in his *Derashot ha-Ran,* #11, the fourteenth century scholar whose work is discussed in chapter 9.

Chapter 3. Halakhah and Governance

1. See Isaiah Gafni, "Court Proceedings in the Babylonian Talmud," *Proceedings of the American Academy for Jewish Research* 49 (1982): 23–40 [Hebrew]; See also Shalom Albeck, *Rabbinical Courts in the Talmudic Era*, (Ramat Gan: Bar Ilan University Press, 2nd ed., 1987) [Hebrew]. For a more skeptical take on the scope of rabbinic authority in the earlier parts of the rabbinic era, see Hayim Lapin, *Rabbis as Romans: The Rabbinic Movement in Palestine 100–400 CE* (Oxford; New York: Oxford University Press, 2012), 98–125.

2. The concept is referred to as *"hefker beit din hefker,"* which enables a court to declare certain property ownerless. It is discussed in several talmudic sources including b.Gittin 36b.

3. Catherine Hezser, "Social Fragmentation, Plurality of Opinion, and Nonobservance of Halakhah: Rabbis and Community in Late Roman Palestine," *Jewish Studies Quarterly* 1 (1993–1994): 234–251; Seth Schwartz, *Imperialism and Jewish Society: 200 BCE–640 CE* (Princeton: Princeton University Press, 2001), 101–162; see also Lapin, *Rabbis as Romans*.

4. *Terumah* is a small percentage of produce given to a *kohen* (priest). It can only be eaten only by a kohen and his household in a state of ritual purity that exceeds the standards that apply to ordinary food.

5. For the former opinion see Yitzhak D. Gilat, *Studies in the Development of the Halakhah* (Ramat Gan: Bar-Ilan University Press, 1992), 290–291 [Hebrew]. For the latter, see Carl M. Perkins, "The Evening Shema: A Study in Rabbinic Consolation," *Judaism* 43:1 (1994): 28–29.

6. Avraham Walfish, "Approaching the Text and Approaching God: The Redaction of Mishnah and Tosefta Berakhot," *Jewish Studies* 43 (2005-2006): 44–46.

7. Hayim Lapin, *Early Rabbinic Civil Law and the Social History of Roman Galilee: A Study of Mishnah Tractate Baba' Meṣi'a'* (Atlanta: Scholars Press, 1995), 1–34 and 213–217.

8. Yaakov Elman, "Order, Sequence, and Selection: The Mishnah's Anthological Choices," in *The Anthology in Jewish Literature*, ed. David Stern (Oxford; New York: Oxford University Press, 2004), 53–80; H. L. Strack and G. Stemberger, *Introduction to the Talmud and Midrash*, Markus Bockmuehl trans. (Minneapolis: Fortress Press, 2nd ed., 1996), 135–38.

9. Gershom Scholem, "Revelation and Tradition as Religious Categories in Judaism," *The Messianic Idea in Judaism and Other Essays on Jewish Spirituality*, Henry Schwarzschild and Michael Meyer trans. (New York: Schocken Books, 1971), 288–89.

10. The Tosefta is a cousin-text to the Mishnah which deals with roughly the same topics, albeit in a more loosely edited format. Scholars debate whether Tosefta is more of a "rough draft" of what became the Mishnah, or whether it was compiled after the Mishnah to preserve materials edited out of the mishnaic text. Further, whether either work was initially produced as a unity is also open to debate, and a case-by-case assessment may be warranted. For a recent discussion of different scholarly theories on the Tosefta, see Moshe Simon-Shoshan, *Stories of the Law: Narrative Discourse and the Construction of Authority in the Mishnah* (Oxford; New York: Oxford University Press, 2012), 97–99 and 247 nn. 1–8. See also Robert Brody, *Mishnah and Tosefta Studies* (Jerusalem: Magnes Press, 2014), 111–114, and Paul Mandel, "The Tosefta," *Cambridge History of Judaism* (Cambridge: Cambridge University Press, 2008), 4:316- 335.

Chapter 4. Halakhah as Torah

1. See sources collected in the *Mesivta* edition of the Talmud (Brooklyn: Oz ve-Hadar) to Sanhedrin 45a in Sanhedrin Vol. 2, p.264 of the *Likutei Biurim* section.

2. See Maimonides, *MT*, The Laws of Murder, 9:11–17. For example, the body must be found on the ground rather than in the water, buried underground, or hung from a tree.

3. As in Genesis 2:7 which relates how God animated man by breathing life into his nostrils.

4. See the Annotations of Gra of Vilna on *Shulḥan Arukh*, YD § 246.

5. For example, Maimonides, *Commentary to the Mishnah* on Sotah 9:15. See also sources collected in the *Mesivta* edition of the Talmud on Menaḥot 99b in Menaḥot Vol 5, pp. 168–69 of the *Likutei Biurim* section. A number of conceptual and historical analyses of the issue can be found in *Judaism's Encounter with Other Cultures: Rejection or Integration?*, Jacob J. Schacter ed. (Northvale, N.J.:Jason Aronson, 1997).

6. See Martin Jaffee, "Rabbinic Authorship as a Collective Enterprise," in *The Cambridge Companion to the Talmud and Rabbinic Literature,* Charlotte Fonrobert and Martin Jaffe eds. (Cambridge: Cambridge University Press, 2007).

7. Jonathan Rosen, *The Talmud and the Internet: A Journey Between Two Worlds* (New York: Farrar, Straus & Giroux, 2001).

8. m. Yadayim 3:5 and 4:5–6, as well as b.Shabbat 115a-b. See also Ḥayyim Naḥman Bialik, "Halakhah and Aggadah," in *Revealment and Concealment* (Jerusalem: Ibis Editions, 2000), 56–57.

Chapter 5. Halakhah as Theology

1. Marshall McLuhan, *Understanding Media: The Extensions of Man* (Cambridge, Mass.: MIT Press, 1964), 7.

2. This passage has been analyzed by Emmanuel Levinas in *"Model of the West"* in *Beyond the Verse: Talmudic Readings and Lectures* trans. Gary D. Mole (Bloomington, Ind.: Indiana University Press, 1994), 13–33.

3. Samuel Eidels (Maharsha) (Poland;1555–1631) offers a textual basis for this comparison based on Ps. 119:117, "I will occupy myself with Your statutes *continually* (תמיד)," the same word used to describe the continual placement of Bread of the Presence. Maharsha to Menaḥot 99b.

4. In his work *Sefat Emet*, R Yehudah Aryeh Alter (Poland; 1847–1905), argues that even the majority view in the Mishnah which argues with R. Yose regarding the showbread adopts a more flexible stance relating to Torah study. See *Sefat Emet* (Jerusalem: Mir Publications, 1996) Vol. 3 on Menaḥot 99b.

5. This reading streamlines the approach of Rashi and Tosafot to Menaḥot 99b. Rashi understands the Talmud's conclusion as attitudinal—though Torah study may be a constant obligation, it should be viewed as a labor of love. Tosafot by contrast, read it as minimizing the scope of obligation thereby leaving room for human accomplishment.

6. I want to thank Elli Fischer for this insight. Later, I saw that Isaac Minkovsky (Pinsk,

Belarus; 1788–1851), similarly raises the issue of how the latter *amora* argues on earlier authorities. See *Keren Orah* on Nedarim 8a (Bene Brak: Ohr ha-Hayyim, 2004), Vol. 2:387.

7. See also Keren Orah on Menaḥot 99b Vol.5:516-517 who understands the competing approaches as speaking to different personalities.

8. See t.Ḥullin 2:22 ; b.Avodah Zarah 27b; y.Avodah Zarah 2:2; y.Shabbat 14:14 and parallels. In b.Berakhot 56b, ben Dama also appears asking his uncle a question. Further, one version of t.Shevuot 3:4 (Tzukermandel) records ben Dama as presenting a rejected halakhic argument to his uncle, though other versions cite ben Zoma. A ben Dama is also featured in the context of the ten martyrs memorialized in the Yom Kippur liturgy, though it is unclear whether this refers to R. Ishmael's nephew.

9. This source is discussed in Ḥayyim N. Bialik, "Halakhah and Aggadah," in *Revelation and Concealment* (Jerusalem: Ibis Editions, 2000), 64.

10. The question of carrying weapons for self-defense is discussed elsewhere in the Talmud, e.g., b.Eruvin 45a.

11. b.Berakhot 57b. For examples in Hasidic thought, see Levi Yitzḥak of Berdichev (Ukraine; 1740–1809), in his *Kedushat Levi* (Jerusalem: Institute for Publication of Works of Musar and Hassidut, 1964) on Ki Tisa, "Et Shabtotai Tishmoru," and Jacob Joseph of Polonne (Ukraine; 1710–1784) in his *Toldot Yaakov Yosef* (Jerusalem: Ohr ha-Hayyim, 2007) on Behar, "Behar Sinai."

12. See for example the Aramaic Targum on Psalm 45; See also commentary of R. David Kimḥi (Provence, 12th century), on Psalms 45:1.

13. For the halakhic matter see *Shulḥan Arukh*, OḤ . §301:7. For the theology, see Maimonides *MT*, Laws of Repentance 8:7 and 9:2 (adopting R. Eliezer's minimalist view), as contrasted with Naḥmanides' maximalist and utopian vision of the messianic era outlined in his *Commentary to Torah* on Lev. 26:6 and Deut. 30:6. Fuller treatment of this issue can be found in Joseph Sarachek, *The Doctrine of the Messiah in Medieval Jewish Literature* (New York: Hermon Press, 2nd ed., 1968) and Yehudah Chayoun and Yaakov Mordechai Rapoport, *When Moshiach Comes: Halachic and Aggadic Perspectives* (Southfield, Mich.: Targum/Feldheim, 1994). Note also that both R. Moshe Feinstein and R. Shlomo Goren wrote responsa engaging in both the technical and theological aspects of this issue. See *Igrot Moshe,* OḤ v. 4 §75:3 and *Meishiv Milḥama* §2:61 respectively.

14. Indeed, it is cited independent of the context of prayer laws in Midrash Tanḥuma, *va-Yetze,* §19 (Solomon Buber Edition, Vilna: Romm, 1913).

15. Moshe Halbertal, "The Limits of Prayer: Two Talmudic Discussions," *Jewish Review of Books* 2 (Summer 2010): 44.

Chapter 6. Halakhah as Education

1. Robert Cover, "Nomos and Narrative," *Harvard Law Review* 97 (1983): 13.

2. This sugya was analyzed by Emmanuel Levinas in his *Nine Talmudic Readings*, Annette Aronowicz trans. (Bloomington, Ind.: Indiana University Press, 1994): 94–119.

3. Echoes of this approach are found in *Tur* which rules that when the prevailing background

custom calls for the employer to supply food even in the absence of express stipulation, and the employer expressly promises food to the workers, the employer is understood to have promised a more elaborate meal than the local baseline. See *Tur, ḤM §331:2*. This approach to contract interpretation is quite different from how parallel questions are analyzed in American law.

4. The Talmud stresses this rationale by claiming that Abraham's feast was *even more lavish* than Solomon's, and that Abraham's progeny should be fed in accord with their inherited status. b.Bava Metzia 86b.

5. See Talmud and Meiri on Kiddushin 20a. See also b.Ketubot 61a.

6. *Arukh ha-Shulḥan, ḤM §331:7.*

7. At times, the Talmud's medieval commentators downplay the normative significance of weak Stage 1 questions claiming they are merely part of the Talmud's dialectical style. See for example, *Tosafot ha-Rosh* on Bava Metzia 48b, s.v. *ka-tani miha*. A more general discussion can be found in Yehuda Brandes, "The Meaning and Structure of the Ukimta," *Netuim* 11-12 (2004):9-38 [Hebrew].

8. While the Talmud does not resolve the question, it concludes that the matter is disputed by tannaim. Since the view of the Mishnah aligns with the "heaven's food" perspective, this view is adopted by later halakhists. Nevertheless, the conceptual tension between the two ways of framing the issue is never fully resolved. According to some, despite lack of initial control over the eating right, the worker fully owns it and may give it to his wife and children once he has taken physical possesssion. See for example, Ḥayyim Soloveitchik (Belarus/Poland; 1853–1918), *Ḥidushei Rabbeinu Ḥayyim ha-Levi al ha-Rambam* on Hilkhot Me'eila 8:1 (Israel 2004). See also Aharon Walkin (Belarus; 1864–1942) in his *Beit Aharon*, (Jerusalem: Makhon ha-Maor, 2003) commenting on Rashi on Bava Metzia 92a, "*le-didei*".

9. I have followed the version of the printed Vilna text. Several medieval authorities, however, record an alternate reading wherein the Stage 2 conclusion associates the sages with a view the Talmud expressly rejects just a few pages earlier. After inquiring why the Talmud associated the sages with a rejected view, these authorities note that "it is the way of the Talmud to cite a *drashah* (teaching) that is more common, or that is closer to the plain meaning of the biblical verse, and there is no insistence that it specifically follow the accepted halakhah. There are many examples of this across the Talmud." See *Shitta Mekubetzet* on Bava Metzia 92a, citing the views of Ramban, Rashba and Ran.

10. Though most halakhic codes record this exemption, the conceptual peculiarity of the ruling leads to more restricted interpretations than the plain meaning of the text would suggest. Some hold that the employer is exempt only from the theoretical punishment of lashes, but he must compensate workers for the deprivation of rights. (See *Tur, ḤM §337*, citing Ramah; see also comments of R. Moshe Isserlis (Rema) on ḤM §337:1). According to others, this exemption teaches that, though the right is "from Heaven," the parties can contract around it. See Ritva on Bava Metzia 88b. Interestingly, this ruling view is not cited by Rif nor does it appear in the main text of the *Shulḥan Arukh* either in HM §§337 or 338. It is however recorded in *Beit Yosef* to §337:2.

11. One example is drawn from the laws of the hacked-calf ceremony encountered in chapter 4. There we saw that the town nearest to the victim's body is required to undertake the ceremony. In discussing an unrelated issue, the Talmud, b.Bava Batra 23b, proposes a "stage 2 conclu-

sion" implying the nearest town is responsible only when the body in found is a mountainous and inaccessible area. But in more traversed locations, the assumption is the body came from the more *populous* town, thereby exempting the closest town from undertaking the ceremony.

This statement significantly alters the fabric of halakhah as presented in Mishnah and Talmud in tractate Sotah, the "home field" of the laws of the hacked-calf. Indeed, Maimonides does not include it in his codification. (see The Laws of Murder 9:6). Over the centuries, halakhists have offered numerous accounts as to why this uncontested statement in the Talmud fails to register in *MT*. (See sources cited in the Frankel edition to *MT*, The Laws of Murder 9:6 at p. 289 of the indices). The simplest answer, however, is that Maimonides understood the Talmud as merely waiving off a "stage 1 assumption," but not as making a normative statement that restructures existing halakhah.

12. See for example, Louis Jacobs, *Studies in Talmudic Logic and Methodology* (London: Vallentine, Mitchell, 1961), 147; David Brodsky, "From Disagreement to Talmudic Discourse: Progymnasmata and the Evolution of the Rabbinic Genre" in *Rabbinic Traditions: Between Palestine and Babylonia*, Ronit Nikolsky and Tal Ilan eds. (Leiden, The Netherlands: Brill, 2014). In a different vein, Daniel Boyarin, *Socrates and the Fat Rabbis* (Chicago: University of Chicago Press, 2009); Richard Hidary, *Rabbis as Greco-Roman Rhetors: Oratory and Sophistic Education in the Talmud and Midrash* (Cambridge: Cambridge University Press, 2017); Barry Scott Wimpfheimer, *The Talmud: A Biography*, (Princeton: Princeton University Press, 2018), 50-72.

13. Maimonides called it the *"masah u-matan shel ha-talmud"* that is, "the give and take of the Talmud." See Robert Brody, "On Maimonides' Attitude Towards the Anonymous Talmud," *Bar-Ilan* 30–31 (2006): 42–43. [Hebrew], and Jacob Levinger, *Maimonides' Halakhic Methodology* (Jerusalem: Hebrew University Press, 1965):155–160 [Hebrew]. An extensive collection of sources on this topic can be found in see Hanokh Albeck, *An Introduction to the Talmuds* (Tel Aviv: Dvir, 1969): 545–556 [Hebrew].

Chapter 7. Halakhah as Aggadah

1. Ḥayyim Naḥman Bialik, "Halakhah and Aggadah," in *Revealment and Concealment: Five Essays* (Jerusalem: Ibis Editions, 2000), 49.

2. Barry Scott Wimpfheimer, *Narrating the Law: The Poetics of Talmudic Legal Stories* (Philadelphia: University of Pennsylvania Press, 2011), 9–13; Moshe Simon-Shoshan, *Stories of the Law: Narrative Discourse and the Construction of Authority in the Mishnah* (Oxford; New York: Oxford University Press 2012), 8–11; Yair Lorberbaum and Ḥaim Shapira, "Maimonides' Epistle on Martyrdom in Light of Legal Philosophy," *Dine Israel* 25 (2001): 123–169.

3. This claim has been most convincingly advanced by Avraham Walfish. See his "Standing Before God as a Halakhic and Theological Idea: A Comparative Analysis of Mishna and Tosefta," in *Rav Shalom Banayikh: Essays Presented to R. Shalom Carmy in Celebration of Forty Years of Teaching*, H. Angel and Y. Blau eds. (Jersey City, N.J.: Ktav, 2012), 365–83; as well as his "Halakhic Confrontation Dramatized: A Study of Mishnah Rosh Hashanah 2:8–9," in *Hebrew Union College Annual* 79 (2008): 1–43; and his "The Poetics of the Mishnah," in *The Mishnah in Contemporary Perspective*, Alan J. Avery-Peck and Jacob Neusner eds. (Leiden, The Netherlands: Brill, 2006), Vol. 2: 153–89.

4. See sources cited in Moshe Benovitz, *A Critical Commentary to the First Chapter of Tractate Berakhot*, (Association for Talmudic Commentary, 2006): 11–13, 20 [Hebrew].

5. This could also mean from when the day is sanctified.

6. The sole exception is #4, which references starlight as *a secondary* timing device. The meaning of this secondary form of identification is analyzed by the Talmud.

7. b. Berakhot 2b. My presentation is indebted to Yehudah Brandes, "An Introduction to Tractate Berakhot," *Asif* 1 (2014): 107–71 [Hebrew].

8. See for example, Carl M. Perkins, "The Evening Shema: A Study in Rabbinic Consolation," *Judaism* 43:1 (1994): 28–29, as well as Brandes, cited above.

9. See Raphael Yom Tov Lipman Heilpern, (Poland; 1816–1879) *Responsa Oneg Yom Tov* (Jerusalem: Bruchman, 2000), Vol. 1 §14. See also Isser Zalman Melzer, (1870–1953) *Even ha-Azel*, Laws of Shema 1:1 Vol. 8, 9-11.

10. Israel Knohl, "A Section that Includes Accepting the Divine Kingdom," *Tarbiz* 53 (1984): 11–32 [Hebrew].

11. Knohl, at 15–17.

12. See *Tur OḤ* §235:1 citing the views of the Geonim, R. Amram and R. Paltoi.

13. See Jacob Katz, "Alterations in the Time of Evening Service (Maariv): An Example of the Interrelationship Between Religious Customs and their Social Background," in *Divine Law in Human Hands: Case Studies in Halakhic Flexibility* (Jerusalem: Magnes Press, 1998): 114.

14. Tosafot to Berakhot 2a.

15. Ra'avan to Berakhot §122. See generally, Katz, "Evening Service."

16. Zerachiah ben Isaac Gerondi, (Ba'al ha-Meor) *Meor ha-Katan*, Berakhot 1b (Rif pagination); Meiri on Berakhot 2a.

17. t.Sanhedrin 1:2. The version cited and analyzed in text is based on the printed Bavli version, though variations appear in the Tosefta and Jerusalem Talmud. For the sake of simplicity, I have omitted some segments of the text.

18. My analysis in this section draws on some of the themes developed in Ḥaim Shapira, "The Debate Over Compromise and the Goals of the Judicial Process," *Dine Israel* 26–27 (2009–2010): 183–228.

19. Jacob Reischer, *Responsa Shevut Yaakov* Vol. 2 §145.

20. Malkiel Tannenbaum, *Responsa Divrei Malkiel* Vol. 2 §133.

21. Joseph Dov Soloveitchik, *Reflections of the Rav*, Abraham R. Besdin ed. (Jersey City, N.J.: Ktav, 1993), 54.

Chapter 8. Thinking Legally

1. Daniel J. Wakin, "Scalia Defends Government's Rights to Deny Art Funds," *New York Times*, Sept. 23, 2005, <http://www.nytimes.com/2005/09/23/nyregion/scalia-defends-governments-right-to-deny-art-funds.html.>

2. See note 13 to Chapter 5.

3. The halakhic discussion centers on the fact that Maimonides sides with the majority opinion regarding the rites of the Bread of Presence, yet rules in accord with R. Yose regarding

recitation of *Shema*. The matter is addressed in R. Abraham de Boton's (Salonika; sixteenth century). *Leḥem Mishneh* to *MT*, Laws of Torah Study 8:1, as well as in the works of *Sefat Emet* and *Keren Orah* cited in notes 4 and 7 to Chapter 5.

4. See respectively, Tosafot to Sotah 10b; Yonah b. Abraham Gerondi's *Shaarei Teshuva* § 3: 139; Ḥezekiah da Silva, *Mayim Ḥaim* to *MT*, Laws of the Foundation of the Torah 5:2; Jacob Ettlinger, *Responsa Binyan Tzion* §172 and our discussion in Chapter 11.

5. b. Ketubot 72b and Rashi and Tosafot therein. See also *Shulḥan Arukh*, EH §115 and super-commentaries to that section of the code.

6. See, e.g., *Arukh ha-Shulḥan*, OḤ §75:7; Yeḥiel Y. Weinberg, *Responsa Sridei Aish* §2:8; Mosheh Lichtenstein, "Kol Isha - A Woman's Voice," *Tradition* 46:1 (2013): 9–24; David Bigman, "A New Analysis of *Kol b'Isha Erva*, (Maale Gilboa: Institute for Jewish Ideas and Ideals, 2009).

7. Reuven Margaliot, *Margaliot ha-Yam* (Jerusalem: Mossad ha-Rav Kook, 1957) on Sanhedrin 75a: *Yamut ve-al tibael lo*.

8. Barry Scott Wimpfheimer, *Narrating the Law: The Poetics of Talmudic Legal Stories* (Philadelphia: University of Pennsylvania Press, 2011), 40–62.

9. Alfasi to Sanhedrin 18b (Rif pagination); *MT*, Foundations of the Torah, 5:9; Rosh on Sanhedrin Chapter 8 §4.

10. Joseph ibn Habib, *Nimukei Yosef* on Sanhedrin 17b (Rif pagination).

11. Rema YD §157:1.

12. See, respectively, *Shakh* (Commentary of R. Shabtai ha-Cohen of Vilna, (1622-1663)) to YD §157:10; *Beit Yosef* to YD §195:17 (indicating this is the view of Maimonides). See also Jacob Reischer, *Torat ha-Shlamim* to YD §195:15.

13. E.g., Moshe Feinstein, *Iggrot Moshe*, EH Vol. 1 §56 and Vol. 2 §14 (New York: Balshan, 1974).

14. Regarding gender-separate schools, see Moshe Feinstein, *Iggrot Moshe*, YD Vol. 1 §137 and Ovadya Yosef, *Responsa Yabia Omer* Vol. 10 EH §23 pp.413-414 (Jerusalem, 2004). As basis for their positions, many point to the stringencies listed by both *Tur* and *Shulḥan Arukh* EH §21:1, which contains the unusually strong phrase: "One must distance himself from women to a very great degree." (צָרִיךְ אָדָם לְהִתְרַחֵק מֵהַנָּשִׁים מְאֹד מְאֹד).

Chapter 9. Transitioning to Law

1. R. Yosef b. Meir mi-Gosh (Ri mi-Gash) on Bava Batra 130. See also Ḥanina Ben-Menaḥem, "The Second Canonization of the Talmud," *Cardozo Law Review* 28:1 (2006): 37–51.

2. See generally, Robert Brody, *The Geonim of Babylonia and the Shaping of Medieval Jewish Culture* (New Haven: Yale University Press, 1998), 155–170.

3. The terms "functional" and "devotional" were first employed by Norman Lamm to describe different models of *talmud Torah*, in his *Torah Lishmah: Torah for Torah's Sake in the Works of Rabbi Ḥayyim of Volozhin and His Contemporaries* (Hoboken, N.J.: Ktav, 1989), 190–192; 205–220. See also Lamm's *The Religious Thought of Hasidism: Text and Commentary* (Hoboken, N.J.: Ktav, 1999), 219–250. Whereas Lamm uses these terms to describe the cognitive aspects of Torah study, (does one study to understand the material vs. to effectuate metaphysical

transformations), my usage focuses on the degree to which study is directed towards articulating functional rules of practice vs. a devotional commitment to the mitzvah of Torah study.

4. See for example the statements of R. Hai Gaon, "We know that the words of aggadah are not like halakhah (*shemuah*). Rather, everyone interprets the verse in whatever comes to his mind, saying, 'it could be,' or 'it is possible.' These are not exact things . . . therefore we are not to rely upon them . . . as they are merely estimations." Cited in B.M. Levin, *Otzar ha-Geonim*, (Jerusalem: Hebrew University Press, 1931), Vol. 4, Ḥagigah §67: 59–60. More generally, see Yair Lorberbaum, "Reflections on the Halakhic Status of Aggadah," *Dine Yisrael* 24 (2007): 33–36, who collects Geonic sources to this effect.

5. Three of the most popular works on aggadah are Jacob ibn Habib's fifteenth century collection titled *Ein Ya'acov*, and the commentaries of Judah Loew ben Bezalel of Prague (Maharal) and Samuel Eidels (Maharsha), both of the sixteenth century. Some of this history is recounted in Chaim Eisen, "Maharal's *Be'er ha-Gola* and his Revolution in Aggadic Scholarship," *Hakira: The Flatbush Journal of Jewish Law and Thought* 4 (2007):140–149 and nn.10–11.

6. See generally, Ephraim E. Urbach, *The Tosafists: Their History, Works and Methodology* (Jerusalem: Bialik Institute, 1955) [Hebrew]. My account of Tosafot reflects the widely studied works that appear on the margin of the standard Talmudic page.

7. Yehudah b. Shmuel ibn Abbas, *Netiv Meir*, cited in Mordechai Breuer, *The Tents of Torah: The Yeshiva, its Structure and its History* (Jerusalem: Shazar Institute, 2003), 74 [Hebrew]. Breuer cites several primary sources highlighting the tension between the two styles of learning. See id. at 105–109.

8. Avraham b. David (Ra'avad), *"Comments to the Introduction of the Mishneh Torah,"* as translated in Menachem Elon, *Jewish Law (Ha-Mishpat ha-Ivri): History, Sources, Principles.* 4 Vols. Bernard Auerback and Melvin J. Sykes trans. (Philadelphia: Jewish Publication Society, 1994), Vol. 3: 1224–25.

9. Moshe Halbertal, *Maimonides: Life and Thought* (Princeton: Princeton University Press, 2013),164–194; Yitzchok Shapiro, "To Know the Forbidden and the Permitted: An Analysis of Rambam's view of the Purpose and Goals of Talmud Study," *Hakirah: The Flatbush Journal of Jewish Law and Thought* 9 (2010): 229–233. See also Shamma Friedman, "Maimonides and the Talmud," *Dinei Israel* 26 (2009): 221–238 [Hebrew].

10. Maimonides, *Introduction to the Mishneh Torah*. See also, Isadore Twersky, *Introduction to the Code of Maimonides (Mishneh Torah)* (New Haven: Yale University Press, 1980), 30.

11. Halbertal, *Maimonides* 197–223; Friedman, "Maimonides and the Talmud,"236–237.

12. *MT*, The Laws of Rebels, Chapter 7; The Laws of Idolatry, Chapter 4.

13. Examples are cited in Ḥanina Ben-Menaḥem, "Maimonides on Equity: Reconsidering the Guide for the Perplexed III: 34," *Journal of Law and Religion* 17 (2002): 35–46. Shimshon Ettinger however has suggested there is more harmony between the cases and the code than Ben-Menaḥem suggests. See Shimshon Ettinger, "Law and Equity in Maimonides and Aristotle," *Law and Equity in the Jurisprudence of Maimonides*, Ḥanina Ben-Menaḥem and Berchayahu Lifschitz eds. (Jerusalem: Center for the Study of Jewish Law, Hebrew University, 2004), 244–252 [Hebrew].

14. Aaron Kirschenbaum, *Jewish Penology: The Theory and Development of Criminal Punish-*

ment Among the Jews Throughout the Ages (Jerusalem: Magnes Press, 2013), 401–416. [Hebrew].

15. Simḥa Assaf, *Punishments in the Post-Talmudic Period* (Jerusalem, 1922), 5–16; [Hebrew] Kirschenbaum, *Jewish Penology,* 341–481.

16. Menachem Lorberbaum, *Politics and the Limits of Law: Secularizing the Political in Medieval Jewish Thought* (Stanford, Calif., Stanford University Press, 2001), 93–123.

17. Sherira Gaon, *Shaar Tzion* 4:1, cited in Assaf, *Punishments in the Post-Talmudic Period*: 53–54.

18. Solomon b. Aderet, *Responsa Rashba* Vol. 4 §311.

19. Solomon b. Aderet, *Responsa Rashba* Vol. 3 §393

20. Nissim Gerondi, *Derashot ha-Rran,* #11.

21. Some readers of Ran understand the powers given to the king as limited emergency powers relevant only to maintaining social order through uses of extra-halakhic punishment. See, for example, Aaron Kirschenbaum, "The Role of Punishment in Jewish Criminal Law: A Chapter in Rabbinic Penological Thought," *Jewish Law Annual* 9 (1991): 123–43; Warren Z. Harvey, "Rabbi Nissim of Girona on the Constitutional Power of the Sovereign," *Dine Israel* 29 (2013): 91–94.

Others however broaden these powers to the legislative arena. These scholars hold that Ran authorizes the king to exercise broad political authority and fashion social policy even in derogation of Torah law. For this approach see Aviezer Ravitzky, "Political Philosophy: Nissim of Gernoa vs. Isaac Abrabanel," *History and Faith: Studies in Jewish Philosophy* (Amsterdam: J.C. Gieben, 1996), 43–75; Ravitsky, *Religion and State in Jewish Thought* (Jerusalem: Israel Democracy Institute, 1998), 11–14, 45–65 [Hebrew]. See also Lorberbaum, *Politics and the Limits of Law* (Stanford, Calif.: Stanford University Press, 2002), 124–149; Gerald J. Blidstein, "Ideal and Real in Classical Jewish Political Theory," 2:1–2 *Jewish Political Studies Review* (1990): 43–66.

22. To take one example, see m. Makkot 1:10 discussed in Chapter 2.

Chapter 10. The Idea of Halakhah in the Codes

1. Joel Sirkes, *Responsa Bayit Ḥadash* (Old Version) §80.

2. Jonathan Eibeschitz, *Urim ve-Tumim* Takfo Kohen §124.

3. Asher b. Yeḥiel, *Responsa Rosh* §31:9

4. Yosef Caro, Introduction to *Shulkhan Arukh.*

5. By way of example, see *Rema,* YD §147:5.

6. Sources for both sides of this issue are collected in *Controversy and Dialogue in the Halakhic Tradition* Ḥanina ben Menaḥem et. al., eds. (Boston: Boston University Institute for Jewish Law, 1991) Vol. 1: 513–559 [Hebrew].

7. *Tur* ḤM §12:6, citing R. Moses of Coucy's *Sefer Mitzvot Gadol* (thirteenth century, France).

8. *Shulhan Arukh,* ḤM §12:20.

9. See commentary of *Prishah* (R. Joshua Falk Katz, Poland (1555-1614)) to *Tur,* ḤM §12:6. Notably, the standard printed versions of the Jerusalem Talmud record Shimon b. Shetaḥ, though *Tur* follows the text of *Sefer Mitzvot Gadol.*

10. See generally, Isaiah Gafni, "Court Proceedings in the Babylonian Talmud," *Proceedings of the American Academy for Jewish Research* 49 (1982): 23–40 [Hebrew].

11. *Bayit Ḥadash* to ḤM§12:6.

12. *Tur*, YD §332 and §333.

13. This approach is hardly limited to *Tur*. In fact, in the very next section of the code, YD §149:7, the commentary *Shakh* makes this point explicitly in distinguishing between the formal rules applicable "as a matter of law" (מדינא), and the more permissive positions that govern in practice (אבל האידנא).

14. *Tur* and *Shulḥan Arukh*, ḤM §97.

15. *Tur*, ḤM §97:17–18.

16. This follows a textual variant cited by R. Tam in Tosafot on Bava Metzia 113a. In adopting this view, *Tur* shifts the law in a more creditor-friendly direction.

17. *Tur*, ḤM §97:26.

18. Note also the debate cited in *Tur* regarding the position adopted in Rif's responsum.

19. *Tur*, 97:28

20. *Shulḥan Arukh*, ḤM §§97; 99.

21. Edward Fram, *Ideals Face Reality: Jewish Law and Life in Poland, 1550–1655* (Cincinnati: Hebrew Union College Press, 1997), 149–163 and Menachem Elon, *Individual Liberty in the Process of Debt Collection in Jewish Law* (Jerusalem: Magnes Press, 1964), 218–227 [Hebrew].

22. *Rema*, ḤM § 97:15. *Bayit Ḥadash*, ḤM §97:28. Fram, *Ideals Face Reality*: 153–155. Elon, *Individual Liberty*: 168–170.

23. *Records of the Council of Four Lands* §112, ed. Israel Helpren (Jerusalem: Bialik Institute, 1945), 45 [Hebrew]. See also, Fram, *Ideals Face Reality*: 54.

24. *Bayit Ḥadash* to ḤM 97:17.

25. *Bayit Ḥadash* to ḤM 97:19.

26. *Bayit Ḥadash* to ḤM §97:28.

27. *Bayit Ḥadash*, "Introduction." See also Noam Samet, *Ketsot Ha-Choshen—The Beginning of 'Lamdanut': Features and Tendencies* (PhD diss., Ben Gurion University, 2016):41–53 [Hebrew].

28. The nearest reference to these issues by R. Joshua Falk Katz, author of *Drishah*, is found in his commentary *Sefer Meirot Eynayim* on *Shulḥan Arukh*, ḤM §107:10, which mentions the possibility of imprisonment in passing.

29. For example, the 1697 edition of Joel Sirkes's responsa maintain no discernable order, whereas the edition published as the "New Responsa" in 1785 was reorganized to follow the section headings of the *Shulkhan Arukh*.

30. *Pitḥei Teshuvah*, (Avraham Tzvi Hirsch Eisenstat (Lithuania, 1813-1868)), on ḤM §97:6.

31. *Kessef Kedoshim*, (Avraham David Wahrmann (Galicia, 1771-1840)), on ḤM §97:6.

32. Samet, *Ketzot Ha-Choshen*: 28–33.

33. Mosheh Lichtenstein, "The Period of the Aḥronim: Trends and Directions" *Netuim*: 16 (2009): 161–62 [Hebrew]. See also Samet, *Ketzot Ha-Choshen*: 64–70. Notably during R. Aryeh Leib's lifetime, the ruling authorities in Galicia consolidated power in the centralized state and reduced the juridical autonomy of the Jewish community. See id. 24–25.

34. Samet, *Ketzot Ha-Choshen*: 26 and 66.

35. R. Aryeh Leib Heller, "Introduction to *Ketzot HaHoshen* Vol. 2. See also Samet, *Ketzot Ha-Choshen*: 66.

36. Shlomo Y. Zevin, *Books and Authors*, (Tziyoni, 1958): 7–8 [Hebrew]; Samet, *Ketzot Ha-Choshen*: 66.

37. *Ḥiddushei Rabbeinu Ba'al Ketzot ha-Ḥoshen—Bava Batra* (Haifa: Pardes Publishing, 2000); *Ḥiddushei Rabbeinu Ba'al Ketzot ha-Ḥoshen—Kiddushin* (Haifa: Pardes Publishing, 1991).

38. *Shulḥan Arukh* ḤM §201.The most comprehensive treatment of the legal and historical aspects of this practice is Ron Kleinman, *Methods of Acquisitions and Commercial Customs in Jewish Law* (Ramat Gan: Bar Ilan University Press, 2013) [Hebrew].

39. For example, despite its practical import, *Ketzot's* commentary essentially skips commenting on the laws governing "transactions of the merchants" in ḤM §201. By contrast, *Ketzot* devotes many pages to the largely dormant laws regarding how acquiring rights in one form of property can be used to obtain rights in another form (*kinyan agav*).

Chapter 11. The Idea of Halakhah in Responsa

1. Haym Soloveitchik, "Responsa: Literary History and Basic Literacy," *AJS Review* 24:2 (1999): 352–53.

2. Shmuel Glick, *A Window to the Responsa Literature* (New York, Jewish Theological Seminary, 2012), 33–36 [Hebrew], and Berachyahu Lifshitz, "The Legal Status of the Responsa Literature," *Authority, Process, and Method: Studies in Jewish Law,* Ḥanina Ben-Menaḥem and Neil S. Hecht eds. (Amsterdam: Academic Publishers, 1998), 72–77.

3. See *Shakh* on YD §196:20 and *Beit Shmuel* (commentary of Shmuel b. Uri Shraga Feivish, Poland 17th century) on EH §130:20; More generally, Glick, *A Window to the Responsa Literature*: 180.

4. See Soloveitchik, "Responsa": 352–53; Elon, *Jewish Law* Vol. 3: 1473 and n. 66.

5. Jacob Reischer, *Responsa Shevut Yaacov* Vol. 2 §187.

6. Yair Ḥayyim Bachrach, *Responsa Ḥavot Yair* §60. For an argument that the story described is a literary fable, see Elchanan Reiner, "A Case that Took Pace in the Holy Community of Worms" *Haaretz*, October 4, 2006, <*http://www.haaretz.co.il/1.1142881*> [Hebrew] (accessed December 11, 2017). Whether we accept Reiner's theory or not, it is clear that the responsum was not written to rule upon an actual case brought before the rabbi.

7. See respectively, Tzvi Hirsch Ashkenazi, *Responsa Ḥakham Tzvi* §93 and Jacob Emden, *Sheilat Ya'avetz* Vol. 2 §82.

8. Israel M. Kagan, *Mishnah Berurah* to OḤ §55:4.

9. See, for example, Yigal Betzalel Shafran, "Genetic Cloning in Light of Halakhah," *Teḥumin* 18 (1998): 150 [Hebrew]. See also Avraham Steinberg, *Encyclopedia of Jewish Medical Ethics: A Compilation of Jewish Medical Law on All Topics of Medical Interest*, Fred Rosner trans. (Jerusalem; New York: Feldheim, 2003), Vol. 3: 513-20, 581.

10. Yosef Dov Soloveitchik, *Responsa Beit HaLevi*, (Bene Brak: Ohr ha-Ḥayyim, 2008), Introduction.

11. Ḥayyim Ozer Grodzinski, *Sefer Aḥiezer*, Introduction (Vilna: S.F. Garber, 1922).

12. Shimon Sofer, *Hitorerut Teshuva* (Jerusalem:Institute for the Publication and Research

of Manuscripts in Memory of Hatam Sofer, 1973) [Hebrew]. This edition is a facsimile of the 1911 edition.

13. Jacob Ettlinger, *Responsa Binyan Tziyon ha-Ḥadashot* §23. This responsum and its surrounding history is analyzed in both Judith Bleich, "Rabbinic Responses to Nonobservance in the Modern Era," *Jewish Tradition and the Nontraditional Jew*, Jacob J. Schacter ed. (Northvale, N.J.: Jason Aronson, 1992), 72–76, and Adam Ferizger, *Exclusion and Hierarchy: Orthodoxy, Nonobservance and the Emergence of Modern Jewish Identity* (Philadelphia: University of Pennsylvania Press, 2005), 90–109, particularly 99–105.

14. See also Gerald Blidstein, "Maimonides' Approach to Karaites," *Tehumin* 8 (1987): 501–10 [Hebrew].

15. See Ferizger, *Exclusion and Hierarchy*: 99–105.

16. Bleich, "Rabbinic Responses", 73, assumes the prefatory note was written by R. Ettlinger himself, while Ferziger, *Exclusion and Hierarchy*, 99–100, offers credible evidence that the note was the addition of Ettlinger's son who published the volume. It remains unknown however whether the son was acting on his father's instructions or of his own accord.

17. R. Ettlinger writes, "as to the sinners of Israel of our time, I do not know how to consider them," and likewise, "it is possible that the Sadducees likewise, who were not used to being among Israel . . . do not act brazenly against the sages," before concluding that "those who are lenient [regarding this wine] have on whom to rely upon."

18. Ferziger, *Exclusion and Hierarchy*, 100; Bleich, "Rabbinic Responses,": 74. See also Samuel Morell, "The Halakhic Status of Non-Halakhic Jews," *Judaism* 19:4 (1969): 455–56, and the extensive treatment the responsum receives in Ovadya Yosef's *Responsa Yabia Omer,* (Jerusalem: 2nd ed., 1986) YD Vol. 1 §11.

19. Ettlinger, *Responsa Binyan Tziyon ha-Ḥadashot*, Introduction. See also Ferziger, *Exclusion and Hierarchy*:100.

20. Elon, *Jewish Law*, Vol. 3: 1485.

Chapter 12. Halakhah's Empire. The Yeshiva and the House of Brisk

1. Joseph B. Soloveitchik, *Gerus and Mesorah—Part 1*, YUTorah Online, MP3 (1975) http://www.yutorah.org/lectures/lecture.cfm/767722/rabbi-joseph-b-soloveitchik/gerus-mesorah-part-1/, Accessed on December 11, 2017.

2. Norman Lamm, *Torah for Torah's Sake* (Hoboken, N.J.: Ktav, 1989), 59.

3. *Nefesh ha-Ḥayyim* §4:11, translated in Lamm, *Torah for Torah's Sake*: 106.

4. See for example *Ohr Elḥanan* (Jerusalem: Yeshivat Ohr Elchanan, 1998), 78 [Hebrew]. The biography recounts how Wasserman (a leading student of R. Ḥayyim Soloveitchik), was in the midst of learning when he was informed of the birth of his child, and likewise, on another occasion, when told of a death in his wife's family. The biographer celebrates that while on both occasions R. Wasserman acknowledged the events, he immediately returned to his learning, "as if no emotionally significant event had occurred to him."

5. H. N. Bialik, "The Talmud-Student," in *Complete Poetic Works of Ḥayyim Naḥman Bialik*, Israel Efros, ed. and Maurice Samuel, trans. (New York: Histadruth Ivrith of America, 1948), 35–57.

6. See Ovadya Yosef, *Responsa Yabia Omer,* OH Vol 1, "Introduction."

7. See Lawrence Kaplan, "The Hazon Ish: Haredi Critic of Traditional Orthodoxy," *in The Uses of Tradition: Jewish Continuity in the Modern Era,* Jack Wertheimer ed. (New York: Jewish Theological Seminary, 1992), 154–155.

8. See Yitzchak Adler, *Lomdus: A Substructural Analysis* (New York: Bet Sha'ar Press, 1989), 119 [Hebrew].

9. Maimonides, *MT,* Laws of Impermissible Mixtures (*Kilayim*) 10:32 and commentary of Ra'avad ad. loc.

10. Hayyim Soloveitchik, *Hiddushei ha-Grah ve-ha-Gri'z al ha-Shas* ("Stencil") (Mishor, Israel), 36 at §60 [Hebrew].

11. See Benjamin Brown, "'Soft Stringency' in the *Mishnah Brurah*: Jurisprudential, Social, and Ideological Aspects of a Halakhic Formulation" in *Contemporary Jewry* 27 (2007): 1–41.

12. Joseph B. Soloveitchik, "Mah Dodekh mi-Dod" in *In Aloneness, in Togetherness: A Selection of Hebrew Writings* (Jerusalem: Orot, 1971), 227 [Hebrew].

13. See Shimon Shkop, *Hiddushei R. Shimon to Bava Kamma* (Jerusalem: Y. Weinstein ed., 2010) § 23:5 [Hebrew]

14. See Meir S. ha-Kohen, *Ohr Sameah (Jerusalem)* to Laws of Divorce 2:15; [Hebrew]; Shimon Shkop, *Sha'arei Yosher* Vol. 2 (New York: Committee for the Publication of the Works of R. Shimon Skop, 1958) §7:7 (p. 221) [Hebrew].

15. Elhanan Wasserman, *Kovetz Shiurim* (Tel Aviv: E.S. Wasserman, 1990) Vol. 2 §23:6 [Hebrew]; see also Yitzchak Adler, *Lomdus:* 126–27.

16. Shkop, *Sha'arei Yosher* §3:3 (p. 155).

17. Id.

18. Yitzhak Zev Soloveitchik, *Hiddushei Maran Ri"z ha-Levi al ha-Rambam* (Jerusalem: Soloveitchik, 1998), 130-132.

19. Elhanan Wasserman, *Kovetz Shiurim* Vol. 2, §27:2 (p. 51) [Hebrew]; Hayyim Shmuelevitz, *Sha'arei Hayyim: Gittin* (Jerusalem, 1989), 179 [Hebrew].

20. Hayyim Soloveitchik, *Hiddushei Rabbeinu Hayyim ha-Levi* (Jerusalem, 2004), to Laws of Sales 22:17 [Hebrew].

21. Shkop, *Sha'arei Yosher* §5:3.

22. Isser Zalman Melzser, *Even ha-Azel* to Laws of Intentional Harms 5:6, Vol. 2, 59b-60a.

23. Yisrael Zev Gustman, *Kuntrasei Shiurim: Nedarim,* (Jerusalem: le-Hasig, Yeshivat Netzah Yisrael, 1997), 197.

24. Soloveitchik, *Hiddushei Rabbeinu Hayyim ha-Levi,* to the Laws of Prayer 4:1.

25. Joseph B. Soloveitchik, *Halakhic Man* (Philadelphia: Jewish Publication Society, 1983), 83.

26. This passage is attributed to R. Hayyim in the writings of his students. See *Haggadah Shel Pesah mi-Beit Levi,* M.M. Gerlitz ed. (Jerusalem: Oraysoh, 1983), 182–83.

27. Soloveitchik, *Halakhic Man:* 19.

28. Id. at 24.

29. Baruch Ber Leibowitz, *Shiurei R. Baruch Ber Leibowitz: Bava Kamma, Bava Metzia* (New York: A.D. Friedman 1990) Vol. 2, *Introduction* 1-7 [Hebrew].

30. Soloveitchik, *Halakhic Man:* 23.

31. *Frigaliment Importing Co v. BNS International Sales*, 160 F. Supp. 116 (SDNY 1960).

32. *Nix v. Hedden*, 149 US 304 (S. Ct. 1893)

33. *Procter & Gamble v. Comm of Revenue and Customs*, [2008] EWHC 1558 (Ch).

34. *Smith v. US*, 508 US 223 (S. Ct. 1993).

35. Soloveitchik, *Halakhic Man*: 24.

36. Id. at 59.

37. For example, Aharon Lichtenstein, *Leaves of Faith: The World of Jewish Learning* (Hoboken, N.J.:Ktav, 2004) Vol.2: 65.

38. Joseph Soloveitchik, "Ma Dodekh MiDod" (New York: ha-Doar, 1963), 22

39. Yitzchak Zev Soloveitchik, *Ḥiddushei Maran Ri"z ha-Levi al ha-Rambam, to Laws of Ḥ ametz and Matzah*, 7:9 p. 14; see also Soloveitchik, *Halakhic Man*: 26–28.

40. Soloveitchik, *Halakhic Man*: 60–61.

41. Id., 19–24

42. For some examples of the modern debate surrounding Brisker method, see *Notes from ATID: Talmud Study in Yeshiva High Schools* (Jerusalem, Academy for Torah Initiatives and Directions, 2007); Shimon Gershon Rosenberg, *In His Torah You Will Labor* (Efrat, Shagar Institute, 2008) [Hebrew]. Yehuda Brandes, *Ma'da Toratekha: Ketubot* 2 vols. (Jerusalem: Maggid, 2009) [Hebrew]; Yair Dreyfuss, "Torah Study for Contemporary Times: Conservatism or Revolution?" in *Tradition* 45:2 (2012); Alan Jotkowitz, "'And Now the Children Will Ask': The Post-Modern Theology of Rav Shagar," in *Tradition* 45:2 (2012)· Chaim Saiman, "Talmud Study, Ethics and Social Policy," *Jewish Law Association Studies* 25 (2014): 225–261. See also the several volumes of Re'em HaCohen's *Derekh Sha'ar Elyon* (Gilui Otniel: Otniel, various years).

43. Joseph B. Soloveitchik, *And From There You Shall Seek* (Hoboken, N.J.: Ktav, 2008).

Chapter 13. The State of Halakhah and the Halakhah of the State

1. Aharon Lichtenstein, "Religion and State: The Case for Interaction," *Judaism* 15:4 (Fall 1966): 387.

2. A summary of the political circumstances can be found in Mark R. Cohen's *Under Cross and Crescent* (Princeton: Princeton University Press, 1994).

3. *Fiddler on the Roof*. Dir. Norman Jewison (United Artists, 1971).

4. This number assumes that Israeli Jews who self-identify as "traditional" do not fully adhere to the traditional halakhic constitution. *Statistical Abstract of Israel 2015*, Table 7.6 (Jerusalem: Central Bureau for Statistics, 2015). On the American side, less than 20% of American Jews view adherence to halakhah as essential to being Jewish. *Religious Landscape Survey* (Washington, D.C.: Pew Research Center, 2013).

5. An expanded review of this topic is found in Aaron Kirschenbaum, *Equity in Jewish Law— Beyond Equity: Halakhic Aspirationalism in Jewish Civil Law* (Hoboken, N.J.: Ktav, 1991).

6. See for example, Antonin Scalia, "The Rule of Law as the Law of Rules", *University of Chicago Law Review* 56:4 (1989): 1175–1188. See also Steven Calabresi and Gary Lawson, "The Rule of Law as a Law of Law," *Notre Dame Law Review* 90:2 (2014): 487–503, who discuss the centrality of this idea in Scalia's jurisprudence.

7. Scalia, *The Rule of Law*: 1179. See also Cass Sunstein, "Must Formalism be Defended Empirically," 66 *University of Chicago Law Review* (1999): 636.

8. *Midrash Rabbah, Ecclesiastes* Chapter. 7.

9. See for example, R. Hershel Schachter, *On Partnership Minyanim,*" http://www.rcarabbis. org/pdf/Rabbi_Schachter_new_letter.pdf. ("In my opinion, not every student in Yeshiva, or even in Kollel, or even those ordained as a rabbi, is permitted to express an opinion in halakhic decision-making."); See also his "Preserving our Mesorah in Changing Times," *Jewish Action*, Fall 2010, as well as the Orthodox Union's 2017 statement regarding female clergy, https://www. ou.org/assets/Responses-of-Rabbinic-Panel.pdf, ("Particularly when navigating multiple sources and competing considerations, years of sophisticated mentoring and significant experience in *psak* are required for a reliable conclusion to be reached.") For further analysis on the difference between learning-ability and halakhic authority, see J. David Bleich, "Lamdut and Pesak: Theoretical Analysis and Halakhic Decision-Making" in *The Conceptual Approach to Jewish Learning*, Yosef Blau ed. (Hoboken, N.J.: Ktav, 2006): 87–114. Online links accessed December 11, 2017.

10. See Emmanuel Levinas, *Nine Talmudic Readings* (Bloomington, Ind.: Indiana University Press, 1994), 94–119.

11. See for example, the responsa of R. Joel Sirkes §80 (cited in the epigraph to Chapter 11) which criticizes those who decide halakhah based on the *Shulḥan Arukh* rather than the Talmud and commentaries. Compare this to the authoritative depiction of the *Shulḥan Arukh* set out by R. Ovadya Yosef in his introduction to his work of responsa, *Yabia Omer 2nd ed.* (Jerusalem: Ḥazon Ovadya, 1986).

12. See note 41 in Chapter 11.

13. See for example *Sedei Ḥemed*, (Warsaw: Shimshon and Isaac Sobalsky): Ma'areḥet ha-Ḥet §92; *Otzar Lashon Ḥakhamim* (Jerusalem: Bialik Institute, 2009): §§1502 and 1504.

14. This topic is usefully elaborated in Arye Edrei, "Law, Interpretation, and Ideology: The Renewal of the Jewish Laws of War in the State of Israel," *Cardozo Law Review* 28 (2006): 187–227.

15. See Michael Walzer, "War and Peace in the Jewish Tradition," *The Ethics of War and Peace*, Terry Nardin ed. (Princeton: Princeton University Press, 1998), 108–09.

16. See Naḥmanides *Comments to Sefer ha-Mitzvot, Forgotten Positive Commandements:* §5.

17. Meir Simḥah ha-Kohen of Dvinsk, *Meshekh Ḥokhmah,* revised edition (Israel: 1990), 317-18.

18. See Edrei, "Law, Interpretation and Ideology" : 224–25.

19. Shlomo Goren, *Responsa Meishiv Milḥamah* (Idra Rabba Pubs.1986) Vol. 3:257 [Hebrew].

20. Id. 246 and 257.

21. Id. 258.

22. Id. 260, citing b. Berakhot 10a.

23. This distinction was popularized by Bruce Ackerman in "Law in An Activist State," *Yale Law Journal* 92 (1983): 1083–1128.

24. See Yeshayahu Leibowitz, "The Crises of Religion and State in Israel," *Judaism, Human Values and the Jewish State* (Cambridge, Mass.: Harvard University Press, 1992), 170.

25. *Shulḥan Arukh* ḤM §2. (This translation is based on reading of *Sema* to that section).

26. For example, James Boyd White, *Heracles Bow* (Madison, Wisc.: University of Wisconsin Press, 1985), 28–48.

27. See Christopher Eisgruber, "Is the Supreme Court as an Educative Institution?," *NYU Law Review* 67:5 (1992): 962–1032; See also Edward B. Rock, "Saints and Sinners: How Does Delaware Corporate Law Work," *UCLA Law Review* 44:4 (1997): 1016, who writes, "Delaware opinions can be understood as providing a set of parables—instructive tales—of good managers and bad managers, of good lawyers and bad lawyers. . . . we come much closer to understanding the role of courts in corporate law if we think of judges more as preachers than as policemen."

28. For example, Richard McAdams, *The Expressive Powers of Law: Theories and Limits* (Cambridge, Mass.: Harvard University Press, 2015); Cass Sunstein, "On the Expressive Function of Law," *University of Pennsylvania Law Review* 144:5 (1996): 2021-53.

29. Robert Cover, "Nomos and Narrative," *Harvard Law Review* 97 (1983): 4–68.

30. For example, *Beyond the State: Rethinking Private Law*, R. Michaels and N. Jansen, eds. (Tubingen, Germany: Mohr-Siebeck, 2008); *Negotiating State and Non-State Law: The Challenges of Global and Legal Pluralism*, Michael A. Helfand ed. (Cambridge, England: Cambridge University Press, 2015).

31. Yehudah L. Maimon, *The Renewal of the Sanhedrin in the Renewed State* (Jerusalem: Mossad Harav Kook, 1951) [Hebrew].

32. Israel Democracy Institute, *A Portrait of Israeli Jews: Beliefs, Observance, and Values of Israeli Jews, 2009*. http://www.avichai.org.il/sites/default/files/portrait-english-full-2009.pdf . Accessed January 9, 2018.

33. Basic Law on Human Dignity, <http://www.knesset.gov.il/laws/special/eng/basic3_eng.htm>. Basic Law on Freedom of Occupation <https://knesset.gov.il/laws/special/eng/basic4_eng.htm>.

34. See Menachem Mautner, *Law and the Culture of Israel* (Oxford; New York: Oxford University Press, 2011); Daphne Barak-Erez, *Outlawed Pigs: Law, Religion and Culture in Israel* (Madison, Wisc.: University of Wisconsin Press, 2007).

35. Barak-Erez, 110–115.

36. Nissim Ben Ḥayyim, "The Majority of the Israeli Population thinks the Rabbinate is Distancing them from Religion," *Kikar Shabbat*, July 14, 2013 [Hebrew.]

37. *2014 Religion and State Index* (Jerusalem: Hiddush, 2014), 23.

Conclusion

1. Judah Loew b. Betzalel (Maharal) of Prague, *Netivot Olam, Netiv ha-Torah* at §§1 and 5 (Israel, 1980).

2. Aharon Lichtenstein, "Study" in *Twentieth Century Jewish Religious Thought*, A. Cohen and P. Mendes-Flohr eds. (Philadelphia: Jewish Publication Society, 2009), 934.

3. For example, the statements of Rabbi Joseph B. Soloveitchik cited in in Lawrence Kaplan, "The Ḥazon Ish: Ḥaredi Critic of Traditional Orthodoxy,": 152–153; Eliyahu Stern, *The Genius: Elijah of Vilna and the Making of Modern Judaism* (New Haven: Yale University Press, 2013),

72–76.; Shaul Stampfer, *Lithuanian Yeshivas of the Nineteenth Century* (Oxford; Portland, Ore.: Littman, 2014),105–109; Chaim Saiman, "Legal Theology: The Turn to Conceptualism in Nineteenth-Century Jewish Law," *Journal of Law and Religion* 21 (2006): 39–100.

4. Menaḥem Friedman, *Ḥaredi Society: Sources, Trends, and Processes,* (Jerusalem: Institute for Israel Studies, 1991) [Hebrew].

5. See Aharon Lichtenstein, "The Ideology of Hesder," *Traditon* 19:3 (1981):199–217, who considers this question as the dean of one such yeshiva.

6. A broader discussion of this trend can be found in Adam Ferziger, *Beyond Sectarianism: The Realignment of American Orthodox Judaism* (Detroit: Wayne State University Press, 2015),185–191.

7. Michael A. Meyer, *Response to Modernity: A History of the Reform Movement in Judaism* (Oxford; New York: Oxford University Press, 1988); Barry Scott Wimpfheimer, *The Talmud: A Biography*, 199-204.

8. https://www.youtube.com/watch?v=S8nNpTf7tNo. Accessed on December 11, 2017.

FURTHER READINGS

AS THIS BOOK AIMS to be accessible to the nonspecialist, overt discussion of prior scholarship and scholarly notations have been kept relatively lean. Rather than compiling a traditional bibliography, I have created a topically organized list of further resources on the book's central themes. It attempts to balance the effect of the listed work on my thinking, the centrality of the work in its field, and the degree to which the work is a natural extension of the core themes of this book. English sources are preferred over Hebrew ones, the latter cited only when nothing comparable exists in English. Where relevant to this book's thesis, I have included some brief editorial notations.

The first few topics are organized in terms of their centrality to understanding the rabbinic idea of law. Thereafter, the list corresponds to the order in which a topic appears in the text. Within each heading, I have generally relied on the chronological date when the work first appeared, even if a different publication date is cited.

Works Particularly Influential in Developing the Thesis of This Book

Joseph B. Soloveitchik, *Halakhic Man*, Lawrence Kaplan trans. (Philadelphia: Jewish Publication Society, 1983). In arguing that analytical-legal study of Torah and adherence to its practice stand at the core of authentic Jewish religious experience, this work sets forth the theological underpinnings of Lithuanian talmudism and the modern yeshivah movement. (Previously published in Hebrew, 1944.)

Robert Cover, "Nomos and Narrative," *Harvard Law Review* 97 (1982): 4–62. One of the first articles in a mainstream American law review that employs halakhic sources to comment on the phenomena of law more generally. Cover emphasizes that law contains not only coercive ("imperial") dimensions but also educative and meaning-creating ("paideic") capacities that make legal discourse a deeper and more normative social phenomenon that the mere assertion of power. Hanina Ben-Menahem, *Judicial Deviation in Talmudic Law: Governed by Men, Not by Rules* (Amsterdam: Harwood, 1991). Emphasizes the distinction between "halakhah to be applied," roughly corresponding to law, and "non-applied halakhah." My work builds on this distinction with the aim of providing an account of "halakhah" that encapsulates both its applied and non-applied elements.

Moshe Halbertal, *People of the Book: Canon, Meaning, and Authority* (Cambridge, Mass.: Harvard University Press, 1997). Outlines how authority and community are constituted through the commitment to a corpus of legal texts that are reverentially studied and debated. Halbertal shows how under such conditions, talmudic language and concepts become the forum through which religious and theological issues are assessed and debated.

Moshe Halbertal, *Interpretative Revolutions in the Making* (Jerusalem: Magnes Press, 1999) [Hebrew]. Describes how talmudic debates over minor points of law often mask value-laden discussions on central philosophical questions.

Methodological Companions

In recent years, scholars of Judaic studies have moved away from seeking to establish the historical accuracy of rabbinic accounts, and see them instead as a method for conveying religious, social, and cultural ideas. Most studies focus on a particular topic or historical period, whereas this book develops a conceptual account of halakhah as a whole. Though there are considerable differences both among these scholars and between them and this book over what kinds of ideas are embedded in the details of rabbinic discourse, nevertheless, important commonalities bind these works together

Beth A. Berkowitz, *Execution and Invention: Death Penalty Discourse in Early Rabbinic and Christian Cultures* (Oxford; New York: Oxford University Press, 2006).

Devora Steinmetz, *Punishment and Freedom: The Rabbinic Construction of Criminal Law* (Philadelphia: University of Pennsylvania Press, 2008).

Ishay Rosen-Zvi, *The Mishnaic Sotah Ritual: Temple, Gender and Midrash*, Orr Scharf trans. (Leiden, The Netherlands: Brill, 2012). (Previously published in Hebrew, 2008).

Barry Wimpfheimer, *Narrating the Law: A Poetics of Talmudic Legal Stories* (Philadelphia: University of Pennsylvania Press, 2011).

Moshe Simon-Shoshan, *Stories of the Law: Narrative Discourse and the Construction of Authority in the Mishnah* (Oxford; New York: Oxford University Press, 2012).

Naftali Cohn, *The Memory of the Temple and the Making of the Rabbis* Philadelphia: University of Pennsylvania Press, 2013).

Sergey Dolgopolski, *The Open Past: Subjectivity and Remembering in the Talmud* (New York: Fordham University Press, 2013).

Expressive Theories of Law and Non-Applied Law

Since the 1980s, legal academics have become increasingly interested in understanding how law telegraphs norms and organizes social behavior even in the absence of the state's formalized mechanisms of enforcement. These concepts are central to understanding the interaction between applied and non-applied halakhah.

James B. White, *Heracles' Bow: Essays on the Rhetoric and Poetics of Law* (Madison: University of Wisconsin Press, 1985).

Robert Ellickson, *Order Without Law: How Neighbors Settle Disputes* (Cambridge, Mass.: Harvard University Press, 1991).

Peter Brooks and Paul Gewirtz, eds. *Law's Stories: Narrative and Rhetoric in the Law* (New Haven: Yale University Press, 1996).

Cass Sunstein, "On the Expressive Function of Law," *University of Pennsylvania Law Review* 144 (1996): 2021–53.

Larry Lessig, "Social Meaning and Social Norms," *University of Pennsylvania Law Review* 144 (1996): 2181–2189.

Robert Cooter, "Expressive Law and Economics," *Journal of Legal Studies* 27 (1998): 585–608.

Richard McAdams, *The Expressive Powers of Law: Theories and Limits*, (Cambridge, Mass.: Harvard University Press, 2015).

Histories and Overviews of Jewish Law

Ephraim E. Urbach, *The Sages, Their Concepts and Beliefs* (Cambridge, Mass.: Harvard University Press, 1987), offers a comprehensive overview to the world and thought of the talmudic sages. (Previously published in Hebrew, 1969.)

Menachem Elon, *Jewish Law (Ha-Mishpat ha-Ivri): History, Sources, Principles,* 4 vols. Bernard Auerbach and Melvin J. Sykes trans. (Philadelphia: Jewish Publication Society, 1994). This magisterial treatise remains the standard reference work in the field. Elon comprehensively documents all major periods, figures, and doctrines of Jewish civil law, and further reference to almost every topic addressed in this book can be found within Elon's pages. Elon however, offers a state-centric account of halakhah that understands its history as leading almost inexorably to laws of modern of Israel. Notably, the four volumes of the work say little about the conceptual relationship between halakhah and aggadah, and almost nothing about the role of devotional Torah study in the development and theory of halakhah. (Previously published in Hebrew, 1973.)

Modern Research in Jewish Law, Bernard S. Jackson ed. (Leiden, The Netherlands: Brill, 1980). A collection of essays by leading twentieth century scholars of Jewish law debating the appropriate methodology for its study. The volume presents debates between historicists and conceptualists, doctrinal and cultural approaches, as well as arguments over whether Jewish law is best understood in state-centric or non-state contexts.

Suzanne Last Stone, "In Pursuit of the Counter-Text: The Turn to the Jewish Legal Model in Contemporary American Legal Theory," *Harvard Law Review* 106: 4 (1993): 813–894. In her response to Cover's "Nomos and Narrative," Last Stone stresses how Cover failed to account for the distinctly religious and spiritual underpinning of Jewish law, and that Jewish law's methods of imposing coercive authority limit its effectiveness to serve as an analogue and counterpoint to American constitutional theory.

An Introduction to the History and Sources of Jewish Law, N. S. Hecht et. al. eds. (Oxford: Clarendon Press, 1996). A collection of essays offering an introduction to the central persons, doctrines and sources Jewish law from the biblical era through modern day Israel.

History and Theology of Torah Study

Norman Lamm, *Torah Lishmah: Torah for Torah's Sake in the Works of Rabbi Hayyim of Volozhin and His Contemporaries* (Hoboken, N.J.: Ktav, 1989), comprehensively analyzes the concept of Torah Lishmah from historical and theological perspectives.

Mordechai Breuer, *Oholei Torah (The Tents of Torah): The Yeshivah, Its Structure and History* (Jerusalem: Shazar Institute, 2003) [Hebrew], offers the most comprehensive historical account of the different approaches to Torah study in the post-talmudic era.

Aharon Lichtenstein, "Why Learn Gemara," in *Leaves of Faith: The World of Jewish Learning* (Hoboken, N.J.: Ktav, 2003): 1–17. An insider's view on analytic Talmud study as religious devotion.

Immanuel Etkes ed., *Yeshivot and Battei Midrash*, (Jerusalem: Shazar Institute, 2006) [Hebrew], a collection of articles on the history of Torah study from talmudic to contemporary times.

Paul Socken ed., *Why Study Talmud in the Twenty-First Century?: The Relevance of the Ancient Jewish Text to Our World* (Lanham, Md.: Lexington Books 2009), a collection of essays from different religious and social perspectives exploring the relevance of Talmud study in the modern era.

Hannah Hashkes, *Rabbinic Discourse as a System of Knowledge: "The Study of Torah is Equal to Them All"* (Leiden, The Netherlands: Brill, 2015), offers a philosophical account of how Torah study constitutes the rabbinic system of knowledge.

Conceptual Introductions to the Talmud and the Halakhic System

Moshe Silberg, *Talmudic Law and the Modern State*, Marvin S. Weiner ed. and Ben Zion Bokser trans. (New York: Burning Bush Press, 1973). (Previously published in Hebrew, 1961.)

Adin Steinsaltz, *The Essential Talmud* (New York: Basic Books, 2006), one of the more popular works intended to introduce the Talmud and talmudic study to beginners. (Previously published in 1976.)

Eliezer Berkovits, *Not in Heaven: The Nature and Function of Halakha* (Hoboken, N.J.: Ktav, 1983).

Ephraim E. Urbach, *The Halakhah: Its Sources and Development* (Givataim: Yad La-Talmud,1986). (Previously published in Hebrew, 1984.)

Introductions to Jewish Law Directed to the Students of American and Western Law

Elliot N. Dorff and Arthur Roset, *A Living Tree: The Roots and Growth of Jewish Law* (Albany: State University of New York Press, 1988).

Samuel J. Levine, "Teaching Jewish Law in American Law Schools: An Emerging Development in Law and Religion," *Fordham Urban Law Journal* 26: 4 (1999): 1041–1050.

Menachem Elon et. al, *Jewish Law (Mishpat Ivri) Cases and Materials* (New York: Matthew Bender, 1999), a casebook for use in a law school setting.

Steven H. Resnicoff, *Understanding Jewish Law*. (New Providence, N.J.: LexisNexis, 2012), a black letter description of the Jewish legal system in the style of a modern law school hornbook.

Chaim Saiman, "Framing Jewish Law for the American Law School Context," *Jewish Law Annual* 89 (2011): 89–119.

J. David Bleich and Arthur J. Jacobson, *Jewish Law and Contemporary Issues* (Cambridge, England: Cambridge University Press, 2015).

David Hollander, *Legal Scholarship in Jewish Law: An Annotated Bibliography of Journal Articles* (Getzville, N.Y.: Hein, 2017).

Traditional Historical-Critical Scholarship of Rabbinic Literature

H. L. Strack and Gunter Stemberger, *Introduction to the Talmud and Midrash* Marcus Bockmuehl trans. (Minneapolis: Fortress Press, 1992). (Built on earlier version published in German, 1920.)

J. N. Epstein, *Introduction to Tannaitic Literature* (Jerusalem: Magnes; Tel Aviv: Devir, 1957) [Hebrew]; and, *Introduction to Amoraic Literature* (Jerusalem: Magnes; Tel Aviv: Devir, 1962) [Hebrew].

Ḥanoch Albeck, *Mevo le-Talmudim* (Tel Aviv: Devir, 1969) [Hebrew].

Martin S. Jaffe, *Torah in the Mouth: Writing and Oral Tradition in Palestinian Judaism, 200 BCE-400 CE*. (Oxford; New York: Oxford University Press, 2001).

Shamma Friedman, *Tosefta Atiqta, Pesaḥ Rishon, Synoptic Parallels of Mishna and Tosefta Analyzed, With a Methodological Introduction* (Ramat Gan: Bar-Ilan University Press, 2002).

Judith Hauptman, *Rereading the Mishnah: A New Approach to Ancient Jewish Texts* (Tubingen, Germany: Mohr Siebeck, 2005).

Robert Brody, *Mishnah and Tosefta Studies* (Jerusalem: Magnes, 2014).

Shaye J. D. Cohen, *From the Maccabees to the Mishnah* (Louisville: Westminster John Knox Press, 2014).

Historicity of Rabbinic Accounts of Sanhedrin Practice and Temple Rituals

Hugo Mantel, *Studies in the History of the Sanhedrin* (Cambridge, Mass.: Harvard University Press, 1961).

Joshua Efron, *Studies in the Hasmonean Period* (Leiden, The Netherlands: Brill 1987).

David Goodblatt, *The Monarchic Principle: Studies in Jewish Self-Government in Antiquity* (Tubingen, Germany: J.C.B Mohr, 1994).

Howard Clark Kee "Central Authority in Second-Temple Judaism and Subsequently: From Synedrion to Sanhedrin," *The Annual of Rabbinic Judaism* 2 (1999): 51–63.

Lester Grabbe, "Sanhedrin, Sanhedriyyot, or Mere Invention?", *Journal for the Study of Judaism in the Persian, Hellenistic and Roman Period* 39 (2008): 1–19.

Joshua Schwartz, "The Temple Cult Without the Sages: Prolegomena on the Description of the

Second Temple Period Cult according to the Sources of the Second Temple Period," *New Studies on Jerusalem*, 14 (2008): 7–19 (English section).

Joshua Schwartz, "Sacrifice Without the Rabbis: Ritual and Sacrifice in the Second Temple Period according to the Sources of the Second Temple Period," Alberdina Houtman, et al. eds., *The Actuality of Sacrifice: Past and Present* (Leiden, The Netherlands: Brill; *Jewish and Christian Perspective Series 28, 2014*), 123–149.

The Social, Historical, and Political Context of Late Antiquity

Hayim Lapin, *Early Rabbinic Civil Law and the Social History of Roman Galilee: A Study of Mishnah Tractate Baba' Meṣi'a'* (Atlanta: Scholars Press, 1995).

The Cambridge History of Judaism, Vol 4: The Late Roman-Rabbinic Period, Steven T. Katz ed. (Cambridge, England: Cambridge University Press, 2006).

The Cambridge Companion to the Talmud and Rabbinic Literature, Charlotte E. Fonrobert and Martin S. Jaffee eds. (Cambridge, England: Cambridge University Press, 2007).

The Oxford Handbook of Jewish Daily Life in Roman Palestine, Catherine Hezser ed. (Oxford; New York: Oxford University Press, 2010).

The Formation of the Babylonian Talmud

David Weiss Halivni, *The Formation of the Babylonian Talmud*, Jeffrey L. Rubenstein ed. and trans. (Oxford; New York: Oxford University Press, 2013) (Based on publications in Hebrew from 1975–2003).

Neil Danzig, "From Oral Talmud to Written Talmud: On the Methods of Transmission of the Babylonian Talmud and its Study in the Middle Ages," *Bar-Ilan* 30–31(2006): 49–112 [Hebrew].

Zvi Septimus, *The Poetic Superstructure of the Babylonian Talmud and the Reader it Fashions*, (*Berkeley*: PhD dissertation., University of California, Berkeley 2011).

Ari Bergmann, *Halevy, Halivni and The Oral Formation of the Babylonian Talmud* (New York: PhD dissertation, Columbia University, 2014).

Moulie Vidas, *Tradition and the Formation of the Talmud* (Princeton: Princeton University Press, 2014).

Construction of the Talmudic Sugya

Louis Jacobs, *Studies in Talmudic Logic and Methodology* (London: Vallentine Mitchell, 1961).

Jeffrey L. Rubenstein, *Talmudic Stories: Narrative Art, Composition, and Culture* (Baltimore: Johns Hopkins University Press, 1999).

Isaiah Gafni, "Rethinking Talmudic History: The Challenge of Literary and Redaction Criticism," *Jewish History* 25:3–4 (2011): 355–375.

Judith Hauptman, "The Three Basic Components of the Sugya: The Tannaitic Passages, the Amoraic Statements, and the Anonymous Commentary," in *Studies in the Redaction and*

Development of Talmudic Literature, Aharon Amit and Aharon Shemesh eds. (Ramat Gan: Bar-Ilan University Press, 2011), 27–38.

Joshua Kulp and Jason Rogoff, *Reconstructing the Talmud: An Introduction to the Academic Study of Rabbinic Literature* (New York: Mechon Hadar, 2014).

Barry Scott Wimpfheimer, *The Talmud: A Biography* (Princeton: Princeton University of Press, 2018), 50–72.

Greek and Rabbinic Modes of Thought

Saul Lieberman, *Hellenism in Jewish Palestine* (New York: Jewish Theological Seminary, 1962).

Lee I. Levine, *Judaism and Hellenism in Antiquity: Conflict or Confluence?* (Seattle: University of Washington Press, 1998).

Daniel Boyarin, *Socrates and the Fat Rabbis* (Chicago: University of Chicago Press, 2009).

Moulie Vidas, "Greek Wisdom in Babylonia," in *Envisioning Judaism: Studies in Honor of Peter Schafer* (Tubingen, Germany: Mohr Siebeck, 2013): 287–305.

Christine Hayes, *What's Divine about Divine Law? Early Perspectives* (Princeton: Princeton University Press, 2015).

Richard Hidary, *Rabbis as Greco-Roman Rhetors: Oratory and Sophistic Education in the Talmud and Midrash* (Cambridge, England: Cambridge University Press, 2017).

From Talmud to Law: The Talmud's Early Commentators

Overview

Talya Fishman, *Becoming the People of the Talmud: Oral Torah as Written Tradition in Medieval Jewish Cultures* (Philadelphia: University of Pennsylvania Press, 2010).

Geonim

Robert Brody, *The Geonim of Babylonia and the Shaping of Medieval Jewish Culture* (New Haven: Yale University Press, 1998).

R. Isaac Alfasi

Leonard R. Levy, "The Decisive Shift: From Geonim to Rabbi Yitshak Alfasi," *Tiferet le-Yisrael* (New York: Jewish Theological Seminary, 2010): 93–130.

Maimonides

Isadore Twersky, *Introduction to the Code of Maimonides (Mishneh Torah)* (New Haven: Yale University Press, 1980).

Moshe Halbertal, *Maimonides: Life and Thought* (Princeton: Princeton University Press, 2013).

Tosafot

Ephraim Urbach, *The Tosafists: History, Works and Methodology* (Jerusalem: Bialik Inst. 1955) [Hebrew].

Aryeh Leibowitz, "The Emergence and Development of Tosafot on the Talmud," *Hakirah: The Flatbush Journal for Jewish Law and Thought* 15 (2013): 143–64.

Between Ashkenaz and Sepharad

Ephraim Kanarfogel, "Between Ashkenaz and Sefarad: Tosafist Teachings in the Talmudic Commentaries of Ritva," in *Between Rashi and Maimonides: Themes in Medieval Jewish Thought, Literature and Exegesis,* Ephraim Kanarfogel and Moshe Sokolow eds., (New York: Yeshiva University Press, 2010): 237–273.

Yehuda Galinsky, "Between 'Ashkenaz' (Germany) and 'Tsarfat' (France): Two Approaches Toward Popularizing Jewish law" *Jews and Christians in Thirteenth-Century France*, Elisheva Baumgarten and Judah D. Galinsky eds., (New York: Palgrave, Macmillan, 2015).

Avraham Rami Reiner, "From France to Provence: The Assimilation of the Tosafists' Innovations in the Provencal Talmudic Tradition," *Journal of Jewish Studies* 65:1 (2014).

R. Nissim Gerondi (Ran) and the King's Law

Gerald J. Blidstein, " 'Ideal' and 'Real' in Classical Jewish Political Theory," *Jewish Political Studies Review* 2:1–2 (1990): 43–65.

Aaron Kirschenbaum, "The Role of Punishment in Jewish Criminal Law: A Chapter in Rabbinic Penological Thought" *Jewish Law Annual* 9 (1991): 123–43.

Aviezer Ravitzky, "Political Philosophy: Nissim of Gerona vs. Isaac Abrabanel," *History and Faith: Studies in Jewish Philosophy*, A. Ravitzky ed. (Amsterdam: J.C. Gieben, 1996): 43–75.

Menachem Lorberbaum, *Politics and the Limits of Law: Secularizing the Political in Medieval Jewish Thought* (Stanford, Calif.: Stanford University Press, 2002).

Aviezer Ravitzky, *Religion and State in Jewish Philosophy: Models of Unity, Division, Collision and Subordination*, Rachel Yarden trans. (Jerusalem: Israel Democracy Institute, 2002).

Warren Z. Harvey, "Rabbi Nissim of Girona on the Constitutional Power of the Sovereign," *Diné Israel* 29 (2013): 91–100.

Sub-Halakhah, Extra-Legal Measures of Enforcement, and the Interaction between Jewish Law and Life

Simḥa Assaf, *Punishments in the Post-Talmudic Period* (Jerusalem: 1922) [Hebrew].

Edward Fram, *Ideals Face Reality: Jewish Life in Poland 1550–1655* (Cincinnati: Hebrew Union College Press, 1997).

Aaron Kirschenbaum, *Jewish Penology: The Theory and Development of Criminal Punishment*

Among the Jews Throughout the Ages (Jerusalem: Magnes, 2013) [Hebrew]. The definitive work on this topic.

History, Theory, and Development of the Codes

Isadore Twersky, "The Shulḥan Arukh: Enduring Code of Jewish Law," *Judaism* 16:2 (1967): 141–58.

Israel Ta-Shma, "Rabbi Joseph Caro and his Beit Yosef: Between Spain and Germany," in *Moreshet Sepharad: The Sephardi Legacy* Vol. 2, Haim Beinart ed. (Jerusalem: Magnes Press, 1992): 192–206.

Edward Fram, "Jewish Law from the Shulḥan Arukh to the Enlightenment," *An Introduction to the History and Sources of Jewish Law*, N. S. Hecht et al. eds. (Oxford: Clarendon Press, 1996): 359–377.

Joseph Davis, "The Reception of the 'Shulḥan 'Arukh' and the Formation of Ashkenazic Jewish Identity." *AJS Review* 26:2 (2002): 251–276.

Yehudah Galinsky, "Ashkenazim in Sefarad: The Rosh and the Tur on the Codification of Jewish Law," *Jewish Law Annual* 16 (2006): 12–23.

Nils Jansen, *The Making of Legal Authority: Non-Legislative Codifications in Historical and Comparative Perspective* (Oxford; New York: Oxford University Press, 2010).

Noam Samet, "Ketsot Ha-Choshen—The Beginning of 'Lamdanut': Features and Tendencies" (Beersheva: PhD dissertation, Ben Gurion University, 2016) [Hebrew].

Responsa Literature

At present, no comprehensive treatment of the topic exists in English. In addition to Elon, *Jewish Law* Vol 3. 1454–68, see the following:

Israel Ta-Shma, "Responsa," entry in *Encyclopedia Judaica*, Vol.17 (New York: Macmillan, 2007): 228–39.

Mosheh Lichtenstein, "The Period of the *Aḥronim*: Trends and Directions" *Netuim:* 16 (2009): 131–174 [Hebrew].

Shmuel Glick, *A Window to the Responsa Literature* (New York: Jewish Theological Seminary, 2012) [Hebrew].

The Brisker Method

Descriptions

Joseph B. Soloveitchik, "Mah Dodekh MiDod" in *In Aloneness, in Togetherness: A Selection of Hebrew Writings* (Jerusalem: Orot, 1971), 227 [Hebrew].

Solomon, Norman, *The Analytic Movement: Hayyim Soloveitchik and His Circle* (Atlanta: Scholars Press, 1993).

Shaul Stampfer, *Lithuanian Yeshivas of the Nineteenth Century: Creating a tradition of learning* (Oxford; New York: Oxford University Press, 2012) (originally published in Hebrew in 1995).

Marc Shapiro, "The Brisker Method Reconsidered" *Tradition* 31 (1997): 78–102.

The Orthodox Forum, Lomdus: The Conceptual Approach to Jewish Learning, Yosef Blau ed. (New York: Yeshiva University Press; Hoboken, N.J.: Ktav, 2006), offers a collection of essays on different facets of the Brisker method.

Chaim Saiman, "Legal Theology: The Turn to Conceptualism in Nineteenth-Century Jewish Law," *Journal of Law and Religion* 21 (2006): 39–100.

Sergey Dolgopolsky, "Constructed and Denied: 'The Talmud' from the Brisker Rav to the 'Mishneh Torah'" in *Encountering the Medieval in Modern Jewish Thought,* James A. Diamond et al. eds. (Leiden, The Netherlands: Brill, 2012): 177–200.

Critiques and Responses

Shimon Gershon Rosenberg (Shagar), *BeTorato Yehegeh* (Efrat: Shagar Inst. 2008) [Hebrew].

David Flatto, "Tradition and Modernity in the House of Study: Reconsidering the Relationship Between the Conceptual and Critical Methods of Study Talmud," *Tradition* 43 (2010): 113–136.

Yair Dreyfuss, "The Torah Study for Contemporary Times: Conservatism or Revolution?" *Tradition* 45:2 (2012): 31–47.

Chaim Saiman, "Talmud Study, Ethics and Social Policy," *Jewish Law Association Studies* 25 (2014): 225–261.

The Halakhah of the State

Yeshayahu Leibowitz, *Judaism, Human Values and the Jewish State* (esp. chapters 14 and 15), Eliezer Goldman ed. (Cambridge, Mass.: Harvard University Press, 1992). (These essays were originally published in Hebrew publications in 1947 and 1952 respectively).

Aharon Lichtenstein, "Religion and State: The Case for Interaction," *Judaism* 15:4 (1966): 387–412.

Izhak Englard, "The Problem of Jewish Law in a Jewish State," *Israel Law Review* 3 (1968) 254–278.

Aviezer Ravitzsky, *Messianism, Zionism, and Jewish Religious Radicalism,* M. Swirsky and J. Chipman trans. (Chicago: University of Chicago Press, 1996). (Previously published in Hebrew, 1993).

Gerald J. Blidstein, "Halakha and Democracy," *Tradition* 32 (1997): 6–39.

Asher Cohen, *The Tallit and the Flag: Religious Zionism and the Concept of a Torah State 1947–1953* (Jerusalem: Yad Ben-Zvi, 1998) [Hebrew].

Yedidia Z. Stern, *State, Law, and Halakha: Part One: Civil Leadership as Halakhic Authority,* (Jerusalem: The Israel Democracy Institute, 2001); Stern, *State, Law, and Halakha: Part Two:*

Facing Painful Choices: Law and Halakha in Israeli Society, (Jerusalem: Israel Democracy Institute, 2003); and Stern, *State, Law, and Halakha: Part Three: Religion and the State: The Role of Halakha* (Jerusalem: The Israel Democracy Institute, 2004).

Aviezer Ravitzsky, "Is a Halakhic State Possible? The Paradox of Jewish Theocracy," *Israel Affairs* 11:1 (2005): 137–164.

Suzanne Last Stone, "Judaism and Civil Society," in *Law, Politics, and Morality in Judaism*, Michael Walzer ed. (Princeton: Princeton University Press, 2006): 12–33.

Daphne Barak-Erez, *Outlawed Pigs: Law, Religions and Culture in Israel* (Madison: University of Wisconsin Press, 2007).

Yizhak Conforti, " 'The New Jew' in the Zionist Movement: Ideology and Historiography," *Australian Journal for Jewish Studies* 25 (2011): 87–118.

Menachem Mautner, *Law and the Culture of Israel* (Oxford; New York: Oxford University Press, 2011).

Suzanne Last Stone, "Law Without Nation? The Ongoing Jewish Discussion," in *Law Without Nations*, Austin Sarat et al., eds. (Stanford, Calif.: Stanford University Press, 2011), 101–137.

Alexander Kaye, *The Legal Philosophies of Religious Zionism 1937–1967* (New York: PhD dissertation, Columbia University, 2013).

Shimon Shetreet and Walter Homolka, *Jewish and Israeli Law—An Introduction* (Berlin; Boston: De Gruyter, 2017).

INDEX